T0326333

THE CHRONICLE OF
GEOFFREY LE BAKER OF SWINBROOK

Geoffrey le Baker's chronicle covers the reigns of Edward II and Edward III up to the English victory at Poitiers. It starts in a low key, copying an earlier chronicle, but by the end of Edward II's reign he offers a much more vivid account. His description of Edward II's last days is partly based on the eyewitness account of his patron, Sir Thomas de la More, who was present at one critical interview. Baker's story of Edward's death, like many other details from his chronicle, was picked up by Tudor historians, particularly by Holinshed, who was the source for Shakespeare's history plays.

The reign of Edward III is dominated, not by Edward III himself, but by Baker's real hero, Edward prince of Wales. His bravery aged 16 at Crécy is presented as a prelude to his victory at Poitiers, a battle which Baker is able to describe in great detail, apparently from what he was told by the prince's commanders. It is a rarity among medieval battles, because – in sharp contrast to the total anarchy at Crécy – the prince and his staff were able to see the enemy's manoeuvres.

Throughout the chronicle there are sharply defined vignettes which stay in the mind - the killing of the Scottish champion on Halidon Hill, the drowning of Sir Edward Bohun, the earls of Salisbury and Suffolk as prisoners carried in a cart, the death of Sir Walter Selby and his two sons, the bravery of Sir Thomas Dagworth against a cobbler's son, the duel between Otho and the duke of Lancaster, John Dancaster and the lewd washerwoman.

Baker writes in a complex Latin which even scholars find problematic, and David Preest's new translation will be widely welcomed by anyone interested in the fourteenth century. There are extensive notes and an introduction by Richard Barber.

THE CHRONICLE OF
GEOFFREY LE BAKER
OF SWINBROOK

Translated by David Preest

Introduction and Notes by Richard Barber

THE BOYDELL PRESS

First published 2012
The Boydell Press, Woodbridge
Paperback edition 2018

ISBN 978 1 84383 691 9 hardback
ISBN 978 1 78327 304 1 paperback

The Boydell Press is an imprint of Boydell & Brewer Ltd
PO Box 9, Woodbridge, Suffolk IP12 3DF, UK
and of Boydell & Brewer Inc.
668 Mt Hope Avenue, Rochester, NY 14620–2731, USA
website: www.boydellandbrewer.com

The publisher has no responsibility for the continued existence or accuracy
of URLs for external or third-party internet websites referred to in this book,
and does not guarantee that any content on such websites is,
or will remain, accurate or appropriate

A CIP catalogue record for this book is available
from the British Library

This publication is printed on acid-free paper

Contents

Acknowledgements

I would like to thank Andrew Rossabi for his help in suggesting solutions to the obscurer parts of the *Chronicle*, and my wife Verity for her unfailing support and for climbing two flights of stairs on a regular basis to deal with my computer problems.

DAVID PREEST

March 2012

Professor Mark Ormrod and Dr Paul Dryburgh have been kind enough to read the introduction and the notes, and to make many useful comments and additions, particularly on the material relating to Edward II's reign. Professor Rodney Thomson looked at the sources cited by le Baker and his general Latin style, to see if this indicated a particular cultural milieu. All of this substantially improved the book, and I am most grateful to them.

RICHARD BARBER

April 2012

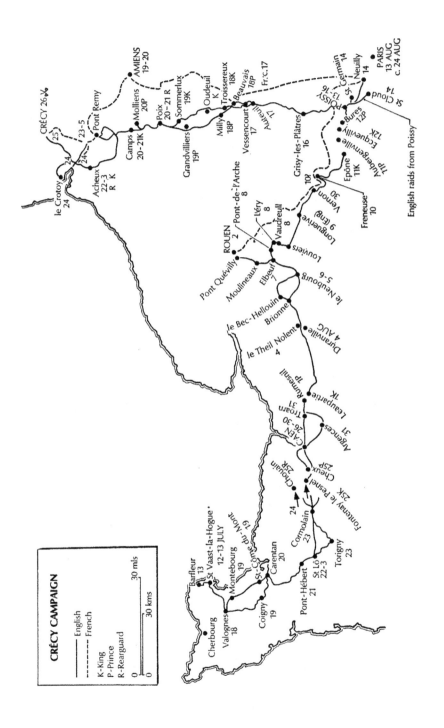

CRÉCY CAMPAIGN

— English
---- French
K-King
P-Prince
R-Rearguard

0   30 mls
0   30 kms

Barfleur 13
St Vaast-la-Hogue 12-13 JULY
Cherbourg
Valognes 18
Montebourg 19
St-Côme-du-Mont 19
Coigny 19
Carentan 20
Pont-Hébert 21
St Lô 22-3
Toigny 23
Cormolain 23
Chouain 24
Fontenay le Pesnel 25K
Cheux 25P
Agences 31
CAEN 26-30
Troarn 31
Leauparti\`e 1P
Rumesnil 1K
Durainville 4 AUG
le Theil Nolent 4
Brionne
le Bec-Hellouin
Moulineaux
Pont Quévilly
Elbeuf 7
le Neubourg 5-6
Louviers
Léry 8
Vaudreuil 8
Pont-de-l'Arche 8
ROUEN 2
Longueville 9 (Eng)
Vernon 30
Freneuse 10
Epône 11K
Aubergenville 11P
Ecquevilly 12K
Bures 12P
POISSY 13-16
St Germain 14
St Cloud 14
Neuilly 14
PARIS 13 AUG c. 24 AUG
Grisy-les-Plâtres 16
Grisy 10R
Vessencourt 17
Auteuil 17
Milly 18P
Troissereux 18K
Beauvais 18P
Fr. c. 17
Oudeuil K
Sommerlux 19K
Poix 20-21 R
Grandvilliers 19P
Molliers 20P
Camps 20-21K
AMIENS 19-20
Pont Remy
Acheux 22-3 R K
CRÉCY 26
25
24
23-5
le Crotoy 24

English raids from Poissy

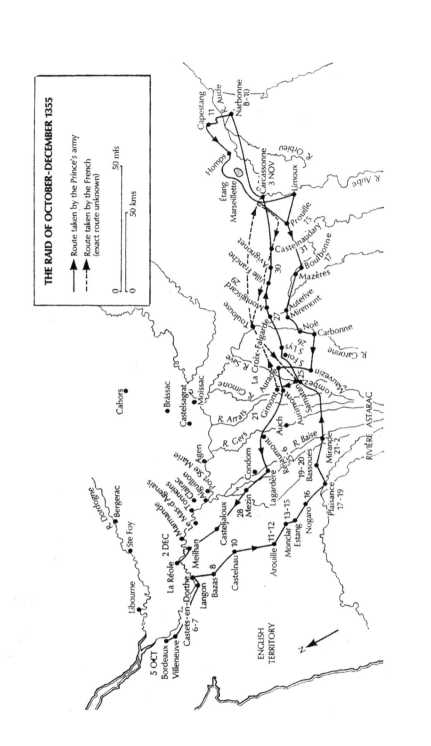

THE RAID OF OCTOBER–DECEMBER 1355

→ Route taken by the Prince's army
⇢ Route taken by the French
(exact route unknown)

50 mls

50 kms

Libourne

R. Dordogne
Bergerac
Ste Foy

Bordeaux
5 OCT
Villeneuve
Castets-en-Dorthe
6–7
La Réole 2 DEC
Langon
Bazas
Castelnau 10
Melihan 8
Arouille 11–12
Casteljaloux
Mezin 28
Monclar 13–15
Estang
Nogaro 16
Plaisance
17–19
Mirande
21–2

Cahors

Brassac

Castelsagrat
Moissac

R. Arrats
R. Gers
R. Gimone
R. Save
R. Baïse

Agen
Port Ste Marie
Aiguillon
Clairac
Le Mas d'Agenais
Marmande
Tonneins

Condom
Lagardère
Réjaumont 6–9
Auch
25

Samatan
Aurimont
Gimont 21
Aurade
La Croix-Falgarde
St Foix 5 Lys
26
Lombez
Mauvezin
Noé
Carbonne
R. Garonne

RIVIÈRE ASTARAC

ENGLISH
TERRITORY

N

Toulouse
Montgiscard 29
Ville Franche
Avignonet
30
Castelnaudary 31
Boulbonne
17
Mazères
Auterive
Miremont
27

Étang
Marseillette
Homps
Capestang 11
R. Aude
Narbonne
8–10

Carcassonne
3 NOV
Limoux
Prouille
15
R. Orbieu
R. Aude
R. Aube

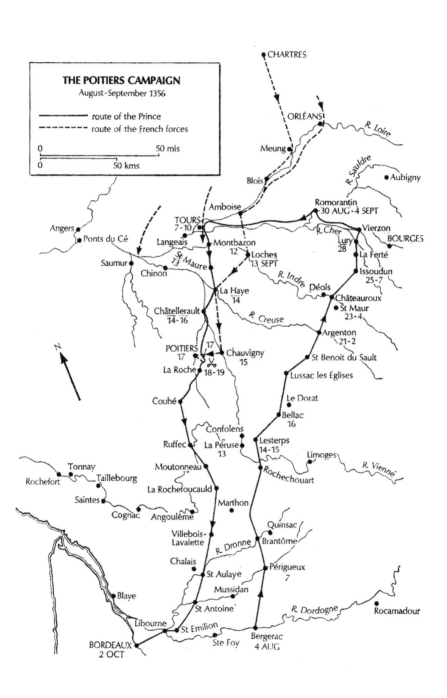

THE POITIERS CAMPAIGN
August–September 1356

——————— route of the Prince
- - - - - - - route of the French forces

0   50 mls
0   50 kms

CHARTRES

ORLÉANS

R. Loire

Meung

R. Sauldre

Blois

Aubigny

Amboise

Romorantin
30 AUG–4 SEPT

TOURS
7–10

R. Cher

Vierzon

Angers

Langeais

Montbazon
12

Lury
28

BOURGES

Ponts du Cé

St Maure

Loches
13 SEPT

La Ferté

Saumur

Chinon

R. Indre

Déols

Issoudun
25–7

La Haye
14

Châteauroux

St Maur
23–4

Châtellerault
14–16

R. Creuse

N

POITIERS
17

17

Chauvigny
15

Argenton
21–2

St Benoit du Sault

La Roche

18–19

Lussac les Églises

Couhé

Le Dorat

Bellac
16

Confolens

Ruffec

La Péruse
13

Lesterps
14–15

Limoges

R. Vienne

Tonnay

Moutonneau

Rochechouart

Rochefort

Taillebourg

La Rochefoucauld

Saintes

Marthon

Cognac

Angoulême

Quinsac

Villebois-
Lavalette

Brantôme

R. Dronne

Chalais

St Aulaye

Périgueux
7

Mussidan

Blaye

St Antoine

R. Dordogne

Rocamadour

Libourne

St Emilion

Ste Foy

Bergerac
4 AUG

BORDEAUX
2 OCT

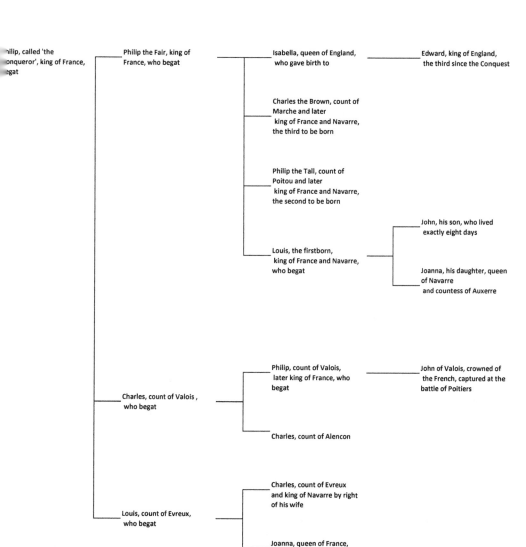

Philip, called 'the Conqueror', king of France, begat

Philip the Fair, king of France, who begat

Isabella, queen of England, who gave birth to

Edward, king of England, the third since the Conquest

Charles the Brown, count of Marche and later king of France and Navarre, the third to be born

Philip the Tall, count of Poitou and later king of France and Navarre, the second to be born

Louis, the firstborn, king of France and Navarre, who begat

John, his son, who lived exactly eight days

Joanna, his daughter, queen of Navarre and countess of Auxerre

Charles, count of Valois, who begat

Philip, count of Valois, later king of France, who begat

John of Valois, crowned of the French, captured at the battle of Poitiers

Charles, count of Alencon

Louis, count of Evreux, who begat

Charles, count of Evreux and king of Navarre by right of his wife

Joanna, queen of France, married to Charles, king of France

Family tree of the kings of France, displayed in order to emphasise Edward III's claim to the French throne

This diagram appears at the end of the Bodleian manuscript of Geoffrey le Baker's chronicle

Abbreviations

Anonimalle *The Anonimalle Chronicle, 1333-1381*, ed. V. H. Galbraith, Manchester 1927

Annales Paulini *Annales Paulini*, in *Chronicles of the Reigns of Edward I and Edward II*, ed. W. Stubbs, 2 vols, RS 76, London 1882-3, i

Brut *The Brut, or, The Chronicles of England*, ed. F. W. D. Brie, 2 vols , EETS Original Series, cxxxi, cxxxvi, London 1906-8

CCR *Calendar of Close Rolls, Edward II-Richard II*, 24 vols, London, 1892-1927

CPR *Calendar of Patent Rolls, Edward II-Richard II*, 27 vols, London, 1894-1916

Chronicon *Chronicon Galfridi le Baker de Swynebroke* ed. Edward Maunde Thompson, Oxford 1889

EETS Early English Texts Society

EHR English Historical Review

Foedera *Foedera, Conventiones, Literae et Cujuscunque Generis Acta Publica*, ed. T. Rymer, 3 vols in 6 parts, London 1816-30

Historia Anglicana Thomas Walsingham, *Historia Anglicana*, ed. H. T. Riley, 2 vols, RS28.i, London 1863-4

Knighton *Knighton's Chronicle, 1337-1396*, ed. G. H. Martin, Oxford 1995

Le Bel *The True Chronicles of Jean le Bel*, tr. Nigel Bryant, Woodbridge and Rochester NY 2010
Chronique de Jean le Bel, ed. Jules Viard and Eugène Déprez, Société de l'Histoire de France, Paris 1904–5, rptd Paris 1977. [Page references to this edition are given in square brackets]

Lewis, Note *Note on the Chronicle ascribed to Geoffrey le Baker, of Swinbrook*, Cardiff 1918.

Murimuth *Chronica Adae Murimuth et Roberti de Avesbury*, ed. E. M. Thompson, RS 93, 1889

Phillips Seymour Phillips, *Edward II*, New Haven and London 2011

Prestwich Michael Prestwich, *Edward I*, London 1988

PROME *The Parliament Rolls of Medieval England*, ed. and trans. P. Brand, A. Curry, C. Given-Wilson, R. E. Horrox, G. Martin, W. M. Ormrod and J. R. S. Phillips, 16 vols, Woodbridge 2005

RS Rolls Series

TNA The National Archives

Page numbers in brackets in the text refer to the *Chronicon* edition.

Introduction

The author

We know very little about Geoffrey le Baker's personal circumstances. He himself tells us that he was from Swinbrook in Oxfordshire, and that he was a *clericus* living at Oseney in July 1347; this information comes from a note at the end of a very short chronicle which he wrote in that year for Sir Thomas de la More.[1] Otherwise, there is a record of him as Geoffrey Pachon from Swinbrook in 1326, described as a chaplain, when he is pardoned for an unspecified offence by Edward II on condition that he helps the king to repel the invasion of queen Isabella, together with a long list of other criminals.[2] If we accept this identification, he reappears as Geoffrey Pachoun, parson of the church of Wishford near Salisbury, who had been convicted as a felon by the Oxford justices, in 1332.[3] This entry could in turn be connected with a complaint by the prior of Stogursey in July 1332 that Robert Fitzpayn and his supporters, including three clerics and Geoffrey le Baker, attacked his property, felling trees and carrying off cattle[4]. Despite Geoffrey's presence at Oseney in 1347, his name does not appear in the records of Oseney Abbey, though he does insert two minor pieces of information about this house in his short chronicle, which would imply a good knowledge of its history.[5] There is also a local item of Oxfordshire news under the year 1350, about the discovery of a curious two headed monster at Chipping Norton.[6] And finally, there are two references to medical works by Galen and Hippocrates which might indicate some knowledge of that subject.[7] He remains a shadowy figure as far as the records are concerned.

Context

However, if we look at the sources for Baker's chronicle, we can place him in some kind of context. Baker uses the chronicle of Adam Murimuth as the basis for the early part of his work, and he draws on the eyewitness testimony of Sir Thomas de la More for details of the abdication of Edward II. These two were probably

---

[1]   *Chronicon*, 173
[2]   *CPR 1324-7*, 331. Pardons, or promises of pardons, of this sort were frequently used to recruit troops: large numbers of such documents were issued after the Crécy campaign. See
George Wrottesley, *Crecy and Calais*, London 1898, pp. 219 ff.
[3]   *CPR 1324-7*, 377; this is either Wishford near Salisbury or Wickford in Cambridgeshire.
[4]   *CPR 1324-7*, 352. Stogursey is in Somerset, near Bridgwater, and Robert Fitzpayn appears
to have been the owner of the castle.
[5]   See *Chronicon*, v, 163, 169.
[6]   See p.94 below.
[7]   See pp. 29, 22 below.

Oxfordshire neighbours, since Murimuth's family may have been from Fyfield in Oxfordshire, five miles north-west of Swinbrook, and the de la More family held lands at Northmoor, seven miles south-east of Swinbrook. Both Murimuth, who was a graduate of Oxford university, and Thomas de la More were connected to John Stratford, bishop of Winchester from 1323 until his translation to Canterbury in 1333; as archbishop, he played a central part in Edward's government; De la More was Stratford's nephew and a member of his retinue.

All these places lie in the hundred of Chadlington, the lordship of which, according to the editor of Baker's chronicle, was in the hands of the Bohun family.[1] Several pieces of evidence point to a connection with the Bohuns. The surviving manuscript of the whole chronicle seems to have belonged to Thomas de Walmesford, rector of Great Leighs in Essex, who was presented to the living by John Bohun, earl of Hereford in 1335. A copy of the presentation is the item immediately preceding the chronicle. There are later additions listing the medicines which the widow of Humphrey Bohun, earl of Northampton and Hereford, required in 1408, and a note of the death of the earl, so the book remained in the possession of someone associated with the Bohuns until at least the beginning of the fifteenth century.

Furthermore, there is very precise detail about the death of an earlier Humphrey Bohun at the battle of Boroughbridge in 1322: Baker goes to some lengths to justify Bohun's appearance among the barons fighting against the king, and then describes how he 'was crossing a bridge and never expecting to find an enemy under his feet when, through a hole in the planking, a Welshman stabbed him in the groin, a private part where soldiers are not usually protected',[2] which no other source mentions, and is very likely to have come from the family itself.

There is one remark that implies that Baker may have been in Gascony, in relation to Henry of Grosmont's appearance before Toulouse in 1345; Grosmont 'did no harm to the inhabitants, except to make them shiver in their shoes, as the besieged afterwards told me'.[3] He also notes at Bannockburn that clerics were present and on the 1355 campaign, something which other chroniclers rarely note.[4]

The story which immediately follows this remark is about the Carmelites of Toulouse, so it is possible that a Carmelite visitor to England might have been the source of the episode, given the other information which came to Baker through Carmelite sources. The Carmelites had a house in Oxford, and Baker also uses a lost charter of the Oxford Carmelites for Edward II's vow to found a Carmelite house at Oxford and endow twenty-four Carmelites to study theology at Oxford if he escaped safely from the battlefield at Bannockburn.

---

[1]   *Chronicon*, viii. I have not been able to find any documentation to support this claim; the lordship of Chadlington is not included in William Bohun's estate at his death (*Calendar of Inquisitions Post Mortem*, London 1921, X 639 ff.).

[2]   See p.13 below.

[3]   See p.68 below

[4]   See pp 8, 111 below; Lewis, *Note*, 6

(9) It seems likely that he had seen the original, as the dates are left out, as if he intended to look at the document again and complete them. Another Carmelite source was a poem written by Robert Baston, a Carmelite friar captured at the battle of Bannockburn in 1314, who was ordered by Robert Bruce to write a poem celebrating the Scottish victory in return for his release. (7) He cites a London Carmelite, Thomas de Lavington, as his source for the death of James Douglas,(37) and also notes the burial of two plague victims from Calais at the Carmelite church in London.(87)

Despite the lack of direct evidence, it does seem likely that Baker belongs in this Oxford circle. He also quotes (58) from the poet nicknamed 'the Anonymous of Calais' by A.G. Rigg,[1] whose verses would seem to have some kind of context in the world of Oxford scholars of the period. The invective of this poet is not unlike the insults which mendicant friars and secular clergy hurled at each other in the 1350s, a controversy which was especially bitter at Oxford. Finally, if Geoffrey was in fact a member of Edward II's Carmelite foundation at Oxford, it might help to explain his very favourable depiction of the late king.

The secular chroniclers of the fourteenth century: Baker and his sources

Baker is one of a group of men at the beginning of Edward III's reign who are a new kind of chronicler. The traditional home of historians up to this period was the monastery, often well-connected and sometimes with an official or semi-official tradition as the keepers of the royal memory. The monks of Saint-Denis fulfilled this role in France, and the long sequence of historian-monks at St Albans had a similar function in England. Adam Murimuth is the first of the secular historians, and was a canon of St Paul's, where another chronicle was also produced by a writer whose name is lost, the *Annals of St Paul's*. This is much more local in outlook, and probably earlier than Murimuth's work; Murimuth seems to have built on it to produce an account which has a national outlook, drawing on his contacts with the clerks who were involved in the diplomatic negotiations of the early years of Edward's reign. He freely admits that his information is incomplete, and that he himself is outside the charmed circle, but he knows how the government works, and has informants in the king's council as well as among the clerks. He incorporates the newsletters which Edward and his commanders used to keep the regency administration informed, and which served to whip up enthusiasm for the military adventures on the Continent.

Baker copies this chronicle with only minor changes up to 1341, and this corresponds to two surviving manuscripts of Murimuth's work which both end in that year.[2] Murimuth's chronicle exists in versions which end in 1337, 1341, 1343 and at his death in 1347. These are sometimes called editions, but

---

[1] A. G. Rigg, *A history of Anglo-Latin literature 1066–1422*, Cambridge 1992, 260.
[2] BL Cotton Claudius E.VII (c.1400) and Magdalene College, Oxford, MS 53 (first quarter of fifteenth century)

since all the manuscripts are more less identical down to 1337, it is more likely that the original was borrowed and copied at intervals.

Baker adds to Murimuth's account at several points. He offers his own assessment of Piers Gaveston's character, and elaborates on the events surrounding his capture and death. And with the birth of Edward III, his narrative becomes much more detailed, and the rhetorical flourishes which characterise the later pages of his work begin to appear. It is in the events surrounding the abdication of Edward II and his subsequent death that his chronicle comes to life. Firstly, he has access to eye-witness accounts of both occasions. The meeting at Kenilworth at which Edward II was persuaded to surrender the crown is, as Baker is at pains to emphasise, described in the words of Sir Thomas de la More, who was present as a member of John Stratford's retinue. There are other major accounts of the occasion in the Rochester chronicle, the Lanercost chronicle, and one of the Canterbury chronicles, and de la More's account differs in points of fact and in emphasis from these, but is undoubtedly what de la More believed to have happened, written at his dictation.[1] This was a public occasion, and a matter of record; the value is in the detailed narrative of how the negotiations proceeded.

The pages describing the death of Edward II are the most famous passage in Baker's work. Here too we have an eye-witness account of the journey from Corfe Castle to Edward's final place of imprisonment at Berkeley. He writes: 'This story was told me by William Bishop who was still alive after the great plague. He had been in charge of Edward's escort, but in hope of the divine mercy he confessed his sin and in contrition repented of it.' This is only part of a much more complex story, and Baker does not claim that Bishop knew more about the other details of Edward's death: Bishop is sometimes said to have been in charge of Edward's guards,[2] but he was actually only responsible for delivering him into the charge of Thomas Berkeley at Berkeley castle. Baker's narrative is drawn from a number of sources, not simply one witness.

Before we look at those sources, we have to take into account the much broader agenda behind Baker's portrayal of Edward's maltreatment, and indeed of the whole period 1324–7. Roy Martin Haines says of this section of the chronicle:

> It gives every appearance of being a piece of propaganda designed to fasten the blame for what happened on particular individuals and thus to deflect it from Stratford and the baronial supporters of Isabella and Mortimer.[3]

---

[1]   For an analysis of the three other major accounts of the interview, in the Rochester chronicle, the Lanercost chronicle, and one of the Canterbury chronicles, see R.M.Haines, *Archbishop John Stratford*, Toronto 1986, 179-86.

[2]   E.g. in Antonia Gransden's excellent account of the chronicle in her *Historical Writing in England c.1307 to the early sixteenth century*, London 1982, 39.

[3]   Haines, *Archbishop John Stratford*, 409.

Baker creates a triumvirate of villains, responsible for Edward's downfall: for
the whole drift of his argument at this point is that Edward is a good king,
perhaps led astray by his favourites, but ultimately brought down by the
vindictive hatred of Isabella, ably seconded by Mortimer, but aided and abetted
by Adam Orleton, bishop of Hereford until 1327, and later bishop of Worcester
and then Winchester. In the parliament of February 1324, Orleton had been
formally accused of helping Mortimer to escape from imprisonment in the
Tower of London in 1323, and so was associated with Mortimer's rebellion at
an early stage, though he does not in fact seem to have been involved in the
escape. He returned to favour when Isabella's coup succeeded, but became
persona non grata with Edward III in 1333 because he was appointed bishop of
Winchester by papal provision, a procedure which eliminated any possibility
of royal patronage or intervention in the election of a new bishop, and which
was to be prohibited in 1351. The offence was compounded because he had
already moved to Worcester in 1327 by provision, and had had to appear before
parliament the following year to explain himself.[1] Furthermore, a quarrel had
arisen between him and Stratford, and he was therefore an obvious associate
to be blamed alongside with Isabella and Mortimer. If Baker was getting his
information from men within Stratford's entourage, they would have been
able to provide him with the necessary details of the three occasions when he
had been summoned before parliament, and would doubtless have supplied
other rumours of his activities. Lesser details, such as the ambiguous message
which was supposed to have signalled Edward's death, were plundered from
earlier histories.[2]

Orleton's reputation, however, was only an accidental target in the broader
aim of Baker's amplification of Murimuth's text, namely the reinstatement
of Edward II's reputation. And the counterpoint to Baker's presentation of
Edward II as a wronged and eventually martyred king is the blackening of
Isabella's character. He consistently rages against her: she is 'the enraged
virago',[3] 'Jezebel' or simply 'the virago', who spends a year plotting her
revenge before she finally 'prepares to drink its cup'. The idea that Edward
II should be revered as a martyr grew up in the 1330s, and culminated in a
formal attempt by his great-grandson Richard II to have him canonized; but
popular opinion, despite the miracles performed at the great tomb erected for
him in Gloucester Cathedral, was divided: Ranulph Higden, writing in the
1350s, said that 'of his life and his deeds there is still strife among the common
people . . . for neither imprisonment nor persecution prove a man a saint, for
evil-doers suffer such penalties; neither offerings nor apparent miracles prove

---

[1]   R.M. Haines, *The Church and Politics in Fourteenth-Century England: The Career of Adam
        Orleton c.1275-1345*, Cambridge Studies in Medieval Life and Thought 10, Cambridge
        1978, 110.
[2]   Haines, *Church and Politics*, 109: it occurs in a continental chronicle in connection with
        the death of Gertrude queen of Hungary in 1213.
[3]   See pages 20, 21, 24 below

a man a saint, because they are but indifferent proofs of holiness, unless they correspond to holiness of life.'[1]

The only part of Baker's narrative which comes from an eye-witness is the details of the journey from Corfe to Berkeley. The rest of the story depends on other sources, some of which may have been written, some oral. The probable date at which Baker started to write is around 1350,[2] and he is therefore describing the events of Edward II's reign very much at second hand, even though he was marginally involved in the politics of the end of that period. By this date, the chronicles he used included not only the evidence which emerged after Mortimer's death in 1330, but also all the tall tales and rumours which had circulated in the meantime. A much more reliable witness, and one to which Baker is probably indebted, is the chronicle known as the *Brut*, one version of which was completed in 1333, just six years after the king's death. The *Brut* account is much more detailed than Baker's, who has summarised it and misunderstood some of it. According to the *Brut*, when Roger Mortimer had decided that Edward had to be put to death, he sent instructions to Thomas Gournay and John Maltravers who were in charge of the prisoner:

> And when they had the instructions they made the king's father [i.e. Edward II] as much at ease as they could at his supper, and he knew nothing of their treacherous intentions. And when it was time for him to go to bed, and the king lay down to sleep, the false perjured traitors, against their fealty and homage [to him], entered the chamber with their henchman and put a great table on his stomach, pressing down both ends of the table on his body, at which he awoke and turned his body over. Then the traitors like savages took a horn and put it in his fundament as far as they could and took a spit of glowing copper and put it through the horn into his body, stirring it often in his bowels. And so they killed him in such a way that nothing could be seen, and then he was buried at Gloucester.[3]

There are shorter versions of the *Brut*, probably written a year or two before this one, which have no idea as to how the king died, and suggest illness, simply grief at the loss of his power and his imprisonment. Two hint at murder, and one suggests strangulation. Adam Murimuth, on the whole more cautious than the *Brut*, says that the king was suffocated, and this could account for Baker's alteration of the story of crushing under a table to the rather curious heavy mattresses heaped on the king.[4] Later versions of the *Brut* offer an

---

[1]   Ranulph Higden, *Polychronicon*, ed. J. R. Lumby, RS 41, London 1882, viii.324-6. See also Phillips, *Edward II*, 601-3.

[2]   See p.xxiv below

[3]   Marcia Lusk Maxwell, 'The Anglo-Norman Prose 'Brut': an edition of British Library MS Cleopatra D.III', Ph D dissertation, University of Michigan 1995, I, 281; my translation.

[4]   For a full list of the fourteenth century chronicles which discuss the death, see Ian Mortimer, 'Sermons of Sodomy: A Reconsideration of Edward II's Sodomitical Reputation' in *The Reign of Edward II: New Perspectives*, ed. Gwilym Dodd and Anthony Musson, Woodbridge and Rochester NY, 2006, 58-60, supplemented by Phillips, *Edward II*, 561 n.232 which adds eight further sources.

accumulation of anecdotes about the king's fate: a version written around 1400 depicts Gournay's unremitting mockery and taunting of the king, and describe how the drink at his last meal was poisoned. When he was attacked in bed, he leapt out naked, and clung to an iron bar, but was dragged away and tortured before he was killed as described in Baker. Like all such dramatic moments, the legend grew with the passage of time.[1]

The *Brut* is also the probable source of Baker's information about the coup against Mortimer and Isabella at Nottingham in the autumn of 1330. Although he could have heard details of this from the Bohun family, because Edward Bohun was one of the participants in the plot, it would have been at secondhand, since Edward was drowned in Scotland in 1335. The *Brut* offers a much less nuanced story than Baker's: the latter claims that the queen was preparing to go to bed, and that Mortimer was in her chamber, implying that they were lovers, whereas the *Brut* has no such incriminating details, and reports that Isabella cried out when Mortimer was arrested, 'Good sirs, I ask that you do nothing other than good to the person of this noble knight, our very dear and well-loved cousin". Her appeal to the invaders is couched in purely formal terms, while Baker has the king hiding behind the door and Isabella addressing her appeal to him personally as he is seized: ' "Dear boy, dear boy, have pity on gentle Mortimer." For she suspected that her son was there, even if she could not see him.' The scene is changed from an attack on Mortimer to a confrontation between the king and his adulterous mother.

It is only in 1346 that Baker begins to be authoritative, often providing material not found elsewhere. His account of the Breton wars of 1342-5 (in common with almost all the chroniclers) is muddled and ill-informed, but for the Crécy campaign he offers one of the four full diaries of the day by day journeys of the army (70-72). Such diaries were clearly in wide circulation, as no less than ten chroniclers have some kind of narrative of the places through which the army marched. There are also three official or semi-official English documents which give the places where the army stopped each night. The fullest of these is the *Acts of War of Edward III*, a narrative of Edward's 'warlike deeds' on the campaign, but this is unfortunately fragmentary.

The purpose of the *Acts of War of Edward III* is clear: to provide a full record of the triumph of the English army in Normandy in July and August 1346, probably with a view to encouraging support for the war against France. Andrew Ayton has argued that the origin of this material could be the report which Bartholomew Burghersh, one of the leaders of the prince's division, presented to parliament on 13 September 1346.[2] All that the parliament records tells us is that

---

[1]   Oxford, Corpus Christi College MS 78, ff.169-170, printed in *EHR*, xliii, 1928, 216-7.
[2]   Andrew Ayton, 'Crécy and the Chroniclers', in *The Battle of Crécy, 1346*, ed. Andrew Ayton and Philip Preston, Woodbridge 2005, 313-4.

Sir Bartholomew, for himself and for his companions, in the presence of the said keeper [prince Lionel] and of the prelates and other great men . . . declared the graces which God had given our lord the king and the great men and others of his company since their arrival at La Hogue in Normandy, such as good towns, castles and prisons, takings of war, both at Caen and in many other places, and also the victory which God gave them at Crécy, where the enemy of France was defeated with all his great host, and the kings, prelates, dukes, counts, barons and knights and other great men of his people were killed, taken and wounded; and how our lord the king had arrived before Calais, and had laid siege there . . .[1]

The problem is that we have one fragmentary copy of the *Acts of War*, missing four pages at one point, and lacking the vital ending which would probably have contained some account of the battle. This was probably compiled from the records of the clerks with the retinues of the king and of the prince of Wales, since it gives different places for the prince's overnight lodging at one point, which the other documents do not. The records of the king's retinue surviving in the so-called 'kitchen journal' are probably the most accurate as to place, since this set of accounts was written up from the daily notes kept by William Retford, the clerk of the kitchen, during the march; there are only two places where the *Acts of War* differs, and one of these is probably because Retford was unsure of the name of the place in question.[2]

We have also a brief diary of the campaign copied at the end of a manuscript of the shorter version of the *Brut*.[3] It is headed 'This is an account of the deeds and damage[4] which our lord did in the kingdom of France', and reads almost like an outline for the *Acts of War*, though the details differ in a number of places. Its style is very much that of the newsletters which Edward and members of his entourage sent home during the campaigns, and seems to have been written at Calais at the end of September 1346, since it ends with the capture of Thérouanne on 19 September and the destruction of the surrounding countryside during the following week. A diary of this kind also exists for the 1339 campaign in Flanders, and was the basis for Edward's official letter home about his exploits. The diaries must have been a deliberate effort to create a record of the army's activities, as a source for such missives, which are less detailed and concentrate on presenting a favourable version of events. They are distinct from the reports home, the 'campaign letters', and much less common. The only other examples for Edward's reign which survive are those for the 1355—56 campaigns. That for the duke of Lancaster's actions in Normandy in the summer of 1355 is included in Avesbury's chronicle;[5] that

---

[1]   *PROME* IV 389. The other business for that day was fairly brief, so there was time for Burghersh to give a detailed narrative.
[2]   TNA E101/390/11.
[3]   BL, Cotton MS Cleopatra D.vii, f.179, printed in *Chronicon* 253.
[4]   *descomfiturs*: i.e. the discomforts he inflicted on the enemy
[5]   Avesbury in *Murimuth*, 462-5

for the prince's raid into Languedoc in the autumn of the same year is quoted in full by Baker towards the end of his chronicle (110-119); and that for the prince's 1356 march to the Loire is given in the *Eulogium historiarum*, compiled in the early fifteenth century.[1]

The kitchen journal and the campaign diary for the Crécy campaign contain 38 and 37 names respectively, but the lists are often different: there are 44 placenames in all; Baker has 48 placenames, of which ten are not in any of the other three records, but three are in Jean le Bel's chronicle. It looks as if Baker had access to a document similar to that in the campaign diary, and that a number of such histories of the campaign may have been in circulation. After all, this was the most dramatic and successful campaign by an English army that anyone could remember, a possible prelude to the conquest of France, and those who had taken part were eager to record their deeds. During the campaign, we have letters from Bartholomew Burghersh, the chancellor of St Paul's (to 'his friends in London'), Michael Northburgh, and Richard Wynkeley, as well as the king's own account written on September 3. There must have been many more besides these; in 1355 Sir John Wingfield wrote personally to Sir Richard Stafford, and reassured him after giving an account of the campaign that Stafford's own men were all safe.

However, what none of these documents is likely to have contained is a substantial account of the battle. None of the surviving campaign letters, which exist from the late twelfth century onwards, ever gives more than the vaguest details of a battle, though they often give the names of those killed and occasionally numbers of the enemy slain. Once we get to the battle itself, we are looking at a much more literary exercise.

In his account of the battle Baker focuses on the prowess of the prince of Wales, and once again looks forward to his victory at Poitiers in so doing; in his best rhetorical Latin, he evokes the prince as warrior and wonders at the heroic deeds of one so young. A quarter of the description of the battle is taken up by this eulogy, and when we strip away the rhetoric from the rest, he has relatively little specific to say about what happened. If we summarise the actual events that he records, they are as follows:

> The English draw up their forces in three arrays and dismount, with their horses in reserve.
> The French arrange their army in nine divisions. Only the commander of the first, the king of Bohemia, is named.
> The Oriflamme and dragon standard are raised.
> The opening shots are fired by the French crossbowmen, and the English archers respond with deadly effect.
> The first division of French cavalry charge and ride over their crossbowmen, because they are largely untrained and assume the victory will be easy.

---

[1] *Eulogium historiarum*, ed. F. S. Haydon, RS 9, London 1863, iii.221-26

The English stand firm behind the pits they have dug to protect their front (which the French never reach), with their archers carefully placed on the wings so that they did not hinder their own troops.

Many French are crushed to death.

The prince fights in the front line, and is hard pressed, to the point of being forced to his knees; a request for help is sent to the king, who sends twenty knights to support him under an unnamed leader. They find him resting and waiting for the next French attack.

The French raise a warcry three times, and make fifteen attacks on the English, but are defeated and flee.

The following day four further French arrays come up; the war cry is raised again, and they attack the English but are defeated.

The only clearly defined episode reported by Baker is the rescue of the prince of Wales: the episode of his being forced to his knees is reported in French chronicles, but not in English sources.[1] He mentions very few names; on the English side, he fails to name the commanders of the second division, or the commanders who shared responsibility for the first and third divisions. He knows very little about the French commanders, and the list of casualties which he provides comes from an English record of the dead, reported with variations in a large number of other chronicles.

The two tactical elements of the English disposition that he reports, the stationing of the archers on the wings of the army and the pits dug to protect the front line, are not found elsewhere, and have caused a great deal of discussion among military historians. The classic view of English tactics at this period is that the archers were deployed exactly as Baker describes, in massed formations on either side, but this view depends to a considerable extent on this one passage. Given that Baker is writing in a generally rhetorical style, his remarks cannot be taken too literally; in the context, he could well mean simply that the archers were posted on the wings of each array. The detail of the pits is also not found elsewhere; it may simply have been such a normal procedure to most soldiers that it was not felt worthy of mention. It was frequently used in the Scottish wars by both sides, and was probably also used at Morlaix in 1342.[2]

As so often with descriptions of medieval battles – and indeed battles down to the twentieth century where large numbers of troops met in a small area – it is almost impossible for a single observer to have an overview of the action. The impression that we get from Baker's account is that the battle was fought largely in a narrow space (hence the crushing of the French knights) and largely by the first division. Almost everything that he notes could have been witnessed by a member of the prince's division, and the one manoeuvre that he mentions, the relief force sent to the prince, would also have been

---

[1]   *Récits d'un bourgeois de Valenciennes*, ed. Kervyn de Lettenhove, Louvain 1877, p.232.

[2]   *Knighton's Chronicle 1337-1396*, ed. and tr. G.H. Martin, Oxford 1995, 42-3; although this is a late source, the passage seems to be based on a contemporary newsletter.

known to such a witness. However, we do not have to look for a link between Baker and such a witness: it seems that there may be a lost common source behind a number of the English chronicles, and that Baker is merely drawing on this. He may have chosen to retain details which other chroniclers ignored, but equally the evidence would suggest that the nature of this lost description was such that it only gave a general view of the battle.

When we move beyond the Crécy campaign, Baker has a certain amount of apparently original material. He gives a full account of the movement of the Black Death, noting that it struck later in Wales, Ireland and Scotland. He describes the symptoms accurately and in considerable detail, and seems here to draw on personal experience. He also shows detailed knowledge of the efforts of the bishop of London and Sir Walter Mauny to provide a new cemetery in London, as well as of the progress of the plague in the west country. On the other hand, his account of events at Calais early in 1350, when a plot to betray the town was foiled by Edward and the prince in person, is a romanticised version of something widely reported by other writers, notably Robert of Avesbury, another of the secular chroniclers who was like Murimuth attached to the archbishop's administration at Canterbury.

Baker and Robert of Avesbury were writing about the same time; Avesbury's chronicle ends just before the battle of Poitiers, and Baker's immediately after it. Their accounts of the years 1351–56 are similar, but Baker writes at greater length, and has a number of episodes which Avesbury omits. Baker describes the sea-battle of the summer of 1350 at some length, but it is mostly picturesque imagination of what a sea-fight would be like; no specific manoeuvres or actions by individual commanders or knights are mentioned. Avesbury, on the other hand, records that the king embarked from Sandwich, and that the battle was fought off Winchelsea. The same pattern continues for the following years: Baker writes in a more literary style, concerned to tell a lively story if he can, and probably at this stage using eye-witness accounts. Avesbury's material, by contrast, is mainly what would have been reported in official letters. Baker appears either to have been in London at this period, or to have had very good information as to what was going on: an example is the episode of the duel between Thomas de la Marche and Giovanni Visconti. The passage on the taking of Guines may have come from someone involved with drawing up the pardon for John Dancaster, the English archer who mounted a freelance attack on the castle using information gained while he was imprisoned there, or even from Dancaster himself. Again, the duel between the duke of Lancaster and Otto of Brunswick was officially recorded in letters from king John, and Baker may have got the story about Otto's inability to control his horse from a member of the duke's retinue.

The accuracy of Baker's information is at its most important and striking in the prince of Wales's 1355–56 campaign and his account of the battle of Poitiers. His style remains literary, but there is ever-increasing factual content. Again, he seems to have had direct access to documents and other information, some of it probably verbal, specific to this campaign. Just before he begins the account of the prince's raid into Languedoc in October 1355, he gives a fairly brief summary of the movements of the king and the duke of Lancaster in the latter half of 1355, which contrasts sharply with the wealth of information at his disposal about the prince. For the latter, he uses a copy of the 'daily diary of the prince's march', on which the official letter included by Avesbury in his chronicle is based. This is fuller and gives more detail than any of the other diaries we have discussed, particularly on the geography of the country and on the physical difficulties of the march. When it comes to the march towards the Loire in 1356, Baker gives a summary which appears to be based on newsletters. He does at one point give details of an attack on Tours by Bartholomew Burghersh which failed because of torrential rain, which is not found elsewhere.

His description of the battle of Poitiers itself is set out in the same way as that of Crécy. It is prefaced by not one but two speeches by the prince, the first to the army as a whole, and the second to the archers. If the structure of the two set pieces on the prince's victories is the same, at Poitiers he has a great deal to tell us about the manoeuvres during the course of the battle and the individual actions of the commanders. As far as we can tell – and his is the only major contemporary account of the occasion – his information rings true, and can only have come from the men who fought there. The difference between Crécy and Poitiers is that the first was a confused, and at times totally uncontrolled, contest, with the French command completely unable to deploy its troops in any kind of order, and the second was a battle in which the various stages were marked by pauses during which the divisions of the French army manoeuvred in full sight of the English, and could be seen as separate units. Unusually for a medieval battle, the prince and his commanders would have had a fairly good idea of what was happening. Furthermore, it was immediately apparent that this was a momentous victory; the French army had withdrawn, and the English encamped that night in relatively good order. The prince's clerks, particularly if there was someone charged with keeping the daily record, would for once be able to compile an account of the battle on the spot, and would have a very strong incentive for doing so. The narrative seems too confident to be the result of diligent research by Baker himself, or by someone else at a later date. There are few other accounts of battles in medieval chronicles to match it and the history of warfare would be much the poorer without his masterly pages on the action at Poitiers.

Date of composition

This brings us to the question of when Baker is likely to have written his chronicle. It is possible that he copied Murimuth and then inserted additional information later, but in my view it is more likely that the complete book was compiled at some point after 1350, and possibly as late as 1357. If the anecdote about William Bishop is not an insertion, this would give a date after 1349, and there is a reference at the birth of Edward prince of Wales in 1330 that the writer hopes to be spared to describe the prince's victories over the French and his capture of the French king. This would imply that the 1330 entry was written after the events of the battle of Poitiers in 1356.

There is further evidence that when Baker had finished his chronicle, he went back and revised it, but only got as far as 1329. In the one surviving complete text, the section dealing with the beginning of Edward III's reign is duplicated from 1327-1329, the second version being copied immediately after the first.[1] Edward Maunde Thompson, the editor of the Latin original, pointed out that this, and the evidence of the other copy of the chronicle, showed that Baker, apparently having completed the text as a single work down to 1356, then planned to separate his work into the two reigns. In the process, the entry for the birth of Edward prince of Wales is duplicated, and what appears to be the later version omits the comment about the writer 'hoping to be spared'. It would seem that the revisions may only have applied to this section, and were an attempt to reshape the part dealing with Edward III's reign as a separate work, with a particular emphasis on the prince of Wales as a military commander. A plausible chronology would then be that having written the short chronicle, he embarked on the longer work, and having taken this down to 1358, began a revised version at 1330. This would place the approximate date of composition between 1347 and 1360.

This is Baker addressing his readers, and preparing the way for the set piece which, one begins to suspect, he has had in mind as the culmination of his chronicle as he revised it. The pointed references forward, at the birth of the prince of Wales and in the praise of his conduct at Crécy, to the crowning glory of Poitiers, and the fact that he had access to particularly good information about the battle, gave a shape to his work which fitted with Baker's eager patriotism, his belief in Edward's claim to France, and his pointed attempt to belittle the kings of France. He claims that Philip of Valois on his deathbed admitted that he had no right to the throne, and he persistently calls both Philip and John 'the crowned one', to imply their usurpation.

Audience and circulation

The audience for such a chronicle is unlikely to have been a chivalric one, notably because it is in Latin. Anglo-Norman chronicles aimed at a knightly audience were the usual medium through which the knights themselves learned their history, and Baker's Latin, difficult and stylish, would not immediately appeal to them. Another writer, Walter of Peterborough, attempted to portray the prince of Wales's expedition to Spain in 1367 in an

---

[1]   See appendix.p. 135 below.

elegiac Latin poem, which gives confused historical details of the action during the battle of Nájéra. He may have been John of Gaunt's confessor, though the evidence is slight.[1] Other Anglo-Latin literature of the period includes a briefer anonymous Latin poem in praise of the deeds of the prince and his men on that occasion; and there are the poems by 'the Anonymous of Calais' on the battles of Crécy and of Neville's Cross in a similar vein, insulting the enemy and rejoicing in the English victory. Such literature may have had its major audience among the secular clergy, who after all provided many of the senior members of the government as well as most of the king's administration, and among a handful of the great nobles and their households. This may have been a restricted circle, but it was a highly influential one.

Baker's chronicle did not enjoy a wide circulation: only two copies survive, one of which was badly damaged in the fire at the former library of Sir Robert Cotton in 1731. The complete copy is Oxford, Bodleian Library MS 761, dating from around 1365-70; it is a miscellaneous volume, and the first eight items are medicinal, all written by the same scribe. This is followed by a legal document relating to Thomas de Walmesford, mentioned earlier, in a different hand, and then Baker's chronicle, his short chronicle, and four other items, in a third hand. The text is in a single column, and occupies fifty folios. It is clearly written, but appears to be the work of a somewhat unreliable scribe, who was working from Baker's own copy with his revisions in progress. The result is at one point that the text is repeated with variations, as noted above. The second manuscript, now British Library Cotton MS Appendix LII, begins in 1327, and its first leaf is rubbed and worn, implying that it is the outer leaf of the work, and did not have the text for the reign of Edward II at the beginning. The damage in the fire shrank the manuscript, and nineteen leaves were lost: two full quires of eight leaves, and three individual leaves. The remaining text, about half of the text for the reign of Edward III, begins with the same text as the second revised version of the opening of the reign in the Bodleian manuscript, followed by a generally more accurate text for the remainder of the period.

Baker's text does not seem to have a wide circulation, since other historians do not appear to have used it; however, it was known to Elizabethan historians including Holinshed and John Stow. For example, Baker's version of Edward II's death appears in both Holinshed's *Chronicles* of 1577 and Stow's *Annales of England*, of 1605, the two most influential history books of late sixteenth century England; and much other material from his book was also incorporated, so that his more dramatic episodes became part of a kind of authorised version of English history. From Holinshed and Stow, his stories were copied and recopied down to the nineteenth century by later popular historians.

---

[1]   Rigg, *A History of Anglo-Latin Literature 1066-1422*, 276

Chronology

One of the problems with Baker's chronicle is his erratic chronology in the years up to 1346. He has adopted the style of Adam Murimuth for reckoning the years of the Christian era, which makes each year begin at Michaelmas, and this leads to considerable confusion. The correct year is given at the head of each page below, while errors in individual dates are indicated in the notes.

Style

Baker's Latin is reasonably fluent and competent, but does not necessarily indicate a university training or much education beyond the level of a grammar school. His use of quotations similarly is that which could be expected of a well-taught pupil at grammar school level, with the exception of two quotations from Galen and Hippocrates, which might indicate training for a medical degree, but are not signioficant enough to be positive. There is nothing, however, to preclude an association with the Carmelite friars of Oxford, as suggested earlier in the introduction.

RICHARD BARBER

A note on the translation

The generously detailed notes and index of Sir Edward Maunde Thompson's edition of the Chronicle were a great aid to translation, as was his inclusion of long passages of Stow's translation of the Chronicle from his *Annales*. The Elizabethan vigour of Stow's language was not to be matched, but I have tried to put into reasonably simple English the idiosyncratic Latin of a writer who sometimes seems more concerned with the cumulative power of his narrative than with clarity.

DAVID PREEST

The Chronicle of Geoffrey le Baker of Swinbrook

In the one thousand three hundred and third year after the birth of the only-begotten omnipotent king Jesus Christ, in the eighth year of pope Boniface, the eighth pope of this name, and in the thirty-first year of the reign of the noble king Edward of Winchester, the son of Henry king of the English, the Scots slew and treacherously manhandled the guardians and officers whom Edward put in charge of the kingdom of Scotland and its castles. So around the time of Pentecost Edward rode across Scotland with an army, and, when he had captured and killed some of the rebels and caused others to flee from the face of the sword to islands or underground hiding-places, he returned to England. After the king had gone away, the Scots came back from their lairs and their exile and laid siege to Stirling castle.[1] The king had entrusted the safe-keeping of the castle to no more than forty Englishmen. When they had used up their food supplies and were eating horses, dogs, dormice and mice, they finally at last surrendered the castle, which they had defended for a long time, with their lives and limbs intact. They could not deal with both the Scots and that one thing which often on its own causes the capture of the strongest castles, namely hunger. Afterwards the king laid siege to Brechin castle and within twenty days took it by storm.

In this year the peace between the kings of England and of France was renewed, and Gascony, which for quite some time had been unjustly held by the French, was restored to the English.[2]

Also in this year on the eve of the feast of the Nativity of the Blessed Mary, pope Boniface, whom I mentioned above, was taken prisoner in Campania, in the town of Anagni from which he originated. This capture was brought about by the king of France through his envoys, Guillaume de Nogaret[3] and Guillaume Deplessis, and with the consent of the household and neighbours of the pope himself. Also the treasure of the church was taken as plunder. [2][4] Indeed the pope himself was forcibly seated and tied to a wild horse, with his face turned towards the tail of the unbridled animal, and, after being exhausted by the excessive speed of his mount, he died a terrible death on 11 October 1303, uttering a sentence of excommunication right up to the ninth degree upon the degenerate sons of the family of the royal blood of France.

---

[1] The siege of Stirling took place in 1299. See F.D. Watson, *Under The Hammer: Edward I and Scotland, 1286-1307*, East Linton 1998.

[2] Aquitaine was restored in May 1303: *Foedera*, I.ii.955.

[3] Chancellor of France. For a detailed account of the whole affair, see A. Duc de Lévis Mirepoix, *L'attentat d'Anagni. Le conflit entre le papauté et le roi de France, 7 Septembre 1303*, Paris 1969, and Joseph Strayer, *The Reign of Philip the Fair*, Princeton, NJ, 1980. The pope was not murdered in the way described, but was freed by the inhabitants of Anagni. However, he died shortly after his return to Rome.

[4] References in square brackets are to the pagination of E. M. Thompson's edition.

In the following year, that is AD 1304, Boniface was succeeded by pope Benedict XI. He was a Lombard by birth and he was elected pope at Rome on 22 October and crowned the following Sunday. He was first a member of the Dominican order and later became cardinal of Ostia. Finally he became pope and excommunicated and proclaimed as excommunicated all who were privy to the capture of his predecessor. He later died on 7 July.

In this year king Edward marched into Scotland and for ninety days vigorously besieged with frequent assaults the castle of Stirling, which was being defended by William Oliphant. When the besieged no longer had the strength to resist, they came out shoeless and with their necks tied with ropes. They prostrated themselves before the king, entrusting their lives and limbs to his mercy, and the king in his piety preserved their lives and sent them to England to be put in prison.

In AD 1305, the first year of Benedict XI and the thirty-third year of the first king Edward after the conquest, the king celebrated the solemn feast of Christmas at Lincoln. He also established judges of trailbaston, who were to punish such malefactors throughout the whole of England. As the judges punished many, the treasury of the king was greatly enriched.[1]

In this year William Wallace, who previously had committed many crimes against the English in Scotland and the parts adjoining it, was drawn, hung and beheaded in London.[2]

Robert Bruce, who was an Englishman by birth, wished to usurp the kingdom of Scotland, by using his wife's rights and without the knowledge and consent of his liege lord the king of England.[3] So, around the time of the Feast of the Purification,[4] he called a meeting of Scottish nobles, which was held in the church of the Franciscans at Dumfries. [3] But at this meeting Bruce slew lord John Comyn, a loyal friend of the king, because he opposed his conspiracy.[5]

Then, on the feast of Pentecost[6] at Westminster, the king decorated Edward of Caernarfon, his firstborn son, with the belt of knighthood, and together with him he made one hundred other men knights.[7] He also endowed his son

[1]   On 'trailbaston', see Prestwich, *Edward I*, 285. Trailbaston was originally designed as 'a commission to make inquiries and arrests, rather than to determine cases'; so many prisoners were taken that corresponding judicial circuits had to be set up to expedite the trials. See also Caroline Burt: ' "The Peace Less Kept"? The Origins, Revelations and Impact of Edward I's Trailbaston Commissions of 1305-7', in *Thirteenth Century England, XII*, eds. J. Burton, P. Schofield, B. Weiler, Woodbridge 2009, 123-37.

[2]   See G.W.S. Barrow, *Robert Bruce and the Community of the Realm of Scotland*, Edinburgh 2005, 193-5.

[3]   The fact that Bruce was English by birth is incorrect, as is the idea that his claim to the throne was through his wife.

[4]   2 February.

[5]   G.W.S. Barrow, *Robert Bruce* (n.5 above), 205-8. For the Bruce family and descent, see Ruth M. Blakely, *The Brus Family in England and Scotland, 1100-1295*, Woodbridge, 2005.

[6]   22 May.

[7]   Other chroniclers give estimates varying from 97 to 297: *Croniques de London*, ed. G. J. Aungier, Camden Society Original Series xxviii, London, 1844, 31; *The Chronicle of Walter of Guisborough*, ed. Harry Rothwell, Camden Society Third Series lxxix, 1957, 367-8.

with the duchy of Aquitaine. Also, on the king's order, Piers Gaveston swore an oath, renouncing the kingdom of England.[1]

Then, around the feast of the Nativity of the Blessed Virgin,[2] the king again invaded Scotland with a large army. For the whole of the following winter and summer he successfully settled many matters which he wished to deal with, but he left behind the heaviest of tasks for his successors when death snatched him away prematurely.

For he left the light of day on the feast of the translation of St Thomas the martyr,[3] in the 59th year of his life, the 35th year of his reign from the death of his father and the 33rd from his coronation, and the 1307th year from the birth of Christ. His body was buried at Westminster on 28 October and awaits the resurrection and the everlasting kingdom.

In the year just mentioned, that is AD 1307, after Edward of Winchester had entered upon the road of all flesh, as I have written above, he was succeeded as king by his firstborn son, Edward of Caernarfon, the second Edward after the conquest. Immediately after receiving his father's crown, he crossed the channel with the intention of improving relations between himself and Philip the Fair king of the French, who had formerly been greatly estranged from him. The fire of the Holy Spirit kindled such a warmth of love between them that on 28 January[4] at Boulogne king Edward joined to himself in marriage Isabella the daughter of the king of France, amid a great crowd of kings and nobles from both kingdoms. Then on 5 February the king of England returned to England with his wife and a great company of nobles, and on 23 February[5] in the same year at Westminster he celebrated Shrove Sunday wearing his royal crown and accompanied by his wife wearing her crown.[6]

I should not omit to mention the fact that, while the king was waiting in France to marry his wife, he was visited by Piers Gaveston, his one time friend but now an exile [4] on his father's order. The king took him back to England from exile and also gave him the earldom of Cornwall and the daughter of his sister as wife, his sister being Lady Joan de Acre, the countess of Gloucester. Piers was ... by birth.[7] He was handsome, nimble, quick-witted, of an inquisitive disposition and fairly well practised in the arts of war. Those in a position to speak about him testify that, while Gaveston was in command

[1]   *Foedera*, i.ii.1010 (26 February 1307). Gaveston was banished because of his undue influence over prince Edward. See Phillips, *Edward II*, London 2010, 100-3, for the relationship between Gaveston and Edward, which Phillips suggests may have been that of sworn brotherhood. There is an extended discussion of Edward's relationships in W.M.Ormrod, 'The sexualities of Edward II', in *The Reign of Edward II*, ed. Gwilym Dodd and Anthony Musson, Woodbridge and Rochester NY 2007, 22-32.

[2]   8 September.

[3]   7 July.

[4]   The marriage was actually on 25 January: Phillips, *Edward II*, 134

[5]   Actually 25 February; see Phillips, *Edward II*, 140.

[6]   i.e. Edward II's coronation took place on this day.

[7]   He was the son of a minor Gascon lord. See J.S. Hamilton, *Piers Gaveston, Earl of Cornwall: Politics and Patronage in the Reign of Edward II*, Detroit 1988, and P. Chaplais, *Piers Gaveston, Edward II's Adoptive Brother*, Oxford 1994. Piers' wife was Margaret de Clare.

of the army in Scottish lands, the heroism of the English greatly scared the Scots and stopped them from plundering and other acts of madness. But when Gaveston was taken from their midst through the envy of those who hated his happy successes, the cunning Scots were wide awake once more and, white hot with rage, launched attacks on the governors, whom the English king had put in command of the castles of Scotland.

Present at Edward's coronation which I mentioned above were Charles, brother of the queen and the future king of France; Charles of Valois, brother of the king of France and the father of Philip the first usurper of the kingdom of the French[1] and the duke of Brittany; also Henry count of Luxembourg who was later emperor. But Piers Gaveston outshone them all in the splendour of his dress and apparel, thus inspiring general resentment and a wicked hatred of his person, in that he challenged prerogatives which pre-eminently belonged to the nobility alone.[2]

In AD1309 and the third year of his reign the king wanted to put to rest the minds of those envious of Piers and to quieten the mutterings of his detractors.[3] So he sent Piers in person with a strong force across to Ireland to deal with the Irish rebels, assigning him a stipend from the king's treasury to be paid by the exchequer there. Lifted high by this appointment, he did achieve some successes, but these only led to his downfall. It was not for long that fortune continued to show him a shining face. The year in which he returned from Ireland[4] to a glad welcome in the king's household had not fully run its course when the feelings of hatred against Gaveston, formerly kept hidden, were now brought into the open. Vehemently expressed in words and signs, they mushroomed among those who thought they would be serving God and benefiting their country, if the foreigner Piers, who by his success was eclipsing the glory of native Englishmen, were to be deprived of life or of a home in England.

---

[1]   Baker is assiduous in his denial of the legitimacy of the French kings throughout his chronicle, calling them usurpers or in the case of John II, 'the crowned one' rather than the king. He consistently portrays Edward as the undisputedly legitimate king of France.

[2]   The hostility to Gaveston on the occasion of the coronation is recorded in the *Annales Paulini* written by one of the clergy at St Paul's. The author claimed that one of the English earls wished to kill Gaveston on the spot (262). He also records several disasters during the proceedings, including the death of a knight when a wall near the high altar collapsed because of the crowd pressing against it (260-1). See Hamilton, *Piers Gaveston*, 44.

[3]   Baker's chronology is confused here, and events up to his death are telescoped. Gaveston was formally exiled on 18 May 1308 (*Foedera*, ii. 44) in response to pressure from the baronial party led by Henry de Lacy, earl of Lincoln, but it was only on 16 June that Edward appointed him lieutenant in Ireland, faced with the prospect of an armed rebellion by the earls. He sailed from Bristol on 25 June.

[4]   He returned after just under a year on 27 June 1309 (Hamilton, *Piers Gaveston* 73). He and Edward campaigned in Scotland in 1310-11, and it was on the way south that Edward placed him in Bamburgh. He was exiled again from 3 November 1311, but returned with the king's connivance in January 1312. Gaveston was besieged in Scarborough castle, and surrendered to the earls on 19 May 1312, at which point Pembroke swore to guarantee his safety.

So, to save Piers from the power of the nobles, the king placed him in Bamburgh castle, claiming that he did this to please the nobles. [5] But even so there was no escape for the pious king himself from the insults and lies of the nobles.

In AD 1311 around the feast of the nativity of John Baptist, Piers for his own safety was recalled from Bamburgh castle and was entrusted to the custody of Aymer de Valence, earl of Pembroke. In the king's presence, the earl looked upon that holiest of things, the sacrament on the altar, and swore that to the best of his ability he would keep Piers safe against all his enemies for an agreed period. Before the end of this period the king aimed to have reconciled Piers with the nobles of the kingdom by some means or other. But Piers' protector was persuaded, both by the jealousy which on great issues challenges loyalty and also by his love for pleasing Piers' enemies, to break his oath that he would take care of Piers. In the end Piers was taken quite against his will by this hostile friend to Dedington manor between Oxford and Warwick. There he was right in the middle of powerful enemies and with no natural hiding place or any man-made castle or fortress, which could separate him from his neighbour, the earl of Warwick. At nightfall Aymer left Piers on his own, and at dawn Guy, earl of Warwick, arrived with a small force and hue and cry. He then took Piers to Warwick castle, and, after discussing the matter with Thomas earl of Lancaster and the earl of Hereford, on 19 June he had Piers beheaded before their eyes at a place called Gaversike.[1] The king committed his body to honourable burial in the church of the Dominican friars at Langley.[2]

In the same year pope Clement V held a council at Vienne, which began on the first day of October and which lasted until Pentecost. During the council the pope condemned the order of the Templars, at the instigation of the king of France, Philip the Fair, who was present at the council. The king hated the grand master of the Templars because of his persistent demand for the money which the first provincial of France had once loaned to the king for the marriage of his daughter Isabella as queen of England. Also king Philip hoped that one of his sons would be crowned as king of Jerusalem, and then also enriched by booty from the destruction of the Templars. For this reason king Philip had the master and many others of that order [6] living in his kingdom burnt to death, and the order and its whole council annihilated. But his scheme did not satisfy his cruel greed, for the pope assigned the lands and possessions of the exterminated Templars to the Hospitallers, and sent to England a cardinal, accompanied by the bishop of Albano, so that they might release the properties from the Templars' control. But these two met with resistance from the heroes of the English, whose forefathers had enriched the Templars with vast estates, and who, when the Templars had been condemned, seized

---

[1]   Blacklow Hill, near Warwick.
[2]   The body was taken by Dominicans to Oxford, but as Gaveston was excommunicate at the time of his death, they did not bury him there. The burial at Langley took place on 3 January 1315. See Hamilton, *Piers Gaveston*, 97-100 for a full account of his death.

the reverted properties for themselves. So the pope's envoys returned home without having accomplished the purpose of their visit.[1]

In AD 1312 in the sixth year of Edward II on the feast day of St Brice the confessor,[2] queen Isabella gave birth at Windsor to a son for the king. In his time he would be called the third Edward after the conquest.[3] He was to be the great conqueror of the French, the terror of the Scots, and the one who by direct line of descent from the royal blood of England and France would inherit both kingdoms. In this year the king had such joy in his baby son and in his queen, whom he loved deeply and cherished tenderly, that, to avoid causing her any uneasiness, he concealed the distress which he felt at Piers' death. But his foresight had its limitations, for he did not know where to find a loyal friend with whom he might share his secret plans or to whom he might entrust his life when it was in danger. For the death of Piers had openly or secretly stopped many nobles from being his friends. Also while the king himself neglected warfare and spent his time on amusements which were sometimes real but sometimes a pretence, and while the nobles of the realm were busy with seizing the moment to put Piers to death, Robert Bruce captured almost all the castles and forts of Scotland, and removed or killed the custodians assigned to them by the king and his father.[4]

In the following year, on the advice and orders of the prelates and other nobles, Hugh Despenser the son was appointed chamberlain to the king in the place of Piers, who had recently been taken from their midst. Unless those competent to speak are generally lying, the king had shown very little love for Hugh the younger up to now and in fact had positively hated him; and that is why the prelates and nobles were more than happy to choose him for this position, although later, when the king became more friendly towards Hugh the son, they came thoroughly to hate him. Happily Hugh the father was still then living. He was a highly virtuous knight, a farsighted counsellor and vigorous on the battlefield.[7] His natural but inordinate love for his son whom he loved from the bottom of his father's heart increased the distress and shame of his death. The son was extremely handsome in physique, excessively haughty in attitude and deeply depraved in deed. It was his spirit of ambition and greed that precipitated him from the disinheriting of widows and orphans to the murder of the highest nobles of the king and the destruction of himself and his father.[5]

[1]   On the suppression of the Templars, see Malcolm Barber, *The Trial of the Templars*, Cambridge 1978, 193-204, 222-3.
[2]   13 November
[3]   From this point, Baker's chronicle diverges from Murimuth in many details.
[4]   The first attempt to take a great fortress, an attack on Berwick in December 1312 failed, but in 1313, Perth, Dumfries, Roxburgh and Edinburgh all fell. See Phillips, *Edward II*, 224.
[5]   On Hugh Despenser the younger, see M. Lawrence, 'Rise of a royal favourite', in *The Reign of Edward II*, 205-19, and Phillips, *Edward II*, 363-8.

In AD 1314 and the seventh year of the reign of the king, the knights of England were unable to endure the losses inflicted upon them in Scotland by Robert Bruce and the traitors who supported his disloyal conspiracy against the king of England. So, on the eve of the nativity of St John Baptist, they assembled under the leadership of the king near the town of Scotland called Stirling by the natives. The might of England, which up to then had always fought their battles from horseback, brought with them numbers of charging war-horses and much gleaming armour and a large force of fighting men. Their rashness was very presumptuous for they flattered themselves into expecting the victory which the General of the universe usually gives to those who despair of the strength of their forces. They were so confident their victory was assured that they had had brought with them, besides the supplies, necessary for war, of horses, weapons and food, also the silver and golden vessels with which in time of peace men are accustomed to enrich the banquets of the princes of the world.

Those present then never before or afterwards ever saw so many nobles entrusting to the sole favour of Mars the god of war such a finely equipped force swollen by so much pride. That poor Carmelite friar Robert Baston, who was present at the battle and captured by the Scots, has sorrowfully lamented this confidence in his epic poem about the campaign.[1] You would have seen the English that night not living like angels[2] but dripping with wine, drunkenly belching, and bellowing 'Wassail' and 'Drinkhail' louder than usual. On the other side you might have seen the silent Scots keeping a holy watch by fasting, but with their blood boiling with a fervent love for the liberty of their country, which, although unjust, made then ready to die on her behalf.[3]

The next day the Scots occupied the most suitable place on the battlefield for victory and dug ditches three feet deep and wide which extended in a long line from the right to the left wing of their army. These they covered with a thin [8] mesh of branches and reeds or wickerwork hurdles. Then above this mesh they laid turves and grass, so that men on foot could get across this area if they remembered to be careful enough, while it was not strong enough to bear the weight of cavalry.

The Scots, with their army in its usual divisions, stood drawn up in a solid array not far from the ditch between themselves and the English, which they had devised, I will not say as a trap, but as a precaution. Their leader the king had forbade any of them to mount their war-horses. On the other side, as the English army advanced from the west, the rising sun shone on their golden helmets and polished shields, and, since its golden rays were dazzling the

---

[1]   Robert Baston's poem is printed in *Joannis de Fordun Scotichronicon,* ed. Walter Goodall, Edinburgh 1759, ii. 250-5.

[2]   'Anglorum non angelorum': a reference to pope Gregory's remark on seeing the English slaves at Rome – 'Non Angli sed angeli'. This in turn is a paraphrase of Bede, *Historia Ecclesiastica,* book ii, ch.1.

[3]   The standard account of the battle is G.W.S. Barrow, *Robert Bruce and the Community of Scotland,* third edition, Edinburgh 1988, 209-229. See also Phillips, *Edward II,* 228-235 and Aryeh Nusbacher, *Bannockburn 1314,* Stroud 2005.

vision of the English troops, Alexander the Great in such a position and at such a time would have delayed the battle for at least an hour, and would have waited until the midday sun was on the right hand before deciding the issue. But the pity of it! The impetuous, stiff-necked English, preferring death to a postponement of the conflict, drew up in the front line the division of those riding war-horses and large coursers. These failed to notice the Scottish ditch, which, as I have said, was disguised by a thin covering. In the second array were the foot-soldiers, together with the archers who were kept in reserve for when the enemy fled. In the third array came the king and his bishops and other men of religion, including that cowardly knight Hugh Despenser.

The horsemen of the front line advanced upon the enemy but they fell, thrown headlong from their horses, as the forefeet of their tottering mounts pierced the woven coverings and became fixed in the ditch. They could now see that they were exposed to every cruel attack of their enemies falling upon them from above, and indeed, as the English collapsed, the enemy were upon them, killing and capturing and sparing only the rich for ransom. It was there and then that Gilbert, the earl of Gloucester, fell. The Scots would willingly have put him aside for ransom, if they had recognised him by his coat of arms, but he was not wearing it that day. The earl was accompanied on death's journey by Edmund Mauley, Robert Clifford, Payn Tybetot, Giles de Argentine and many other knights. But among those kept for ransom were Humphrey[1] de Bohun earl of Hereford, John Segrave, John Clavering, William Latimer and almost three hundred knights. In this disastrous slaughter some met their death because the archers' unit did not have a suitable station given to it. At that time the archers [9] were generally stationed behind the infantry, whereas now the practice is to put them beside it. When the archers saw the Scots making their savage attack on the men who had fallen into the ditch, some shot their arrows into the sky, only for these to fall harmlessly among the helmets of the enemy, but others, who shot their arrows straight ahead, killed a few Scots in their chests but many English in their backs.[2]

So yesterday's pomp and swagger came to nothing. The king and his bishops and the Despenser took to their heels, seeking safety in flight, but no human skill or speed of horses or hiding places could have kept them safe from capture by the Scots, if Christ, who passed through the middle of the Jews unrecognised,[3] had not listened to the prayers of his mother and rescued the king from Scottish lands. Indeed not only the king himself but also those who fled with him later admitted this. While the king was fleeing in great peril, he vowed to God and to the Virgin, the mother of her beloved, that

---

[1]   Baker wrongly calls him Wilfred.
[2]   This was one of the major reasons for the English defeat. At Falkirk in 1298, the English archers had been brought into play, firing from the flanks to break up the Scottish schiltrons, tight formation of spearmen which the cavalry charges were unable to penetrate and which were the cause of most of the English casualties.
[3]   John 8:9

he would found a monastery fit for habitation for her poor Carmelites, who would be given the special distinction of the name of the mother of God: the king himself would help with the necessary expenses for the twenty four brothers sent there to study theology. The lord pope John XXII approved the vow and the king fulfilled it, assigning to these brothers the free and perpetual alms of his palace at Oxford, although Hugh Despenser argued against it.[1] This happened in theyear of his reign and also in theyear of the lord pope John.[2]

In AD 1315 the Scots under the command of Edward Bruce, who had himself named as king of Ireland by his men, invaded Ireland with unfurled banners, but they were killed in great numbers together with their pseudo-king by those fighting under the banner of lord John de Birmingham, who was then the justiciar of the king of England.[3]

At the same time England endured widespread plague and famine, with a quarter of corn now costing 40 shillings sterling.[4]

In AD 1316 in the first year of lord pope John XXII two cardinals were sent to England and Scotland to arrange peace between the kingdoms. After a discussion with the English king they were travelling towards Scotland, when, in the diocese of Durham, they were attacked and robbed by the knight Gilbert Middleton, who later was hung and divided into quarters [10] for this. Robert Bruce refused to allow these special envoys to enter Scotland, and in return for this the two cardinals excommunicated Robert and his followers and put the kingdom of Scotland under ecclesiastical interdict. When the cardinals were finally returning through England to the Roman curia, as compensation for what they had lost to the robbers they received double the amount from the king and the nobles of the land, who had collected it on their own initiative.[5]

In AD 1317 Robert Bruce forcefully took the castle and town of Berwick, killing nobody who was willing to obey him.[6]

<hr>

[1]   Established in the old palace of Beaumont, otherwise known as King's Hall, in 1317.
[2]   Blanks in original MS. Baker had evidently seen the original deed, which no longer survives, so the dates cannot be completed.
[3]   Edward Bruce was in Ireland for three years; he was defeated and killed near Dundalk in October 1318. See Colm McNamee, *The wars of the Bruces: Scotland, England and Ireland 1306-1328*, East Linton 1997, and Sean Duffy (ed.), *Robert Bruce's Irish Wars: The Invasions of Ireland, 1306-1329*, Stroud 2002.
[4]   For which see Ian Kershaw, 'The Great Famine and Agrarian Crisis in England, 1315-1322', *Past & Present*, lix, 1973, 3-50.
[5]   This account and the following three paragraphs are taken from Murimuth, 27-32. Baker simply omits the reports of church affairs in his source, concentrating on English affairs.The cardinals were Luca di Fieschi and Gaucelin d'Eauze, cardinals of St Mary in Lata and SS Marcellinus & Peter. See Michael Prestwich, 'Gilbert de Middleton and the attack on the Cardinals, 1317', *Warriors and Churchmen in the Middle Ages: essays presented to Karl Leyser*, ed. T. Reuter. London 1992, 179-94
[6]   Berwick was betrayed to the Scots on 2 April 1318.

Also in August of the same year on open ground near Leicester the king and the earl of Lancaster were reconciled with kisses and many embraces of each other. They had been mutual enemies ever since the death of Piers Gaveston, to the great danger of the kingdom and the applause of the Scots.[1]

In the autumn of AD 1318 the king ravaged a great part of Scotland and settled down to besiege Berwick castle. But the Scots invaded England and laid waste the country as far as York, looting and burning as they went. The news of this misfortune recalled the king to the defence of his own kingdom, while the Scots returned to their own land, avoiding the king and going by another route.[2]

In the June of AD 1319 the king of England crossed the Channel and met Philip the king of France at Amiens. He received back from him the countship of Ponthieu, which the French king had seized just after becoming king because Edward had not paid him homage.[3]

In AD 1320, the fourteenth year of the reign of king Edward II, there arose a lamentable split between the king and his loyal subjects on the one hand and the earls of Hereford and Lancaster and the other barons on the other. There also began that civil war which escalated from the destroying of the barons to the deposition of the king and the disinheriting of almost all the royal blood. For out of envy, the barons of the land had become white-hot with hatred against Hugh Despenser the younger, the chamberlain of the king. There were those among them who had said that Hugh was a second king, or worse, the ruler of the king, and that, like Piers Gaveston, he had bewitched the king's mind. He had so far presumed on his friendship [11] with the king that he had often prevented some of the nobles from speaking with him. Also, when on occasions some of them were speaking to the king on various personal matters, the kind attention of the king would be turned elsewhere and Despenser himself would give them answer. Merely claiming that it would inconvenience the king to do so, he would flood them with unwelcome replies which were contrary to their wishes. I admit the truth of these things to Hugh's discredit, but I do not go as far as the chattering crowd who knew how

---

[1]   'The kiss of peace between Edward and Lancaster and the Treaty of Leake brought to an end one of the most prolonged periods of tension and certainly the most tortuous set of negotiations since 1307.' Phillips, *Edward II*, 290-321 gives a full account. The date of the reconciliation was 7 August 1318.

[2]   Despite major preparations for the expedition, which reached Berwick on 7 September 1319, the campaign was a failure, partly because of the defeat of the York militia at Boroughbridge on 12 September.

[3]   Edward performed homage for Aquitaine and Ponthieu in the cathedral at Amiens on 30 June 1320.

to describe him as worse than he was by using their imaginations and indeed in their words to make his misdeeds more awful than the actuality.[1]

For such and similar offences, of the sort often given by a king's ministers, Hugh began to be deeply hated by the nobles of the kingdom. Burning with a furious desire for revenge and in their hatred of Hugh the son and his followers, the nobles seized all the estates of Hugh the father that they found in the principality of Wales and the marches, ransacked the lands and other goods of both of them that they found in England, and also under oath made a conspiracy to kill both Hughs and any other friend of theirs, with the exception of those revered because of their royal blood.

The leaders of the conspiracy were the earl of Hereford, Roger Mortimer, Maurice Berkeley, Bartholomew Badlesmere, Roger D'Amory and Henry Tyes. The earl of Pembroke was on their side in secret, but the earl of Lancaster supported them ardently and openly. Hugh thought that their furious anger could be cooled by the passing of time and so he absented himself for a while and on the king's order took to a ship and lay in hiding, now across the sea, and now on the sea itself. Finally in a parliament held in Westminster both the Hughs were banished, with the sentence being passed against them in their absence. The king was not in agreement but did not dare to voice his opposition in fear of civil discord.[2]

In 1321 around the feast of St Michael when the queen, lady Isabella, came on a journey to Leeds castle in Kent and wished to spend the night there, she was firmly denied entrance.[3] The king regarded the rejection of the queen as tantamount to contempt of himself, and ordered the people round about and the men of Essex and some Londoners to lay siege to the castle. Bartholomew Badlesmere was the keeper of the castle, but he left his wife and children there with some servants who would be able to defend it, [12] and himself set off with other barons to destroy the rich properties of Hugh. But as the king pressed on fiercely with the siege of the castle, while those shut inside it despaired of its safety, the earls and barons who were laying waste to Hugh's property, supported by a large company of armed men, came to Kingston on the eve of the feast of the apostles Simon and Jude.[4] From there they sent the lords of Canterbury and London and the earl of Pembroke as messengers to the king, asking that he should give up his siege of the castle and promising that after the next parliament they would surrender and return the castle to

---

[1]   Despenser's high-handed activities in pursuit of the inheritance of his wife, Eleanor de Clare, and the establishment of a powerful lordship in the Welsh marches based on her lands, were the immediate cause of the rebellion.

[2]   The parliament took place on 14 August 1321, by which time the Despensers were already out of England. *CCR 1318-23*, 494; Phillips, *Edward II*, 393.

[3]   Edward apparently sent her there in the hope that she would be refused entrance, and he would thus have an excuse to attack Badlesmere.

[4]   Edward summoned troops from the counties around London on 16-17 October, and arrived to press the siege on 25 October: (Baker's date is 27 October) *CCR 1318-23*, 504-5; *Foedera* ii, i, 457-8; *CPR 1321-4*, 29; TNA E 101/378/11.

the king. But as the king did not think that the guardians of the castle could hold out much longer and as he was exasperated by its rebellious inmates, he was unwilling to listen to the pleas of the barons. Finally, when the barons had departed elsewhere, the castle after much labour was captured and six of the braver men found in it were hanged without delay. The wife and sons of Bartholomew Badlesmere were sent by the king to the custody of the Tower of London.

On the following nativity of our Saviour the king celebrated Christmas at Cirencester and then gathered an army and set off for the Welsh marches. He went down the hill to Gloucester, which was occupied by some barons prepared for rebellion, and then led his army via Worcester to Bridgnorth. The castle there was held against him for some time but in the end the king took it forcefully by storm. Some of the defenders were killed. Others he put to flight and outlawed, while confiscating all their possessions that could be found anywhere in his kingdom. The king next advanced to Shrewsbury, where both Roger Mortimers gave themselves up to whatever respect and peace terms they could get from the king's majesty. He sent them both to custody in the Tower of London. Maurice de Berkeley and Henry Audley, who like the Mortimers submitted to the king, were sent by him to Wallingford castle. The earl of Hereford, Gilbert Talbot and Roger D'Amory and all their followers took themselves to the earl of Lancaster who was waiting for them in northern parts.

After these events,[1] at a council held in London presided over by the archbishop, it was pronounced by the prelates of the province of Canterbury that the processes of exile against the two lord Despensers were an error and null and void in law. The prelates with the council then decreed that the exiles should be restored to their former honour.

[13] In AD 1321[2] the barons offered no peace terms to the king but persisted in their rebellion against the laws of the land. Without consulting the king and against his wishes, they collected together a force of armed knights serving under their unfurled banners. So the king recalled his army and about the end of February moved his troops northwards. The barons showed spirit and waited for his arrival, but, after some sort of battle at Burton on Trent[3] between the king's battle array and that of the earls of Lancaster and Hereford, the earls fled from the superior power of the king, which in the following week was considerably increased by many men from Humberside under the command of Andrew Harclay.

---

[1]   This is incorrect: the archbishop of Canterbury declared the action against the Despensers unlawful on 1 January 1322, and the Mortimers did not surrender until three weeks later.

[2]   1322

[3]   There were three days of skirmishes in early March. Harclay did not actually join up with Edward, but was still acting independently when the battle at Boroughbridge took place. Edward met Harclay and his captives at Pontefract on 21 March.

Then the resolve of the barons wavered, and some of them suggested that they should throw themselves on the king's grace and mercy and promise him the reverence and submission due from them. But this advice was hateful to the earl of Lancaster. He felt such security from his close relationship with the royal blood that no mishap frightened him from his purpose because he was afraid of none, especially since he claimed that he had taken up arms not against the king but against that traitor to the kingdom, Hugh Despenser.

The earl of Hereford, Humphrey de Bohun, was also against surrender. Ever a fighter, he possessed strength of body, fearlessness of spirit and some wisdom in counsel, and he was driven to continue with the revolt they had begun because he was afraid for the dangers surrounding the ordinary soldiers who were following him, whether he was right or wrong. For these people, so he thought, could not be reconciled to the king and the Despensers without the punishment of death or a completely impoverishing ransom. So the chivalrous earl, because of his innate goodness, chose to be defeated in war and to die what seemed to him a good death, rather than to have his god-fearing mind long tortured by the carrying off of his fellow-soldiers or their wasting away in prison or exile or their punishment by death.

At length on 16 March martial frenzy stirred up both sides, and the standards of the barons under the leadership of the earls advanced to confront the standards of the king. Would that tenfold that number of banners had been unfurled against the enemies of Christ by the king and earls fighting on the same side, rather than have Englishman raging against Englishman, kinsman against kinsman, relative against relative and knight against general. The two sides joined battle at Boroughbridge, and there [14] – the pity of it! – the chivalrous earl Humphrey was crossing a bridge and never expecting to find an enemy under his feet when, through a hole in the planking, a Welshman stabbed him in the groin, a private part where soldiers are not usually protected. On that field the king took prisoner the earl of Lancaster and with him barons, baronets and ninety knights. Five squires, various followers and others who were powerless to carry on the war were driven in flight from the battlefield, and there were some knights hidden among their number. In the presence of the justiciars of the kingdom, Sir Andrew Harclay and others, the prisoners were accused of schism and rebellion. When they had been lawfully convicted of conspiracy against the king's person, they were punished in various ways by the verdict of the law, so that their acquittal should not provide an incentive for others in the future to commit the same offence.

The principal perpetrator of this great disaster, Thomas earl of Lancaster, whose noble birth and immense wealth had attracted others to support him in the belief that he was immortal, was sentenced by a public court on the sixth day after the king's triumph to death by hanging.[1] But the God-fearing

---

[1] The trial was a mere formality: an indictment (printed in *Foedera*, ii.i, 478-9) was read out, and Lancaster was not allowed to speak in his defence before being sentenced. See Phillips, *Edward II*, 409, 411.

king did not allow his kinsman to be disposed of by a death so shameful, and mercifully reduced the penalty for his treason to execution. Of the number remaining, eighteen were drawn and hung in different parts of England and five were sentenced to be fugitives in exile. The king in his mercy spared a crowd of others who had been thrown into the squalor of a gaol and set them free in return for a ransom.

In AD 1322 at a parliament held at York after Easter, Hugh Despenser the father was made earl of Winchester, and the king, having assembled a great army, invaded Scotland on the feast of St James.[1] The Scots knew in advance about the arrival of the enemy. Abandoning some of their people but taking with them across the sea all whom they could easily transport, they stripped the land of food supplies and left it to the English. The king rode over their country without any opposition, and then, as his army was struggling through lack of food, sent it back to England. As soon as they heard of this, the Scots crossed the sea again. Hiding by day and pressing on by night, they pursued the king to Blackmoor forest[2] and by night besieged and assaulted the place where the king was staying. But the king with a few others slipped through their net to the south, although many of his army were taken prisoner. These included the earl of Richmond and the lord of Sully, the envoy [15] of the king of France. The Scots laid waste the whole swathe of the country as far as York, looting and burning as they went, and depopulated the town of Ripon. In return for the offer and immediate payment of £40 sterling they turned aside from the town of Beverley and left it intact. Finally they returned to their own country. In the June of the following year a truce was made with the Scots to last for thirteen years.[3]

In AD 1322 Philip the son of Philip, king of the French, entered upon the way of all flesh[4] and his brother Charles took the crown of his brother's kingdom. Charles sent Andrieu de Florence and another knight to England to summon king Edward to present himself to the new king of the French and to do him homage for the duchy of Aquitaine and his other lands in the kingdom of the king of France.[5] Although Hugh Despenser and Robert Baldock, as they themselves thought, had made it sufficiently clear to the envoys with prayers and deeds of kindness that they should not tell the king the reason for their arrival, nevertheless the envoys, as they withdrew, advised the king, as if making a suggestion, that he should at that time present himself to the king of France to do him homage. On the strength of this advice or rather summons, Andrieu de Florence, who was Charles'

---

[1]   25 July.
[2]   Blackhow Moor near Byland, on 14 October.
[3]   A reference to the controversial truce of Bishopthorpe, formally ratified by the English royal council on 30 May 1323: *Foedera*, ii, i, 521.
[4]   Philip V died on 3 January 1322.
[5]   The embassy arrived in July 1323:. Phillips, *Edward II*, 456.

notary, drew up a public document, without king Edward's council being aware of it, by which the king of France, by a legal process made against king Edward, obtained possession for his own use of some lands from the duchy of Gascony and also the countship of Ponthieu, while the king of England still thought, just as he had been informed, that the summons brought by the envoys had no legal validity.

It was Charles of Valois, the uncle of king Charles, who took possession of these lands for the king of France. He had a very deep hatred of the English. He used as excuses the disobedience of the king of England as duke of Aquitaine and his failure to do homage, and, performing a mission he himself had sought, he took possession with a large army of the countship of Ponthieu and the whole Agenais as dominions for the use of the king his nephew.[1] Finally Charles went to the town of La Réole and found it defended by Edmund of Woodstock, the brother of the king of England, earl of Kent. In the end they agreed upon a truce which would last as long as it took for the kings to discuss peace, and, when the town also had been given back, both sides went home.

In AD 1323 Roger Mortimer, who, as I said earlier, had at one time been imprisoned in the Tower of London, now escaped from it with the help of traitors [16] who bribed the guards.[2] He slipped away to France where, as an exile and an enemy of the English themselves, he turned to Charles of Valois and joined forces with him, thus being preserved by the sower of tares[3] for a new conflict and unhappy civil war.

During the next Lent at a parliament in London a case was brought by lawyers from Herefordshire against Adam, bishop of Hereford.[4] He was accused of having once given support to the followers of Roger Mortimer, those enemies of the king, by supplying them with horses and weapons and helping Roger to escape. As the bishop himself refused to reply to this allegation, this bishop, or rather traitor, was stripped of all his temporalities on the authority of the king. Adam conceived a bitter hatred against the king and his friends as a result. He had a great deal of natural cunning, very much experience of worldly wisdom and was capable of committing large-scale

---

[1] The French invasion of Aquitaine began on 14 August 1324, and the truce was agreed for six months on 22 September. Phillips, *Edward II*, 464-5.

[2] He persuaded the deputy constable to drug Stephen de Segrave, the constable, and escaped with his help on 1 August 1323, crossing to France immediately afterwards. *Knighton*, 429; *Annales Paulini*, 305-6; *Murimuth*, 40; *Chroniques de London*, 47.

[3] Matthew 13:25.

[4] Adam de Orleton was suspected of sympathising with Mortimer, whose lands lay in his diocese. He claimed privilege of clergy, i.e. that he could only be tried in a church court. The verdict was said to have been on the specific order of Edward II. See Phillips, *Edward II*, 452-3 for details;also G.A. Usher, 'The Career of a Political Bishop: Adam de Orleton (c. 1279-1345)', *Transactions of the Royal Historical Society*, Fifth Series 22 (1972), 33-47. The trial proceedings can be found in *Parliamentary Writs and Writs of Military Summons, Edward I and Edward II*, ed. F. Palgrave, Record Commission, London 1827-34, ii. ii, appendix, 244-9.

crimes, and now I must tell the story of how the bishop drank the poison of the anger aroused in him and plotted to overthrow the king and to remove many of the nobles.

The old hatred of the nobles of the kingdom against the two Hughs (the earls of Winchester and Gloucester)[1] had somewhat died down after the king's victory at Boroughbridge, or, more accurately, had been hidden in the nobles' fear of the king's power. But now for clearer reasons than of old it resumed its strength, though still not proudly erect but creeping along the ground. For although the king in his mercy, as I have said, had pardoned many nobles who had taken up arms against him under the earl of Lancaster, the earls of Winchester and Gloucester, who played as they pleased with the apparently bewitched mind of the king, confronted the nobles with the death they deserved, and the nobles thought death inescapable unless they won the favour of the two Hughs. So many of them, in return for a promise that their lives would be saved, often named the two earls and sold to them various of the finest manors of their inheritance, not as cheerful donors[2] but sadly and of necessity. So they made the two earl Hughs hated by everybody, not only because the king loved them more than all the others but because, being driven on by their proud, ambitious spirits, they were pauperising high-born knights by demanding cruel ransoms, and were disinheriting their sons by knocking down their fathers' [17] estates for nothing.

Everybody thought that the enduring of three kings in England at the same time was a burden too big to be borne. Many loved the king greatly, but many more hated the two Hughs out of fear, for

'We all desire the death of him we fear.'[3]

The bishop of Hereford hated the Despensers because he had been stripped of his temporalities. Henry Burghersh, bishop of Lincoln, had been decorated with the mitre as the king's appointment, but he knew he was guilty of the same crime as the Adam whom I mentioned earlier, and so was extremely afraid and in consequence hated the Despensers. Also all the friends of the knights and the two bishops were against the Despensers. With their minds weighed down by a sickening sorrow, they were ready for the fury of rebellion and it was only their reverence for the king's peace that held back their hands.

In addition to this, the Despensers very quickly aroused the feminine anger of the queen against themselves. She was very ready to commit any crime against them, when they lessened the household of the royal consort through their greedy decisions and orders, fixed within precise limits the

---

[1]   Hugh Despenser the younger married Eleanor, co-heir of Gilbert, the deceased earl of Gloucester and acquired considerable lands in the lordship, but was never formally created earl. Baker is probably picking up local references to him by that title; the niceties of the creating of peers were outweighed by his evident political power, and he behaved as if he were indeed earl.

[2]   2 Corinthians 9:7.

[3]   Ovid, *Amores* II. ii. 10.

amount of money she was allowed, and said she would be living upon smaller supplies of food than before.[1] So, now that a woman's insatiable greed had been frustrated of its desires, or at any rate a wife's excessive spending had been checked (and the female sex is always indulging in the one or other of these), the queen blazed up in anger not only against the Despensers but also against her husband, who in his decisions was copying them more than herself.

Her lament was that she, who was of the royal blood of France, or, more than that, the daughter of a king and the only sister of three successive kings in Louis, Philip and then Charles, now found herself married to a king who was a miser. The promise had been that she would be queen, but she had become no better than a maidservant, receiving her wages from the Despensers, whom she hated with a more than perfect hatred. Now she wanted to exchange complaints about her husband with her brother the king of the French. Now she wanted a secret consultation with her uncle Charles of Valois, a man capable of plotting any crime, about how she might be revenged on the Despensers and might incline the mind of the king her husband to listen to her instead. She cursed the wide sea which separated the shores of Normandy from England. She nodded her approval of a dried up sea or at least a wide safe bridge, so that she might carry in person the letters which she frequently sent to her brother and uncle.

While the queen was angry at these restrictions and others unmentioned, who was it that consoled her but the one who had himself been harmed by these same [18] Despensers whom she cursed, namely the bishop of Hereford. With him she bewailed their common misfortunes, and at other times expressed the thoughts of a heart about to break. When at last she did perhaps fall silent, more worn out by tears than by complaints, that cunning bishop did not allow her to finish the tale of her grievances, but with sighs and some tears which were real for his own case but fictitious for the injuries of the queen, he invoked a fake compassion and did not allay but increased the indignation with which the virago was swelling.

The bishop of Lincoln was privy to the secrets of them both. He knew in which hole to find the fox, and he would soothe the queen and comfort her with clever arguments. It was with his agreement that the bishop of Hereford built a new argument in the heart of the queen, by telling her of all the answers she would receive to her prayers if she went to her brother and uncle in France and implored their help against the Despensers. The queen applauded this prayer idea as being practical and definitely capable

---

[1]   Her lands in the West Country were seized by the king in September 1324 allegedly because the French might use them as a landing–place for an invasion; Isabella was given an allowance in lieu of the revenues which was smaller than her income from the confiscated fiefs. *The War of Saint-Sardos (1323-25): Gascon Correspondence and Diplomatic Documents* , ed. P. Chaplais, Camden, 3rd series, lxxxvii (London, 1954), 129-32.

of accomplishing the end she desired, and so she looked for an opportunity to cross the Channel.[1]

As I have touched on earlier, the kings of England and France had agreed to discuss peace terms at this time, and it was necessary to appoint a competent envoy for these negotiations. The king wanted to cross the seas himself for this important business, but he was dissuaded by the earls of Winchester and Gloucester, who were afraid that, if they were deprived of his company, they would fall into the hostile hands of men near them, by whom they knew they were hated. Furthermore they did not dare to cross the sea with the king themselves, because they were well aware that the king of France hated them because of the actions of his sister and the strong poison from Roger Mortimer. All this time the queen herself was exerting great pressure. She was talking sweetly to the king and, like a sensible woman, winning over the other nobles to her side and promising them peace between the kingdoms. As the two bishops were also secretly urging the king's counsellors to accept her scheme, while the majority of the nobles were in favour of it, the queen was entrusted with the embassy which she so greatly desired.[2]

In AD 1324 queen Isabella, the only sister of her only brother the king of France, presented herself at his court. They exchanged the precious glances and kisses for which they had longed. While the queen was the link between two kings, namely her brother and her husband who was duke of Aquitaine and count of Ponthieu, the king her husband spent the whole of Lent and the summer in Kent, so that there might be an easy exchange of messages between himself and the queen, while Isabella was handling the matter for which she had come to France.

In the end [19] the French parliament agreed that, if the king of England would hand over his right to the duchy of Gascony and the countship of Ponthieu to Edward his firstborn, the king of France himself would ensure that the son of the king of England had full possession of the duchy and the countship: he himself would be content with the homage which he would get from the new duke, Edward his nephew. King Charles sent letters patent on these matters, and he also sent other letters concerning safe conduct for the journey of the king's firstborn son to France.[3]

There were many discussions on these issues in England at London and Dover. Some suggested that the king in his own person should cross the sea,

---

[1] 'The claim by Geoffrey le Baker that Adam Orleton, the disgraced bishop of Hereford, somehow engineered her departure as the first part of a carefully stage-managed plot to bring about the downfall of Edward II has been shown to be entirely spurious.' Phillips, *Edward II*, 484. Henry Burghersh, bishop of Lincoln, had been involved with the opposition to the king in 1321-2, and had been deprived of his lands, but was equally no part of a plot against the king.

[2] Isabella is described as departing 'joyfully' by the author of *Vita Edwardi Secundi*, ed. and tr. W. R. Childs, Oxford 2005, 228-9. She crossed to Wissant on 9 March 1325. The date in the following sentence should be 1325.

[3] Peace terms were agreed between Isabella and Charles IV on 31 May 1325; Charles's letters were drawn up on 4 September: *Foedera* ii.i 602, 606.

and such people pointed out that many misfortunes could befall the king's son, while he was exposed to Gallic guile and greed and deprived of the protection of his father and the English. 'Who' they asked 'will stop the French king from marrying off the lad to whatever ill-matched partner he likes, or from assigning to him a carer or tutor?' Although these people gave sound and truthful advice, the earls of Winchester and Gloucester did not agree with them, because they did not dare either to cross the sea together with the king or to stay in England while the king was abroad for the reasons I mentioned earlier. Also the bishop of Lincoln was strongly on the side of the earls to their own destruction. For he was hoping that the scheme hatched between himself and the queen and the bishop of Hereford could be brought to completion (I have in part touched on this matter already). The king put too much trust in the earls, and as he was afraid that, if he went abroad himself, the nobles and barons might again rise in fury to eliminate the earls and so reawaken the civil war which had now been put to sleep, he gave his assent to those who suggested that he should send his son.

So the king drew up a charter for his son concerning the duchy and the countship. They were to be held in the possession of his son and his heirs as kings of England, with the rider that if his son died while his father was still alive, those lands should revert to the control of the father. The king also took care to insert conditions which prevented the French king from being able to marry off his son or to put him under any tutor or carer that he liked. This charter was drawn up at Dover with the consent of the prelates and other nobles of the kingdom on the day after the feast of the nativity of the blessed [20] Mary in the eighteenth year of the king's reign.[1] On the Thursday following Edward, the firstborn son of the king, began his voyage, having with him Walter the bishop of Exeter and a sufficient number of other nobles. Then around the feast of St Matthew he did homage to the French king his uncle, with declarations being made on both sides.

The queen had now completed the mission for which she had been sent to France, and immediately after the feast of St Michael her husband wrote to her with instructions that she should speedily bring back their son to England. His wife wrote back to say that her brother the French king loved them so much that he was keeping them with him against their wills. So she sent back a large part of the retinues of both of them, but for the rest of that year she herself was busy with those particular matters for which she had purposely journeyed to France.

Walter the bishop of Exeter was not ordered to return to England. But he came back privately, as he could see that he had been totally excluded from the proceedings of the secret council of the queen, and that Roger Mortimer and other exiled enemies of the king their lord had usurped his place as her friend.[2] The English were worried that the queen delayed in France and

---

[1]   9 September 1325. The charter is printed in *Foedera*, ii.i 607-8, dated Dover 10 September 1325. The future Edward III crossed on 12 September.

[2]   See F. D. Blackley, 'Isabella and the bishop of Exeter', in *Essays in Medieval History presented to Bertie Wilkinson*, ed. T. A. Sandquist and M. R. Powicke, Toronto 1969, 220-35.

to the displeasure of the king was keeping their son outside the kingdom. Some declared that the two of them were being detained against their wills. Others guessed that she had found comfort in the unlawful embraces of Roger Mortimer, and was just as unwilling to return to England as was Mortimer and the other English exiles whom she found in France.[1] But all the time, while these and other different reasons for her delay were being put forward, some of them false and others half true, the bishops of Lincoln and Hereford, who knew of the plot for whose completion the enraged virago was waiting, kept hidden the secrets of their hearts.

The queen had now spent a year plotting her revenge, and finally on the advice of her lovers she prepared to drink its cup. At the end of the year she went to the lands of Hainault[2] and without any discussion with the nobles of England she married off her son, who was loved and feared by the whole world. She joined him in marriage to Philippa, the daughter of the count of Hainault. The marriage may have taken place without any consultation, but it was blessed in the future by the successful production of many noble children, as will be revealed when it happens.[3] The queen collected from Hainault and [21] Germany an army of soldiers who were told that they would be paid their wages out of the dowries from the new bride. The knights in command of the army were John, the brother of the count of Hainault,[4] and Roger Mortimer, who by this time was the most secret and the most influential person in the queen's private household.

They directed their fleet towards the shores of England and, on the Friday before the feast of St Michael,[5] the wind they had prayed for carried them to the port of Orwell. There they were met by their allies, the earl of Norfolk[6] and Henry earl of Leicester[7] together with a headstrong crowd of barons and fellow knights. Nor were their ranks devoid of prelates, who had broken faith and joined those who were leading them against their country and the lord of that country. For the criminal devisers of this wicked plot met their pupil, who herself was skilled in the weapons of crime, on the appointed day. As leaders in chief of this army, they were not in charge of lambs or sheep but of

[1]   On 8 February 1326, Edward publicly accused Isabella in a proclamation of following the advice of Mortimer and other rebels; and on 18 March he wrote to his son accusing Isabella of consorting with Mortimer 'within her lodgings and elsewhere': *Foedera*, ii.i 619, 623.

[2]   Probably at the end of August 1326. Le Bel, 26-27 [13-17]

[3]   The situation was not as simple as Baker makes out. Edward II had explored plans for a marriage between Edward and a daughter of the count of Hainault as early as 1319, but had broken them off in favour of an alliance with one of the Spanish kingdoms. Joanna countess of Hainault was Isabella's cousin, and they had met in Paris in December 1325. The couple were betrothed, not married, on 27 August 1326: the marriage itself took place in York on 27 January 1328.

[4]   John of Beaumont.

[5]   27 September 1326. However, the actual date of her landing was 24 September: *Annales Paulini*, 313-4.

[6]   Thomas of Brotherton, Edward II's half-brother.

[7]   Younger brother and heir of Thomas, late earl of Lancaster: he was formally acknowledged as earl of Lancaster on 3 February 1327.

cruel, fanged wolves, and they were less shepherds than tyrants. There the two elders, whose wickedness was that of the Babylonians against Susanna but on behalf of Jezebel, yes, those priests of Baal, pupils of Jezebel,[1] I mean the bishops of Lincoln and Hereford and also the bishops of Dublin and Ely,[2] assembled a great army together with the queen.

The task of speaking was entrusted to that eloquent traitor, the bishop of Hereford, and at a plenary parliament of the conspirators he proclaimed that it would be expedient for the kingdom for the king to be ruled and kept in check by the advice of the great number of nobles there gathered; also that something should be done about the irremovable ill-feeling between the queen and the earls of Winchester and Gloucester which had been brought about by their own wishes. But they all agreed that the king was a most loyal supporter of his friends and would never of his own free will send away from the security of his presence his friends the earls, whom the queen had been furiously eager to kill, and also that in his own judgment he was protecting innocent people from the arbitrary actions of the envious. So in the end they showed caution on these important matters and agreed under oath that they should make for the king's presence with their army.[3]

The queen's bishops sent letters from the army to their fellow bishops and other friends, telling them that the French king had sent so many dukes, earls and barons with their largest forces to protect the rights of the queen his sister that England barelyhad enough food to feed them. [22] The people of England, a needy flock without a shepherd, were consumed with fear, expecting the triumph of the one party, but ready to submit to the power of the stronger. Also a false report, starting from the army, had spread like wildfire throughout all parts of the kingdom that the pope at Rome had absolved all the English from their sworn loyalty to their king, and would thunder out a sentence of excommunication against all those who bore arms against the queen. As confirmation of this lie two cardinals were invented who were said to have brought the news of it and to have joined the queen's forces.

In 1326, the eleventh year of the pontificate of pope John XXII and the twentieth and last year of Edward as king of England, the practice of civil war, which was not unknown in England, was renewed by the army I have described, although this war could not last for long. For the king and the earls concluded, as the traitors' army advanced to meet them, that they were not strong enough to put up a fight, and so made vain attempts to find the

---

[1]   Jezebel was a worshipper of Baal (1 Kings 18); there is a wordplay on 'Jezebel' and 'Isabella', though Baker does not actually name her in this passage.
[2]   Alexander Bicknor, archbishop of Dublin, and John de Hotham, bishop of Ely.
[3]   There does not appear to be any other evidence for this 'parliament', and the substance of the supposed speech may derive from the letters sent out by Isabella to London and other major towns immediately after her landing. The proclamation issued by her at Wallingford on 15 October bears some similarity to Baker's report: Foedera, ii.i 645-6.

protection of defensible positions, just as if they were thinking of flight. The king indeed heard from his scouts that almost the whole population of the kingdom had joined his wife in terror at the false rumours, and so he made for Wales with the two earls and Robert Baldock and a few others from his private household.[1] He then sent the earl of Winchester to guard the town and castle of Bristol, while he himself came to Chepstow with the earl of Gloucester, master Robert Baldock and just a very few others. There he boarded a ship, intending to sail to Lundy island.[2]

Lundy is an island in the river Severn, extending two miles in both directions. It is rich with pastures and oats, and produces an abundance of rabbits. There are pigeons and also sparrows, called the birds of Ganymede by Alexander Neckham,[3] with nests for their young. The island also supplies its inhabitants with fresh water bubbling up from springs, although it is itself completely surrounded by the bitterest salt water. It has only one landing place, where two men can just about go on foot side by side. Everywhere else an approach is blocked by high cliffs which jut out in fearsome fashion. So here was an island which, as I have said, was rich in natural supplies of food, and it was in fact furnished with an abundance of wine, olive-oil, honey, corn, malt, fish, salted flesh and coal from under the ground. But when the king wished to [23] sail to it, he was completely stopped by a contrary wind. So with difficulty he skirted around the savage storms at sea and landed in Glamorgan. He marched to the abbey and castle of Neath, but there he stayed put in hiding, bitterly upset because the promises of the Welsh that they wanted to share life and death with him turned out to he false.

The queen, who was now a woman in a very powerful position, gave orders for her army to advance and hunt down the king. It set off under the banner of their son, who was at war with his father, not because he was evil by nature but because he had been badly advised. The army arrived at Oxford, and there, before the university and in the presence of the queen and of the youthful but malleable duke of Aquitaine, Roger Mortimer and their other satellites, the principal plotter of this great disaster, I mean Adam the so-called bishop of Hereford, preached in public about the arrival of the queen and the cause of the army. He took as his text, 'I am grieving for my head,'[4] and interpreted it as showing that a head, which was too weak ever to be bound up by any strength-giving bandages of Hippocrates,[5] had perforce to be removed. Then the army advanced to Gloucester, where its numbers were notably increased by many coming from the north to help the queen.

---

[1]   Edward left London on 2 October, and was at Chepstow on 16 October. The king's movements can best be traced in the account book of his chamber: Society of Antiquaries MS 122, ff. 88-90.
[2]   He embarked on 20 October. His intended destination was probably Ireland where he might have found support and a base for a counter-attack: Phillips, *Edward II*, 510-12; Society of Antiquaries MS 122, f. 90.
[3]   See Alexander Neckham, *De naturis rerum* ch.xlvi, ed. T. Wright, RS 34, London 1863.
[4]   . 4 Kings 4:18 in the Vulgate Bible (2 Kings 4:19 in the King James Bible).
[5]   Hippocrates wrote a work *On the injuries of the head*.

In this situation the crowd at London, in their desire to please the queen and Roger Mortimer, on 15 October in the middle of the city ran riot and seized and beheaded Walter, the bishop of Exeter of happy memory. They also savagely put to death various other men loyal to the king, for no other reason than that they were faithful followers in the king's service. Indeed they brought the head of the bishop to the queen who was watching over her army at Gloucester, thinking it a sacrifice well pleasing to Diana. They also entered the Tower of London and released all the prisoners, and in the same way by a public edict of the queen almost all the prisoners throughout the whole of England were set free. Also those sentenced to banishment and exile were pardoned and recalled. In fact so widespread was the apparent goodness and mercy of the queen's party that the people were fired with eagerness for the coronation of a new king who would be less harsh than the old one. Then all who had committed crimes or in some way offended the king's majesty easily obtained the help of high favour from a queen[24] who was giving orders to everybody.

Then the king's ministers throughout the whole land were in a state of confusion about asking for the king's help or calling themselves friends of the king, so frightened and scared was the flock when its shepherd, the king, was being attacked.[1] All the king's ministers who were found in the Tower of London were removed by the people of London, and new ones were appointed in the name of lord John of Eltham, the nine year old son of the king, who was nominated as the guardian of the city and the tower. For all the king's enemies everywhere took the precaution of not committing any act of *lèse-majesté* unless in the name of one of his sons. They reasoned that, if one day the king regained his powers of justice so that he could legally do freely whatever he wanted in the kingdom, his anger would be directed against his own sons as the principal authors of the crimes.

So in the confusion right and wrong collided, and, as there was no distinction between them and a lack of punishment and pardon easily available, all thieves and murderers and criminals of every kind were stimulated to commit their crimes. This unpunished criminality increased so rapidly that, wherever a friend of the king was found, he was robbed of his possessions or deprived of his life, and no punishment followed. The attacker merely needed to reproach his victim for being the king's friend. Under the cover of this disorder criminals found it profitable to add treason to their misdeeds. In this fashion many grew richer or had their liberty given back to them, and if any had been punished as traitors by the king's justice in the past, the now powerful queen generously restored them to their former riches and positions.

The queen left Gloucester and hurried with her army to the town of Bristol, which, as I have said, was held by Hugh Despenser the father.[2] The queen planned to lay siege to both town and castle, if that had been necessary. But

---

[1]   Matthew 9:36.
[2]   Isabella reached Bristol by 18 October.

the desperation which often unlocks the best defended posts compelled that noble earl to entrust himself and all he had to the mercy of that angry woman. So he surrendered the town and its castle to her, and on her entry the virago gave orders for the earl to be put to death in grisly fashion without a trial or the chance to defend himself. That powerful knight was hurriedly bound with ropes, with his arms and shins stretched out in a long line. Then, before the eyes of the living queen, his belly was cut open[25] and his entrails cruelly pulled out and burnt, while the rest of his body was dragged by horses and hung on the common gallows for thieves.

When this had been done, the queen moved towards the Welsh marches and stayed at Hereford for a month. Then she divided her army. She sent Henry earl of Leicester and Rhys ap Howel, a Welsh cleric, with one part to arrest the king and his followers. This earl was the brother and heir of Thomas, earl of Lancaster, whom I have often mentioned. Rhys, who was sent with him, had once been imprisoned in the Tower of London by the king's justice, but had been set free by the power of the queen. Both earl Henry and Rhys had possessions and wide estates near the place in which the king was hiding. Also Rhys knew his whole country very well. In the end the earl and the cleric, but only after heavily bribing some Welshmen, found with the help of Welsh scouts both the king in Neath monastery and Hugh Despenser the son while he was attempting to flee for safety to a deserted spot.[1]

So the king, Hugh earl of Gloucester, master Robert Baldock and Simon Reading were arrested, while the others were let go scot-free. On the authority of the advice of the bishop of Hereford, the king was entrusted to the custody of the earl of Leicester and taken to Kenilworth castle. He stayed there for the whole winter with a reasonable enough retinue, and was guarded not otherwise than a captive king should be guarded.

While the queen, as I have said, was at the head of her army in Hereford, accompanied by the instigator of the whole of her wicked plot, namely the bishop of that city, Edmund earl of Arundel, John Daniel and Thomas Micheldever were beheaded at the instigation of Roger Mortimer, who hated them with a perfect but not prophetic hatred[2]. Later the earl of Gloucester, Hugh Despenser the son, was shamefully shown in chains with his eyes filled with terror, and, with no waiting for the rational decision of any judge, in that same city of Hereford he was drawn, hung, beheaded and divided into four quarters. His head was dispatched to London Bridge and the four quarters distributed between the four quarters of the kingdom.[3]

---

[1]   They were actually discovered in flight from Neath somewhere near Llantrisant on 16 October: *Annales Paulini*, 319; *Anonimalle*, 130-1; *Murimuth*, 49; *Flores*, 234; *Walsingham*, i 183.
[2]   Psalm 138:22.
[3]   He was executed on 24 November 1326. The form of trial followed that of Thomas of Lancaster, in that the court heard only his indictment, and he was not allowed to speak in his own defence.

Simon Reading was also drawn and hung at Hereford, but master Robert Baldock, after much shameful treatment,[26] was put in the prison of the bishop of Hereford where he lived a life of utter misery until the next feast of the Purification. Then it was the bishop of Hereford, the architect of this whole wicked scheme, who had him brought to his house in London. When he had been taken there, the people of London, not without the covert advice of the bishop, seized hold of him and put him in Newgate prison, waiting for an opportunity to be able to number him among the dead as a drawn and hung traitor. But in the end, when they had failed to find any trace of treachery or other felony in him after many investigations, they handled him so savagely that he died from his tortures immediately after Easter in the same year.[1]

It is not improbable that someone will think that the clear or hidden author of such a heinous crime as the seizure and strangling of a cleric and priest of God was the very man who first sent Robert Baldock from the middle of wolves to his own very safe sheepfold of an episcopal prison in order to help a sheep who had been handed over to him for the protection from the wolves which he afforded him.[2] For, after this, he then had him brought from Hereford to his house in London, from his own episcopate to a foreign diocese, from a completely safe place to the mountains of the leopards[3]. Also what is the significance of the fact that the bishop of Hereford, who was himself the most powerful prelate in the province after the worthy archbishop, took no steps to punish with proper care the seizure and strangling of a cleric entrusted to him? I believe that Quintilian says truly of such a matter, 'The murdered man defeats his tormentor,'[4] and for this reason I conceal my complaint under a cloak of silence, although I heard it with the church from the voices of the murdered innocents below the altar of God.[5]

When the queen, the bishop of Hereford and Roger Mortimer had done the deeds I have described and also several others, just as each of them pleased, they came side by side to London. There, shortly after Epiphany, they themselves summoned a parliament, with no one daring to resist them, and at this parliament it was decreed and ordained that a commission should be sent to the king who was under guard at Kenilworth to do what I shall describe below.[6] The members of this commission, representing the whole kingdom, were to be three bishops, two earls, two abbots, four barons, two knights from any county of England, two burgesses from any city and capital town of any county and similarly two burgesses from the ports.

---

[1]   This is confirmed by *Annales Paulini*, 320-1, 324.
[2]   The text is not clear; 'et lupis' should probably read 'ex lupis'.
[3]   Song of Solomon 4:8.
[4]   Quintilian, *Declamationes* xviii.14.
[5]   Revelations 6:9.
[6]   The assembly took place on 12 January 1327, and the commission was appointed the following day. The evidence is complex, and is set out in Claire Valente, 'The deposition and abdication of Edward II', *English Historical Review* cxii 1998, 852-81; Phillips, *Edward II*, 524-33 modifies her account slightly. See also *PROME* IV 2-10 for a detailed discussion of the business of the parliament.

The members of the commission chiefly responsible for transacting the business were the three bishops, John Stratford [27] bishop of Winchester, Adam Orleton bishop of Hereford and Henry bishop of Lincoln.[1] And you, o noble knight, lord Thomas de la More, you who witnessed these things and wrote about them in French and whose poor interpreter I am, you, I say, were in attendance upon the bishop of Winchester and an adornment to the company with the presence of your famous wisdom.[2]

The bishops of Winchester and Lincoln went ahead of the rest on the journey and talked secretly with the king and his keeper, the earl of Leicester, trying to induce the king to resign the crown in favour of his firstborn son. These three quite cleverly got round the king by promising him that he would have no less honour after laying down the honour of his crown than his royal majesty had been accustomed to receive from all previously. They also added with words which adulterated the truth that it would be greatly to the king's credit with God if he were to reject his temporal kingdom for the peace of his subjects,[3] assuring him that his rejection of the crown was the only way to such peace. As priests making such a prophecy they are undoubtedly to be ranked with Caiaphas the priest. From another direction they used threats against him, saying that, unless he resigned the crown, the people would cease to pay loyal homage to himself, would reject his sons as well and instead exalt to the kingship another who was not of the royal blood.

By these and other bullying threats and promises the pious heart of the king was won over, and, not without sobs, tears and sighs, he climbed down and took the bishops' advice. Knowing that a good shepherd lays down his life for his sheep,[4] he was more ready to end his life as a follower of Christ than to look with the eyes of a living body upon the disinheritance of his sons or a lengthy civil war in his kingdom.

Finally that detestable envoy, Adam Orleton of Hereford, brought to the secret quarters of the king the other envoys, whom he placed in order in

---

[1]   On Baker's attitude to Edward II and the tenor of his account of the deposition interview, see Haines, *Archbishop John Stratford*, 178-9. Haines notes that Stratford is not mentioned until 1327, despite the controversy over his promotion to the bishopric of Winchester in 1323 and the important part he played in the events of 1325-6 when he accompanied Isabella to France. The solution to this is probably that his information about Stratford came from de la More, who was probably not in Stratford's service at that point. The account of the interview, as Baker himself says, is de la More's rather than Baker's own view. For an analysis of the three other major accounts of the interview, in the Rochester chronicle, the Lanercost chronicle, and one of the Canterbury chronicles, see Haines, *Archbishop John Stratford*, 179-86.
Nonetheless, the whole of the following passage, down to Edward's death, needs to be read with Baker's agenda in mind; according to Seymour Phillips, his aim was to present Edward II as a kind of royal martyr: see Phillips, *Edward II*, 22, 535. Orleton is the villain of the piece, while Stratford is treated much more sympathetically. Burghersh was almost certainly not part of the mission: see Haines, *Church and Politics* 173-4.

[2]   For Sir Thomas de la More and his connection with Baker, see pp.xiii-xvi above [introduction]

[3]   John 11 49:50.

[4]   John 10:11.

the king's chamber according to their rank, while keeping for himself with everyone's permission the part which he had laid claim to long ago. At length his royal majesty wearing a black gown came out of his inner chamber and showed himself to his servants, but then, being conscious of the reason for which they had come, in the shock of sorrow he lost his wits and collapsed in a heap on the floor. The earl of Leicester and the bishop of Winchester rushed to his aid and just managed to lift up the semi-conscious king. When he had somehow recovered his wits and his strength as before, Adam of Hereford [28] addressed him. With remarkable effrontery he showed no confusion in dealing with the mind of the king and explaining to him why the envoys had come, even though he believed that the king hated him above all other men. Then the bishop of Hereford added that the king should resign his crown to his firstborn son. If he did not do this, he would be forced after his own dethronement to endure the sight of the nobles choosing as king the man they thought fitter to govern the land. After hearing this, the king with tears and lamentations replied that he was deeply sorry that the people of his kingdom had been so antagonised by him that they were tired of his rule, but finally he did also add that he was very pleased that his son was so acceptable to the people that they wished to have him for their king.

The next day, on behalf of the whole kingdom, the same envoys in the person of the knight William Trussel renounced their homage and ties to lord Edward of Caernarfon lately king, and the knight Thomas Blount, the steward at the king's lodging, broke the rod marking his office and declared that the king's household had been dismissed. After this the envoys returned to the parliament in London, and gave a full report of the king's reply, or rather a fuller report than the actual reply.

The people of England, with their usual distaste for the old and their appetite for the new, were happy to accept the king's resignation, and, as I will describe more fully later, with no delay at all they promoted Edward his firstborn, an able lad of eleven years old.[1] For some people the young boy was more to their taste because they hoped that the sheep of the kingdom would be able to fulfil their own desires under so tender a shepherd. Also so much of the dowry of the queen, Isabella of Caernarfon, had been assigned for various purposes that barely a third part of what belonged to the crown remained for the king her son and queen Philippa. Further, Edward of Caernarfon had been entrusted to the custody of the earl of Leicester, and the queen, the bishop of Hereford and Roger Mortimer, now decreed that he should be paid one hundred marks a month, to come from the royal treasury.

And so the noble lord Edward, who had once been king, suffered with patience the loss of his royal crown and liberty out of his love for Jesus Christ, the poor crucified one, and remained in the house of his kinsman, Henry the earl of Leicester, [29] in want of nothing which a monk-like recluse might need. This servant of God, even when he had sunk to the depths, complained

---

[1]   Edward had turned fourteen two months previously.

of no misfortune except that his wife, whom he was not able not to love, did not want to see him, although he had lived a widower from her embraces for more than an year, and that she did not allow their son, the new king, or any of their children to give him the comfort of their presence.

Countless were the songs of love which this second Orpheus sang with pleading voice, but in vain. Imagine how often he wept and complained that such a noble woman and one so beautiful with all the gifts of nature could have drunk the bitter brew of betrayal. Sometimes he did not keep silence and swore to his hearers that since he had first seen his queen he had never been able to love another woman. This love shown by the despondent Edward and his patience in adversity awoke such pity in the earl his guardian and in both their households that they did not omit to send messages of the despairing love of the noble lord for his wife to a heart that was harder than an adamantine anvil. For the queen was stirred not to love by these messages but to anger, for that iron lady in her secret thoughts began to be very afraid that the church, with its customary pity for the pitiful, might one day actually compel her to share again the bed of the husband she had repudiated. For she thought that a man, who, by his endurance of adversity and the rich fragrance of all his virtues, had brought his own enemies, whom she herself had placed as attendants over him, to take pity on him, would be much more likely to arouse the pity of men who did not know him and who were the very pupils of pity.

Driven into a corner by these and other such reflections, the fierce lioness again sought advice from her master, that priest of Baal[1] the bishop of Hereford, and received from him the actual reply that there was no doubt it was a matter of murder, if now the earl was suffering together with his kinsman Edward. So on the advice of her cunning master the bishop, the cruel queen decided that two evil knights, Thomas Gournay[2] and John Maltravers[3], should pick up Edward from his keeper the earl of Leicester and then take him wherever they liked, provided that no friend or neutral was allowed free access to him or came to know where he was spending any length of time. These two villainous traitors [30] were given by orders from on high the power to demand protection from all fortresses, castles or towns for as long

---

[1]   1 Kings 18:19
[2]   Associated with Maltravers in a case of false arrest in 1320; he was tracked down and captured, first in Castile, where he managed to escape, and again in Naples. He was on his way back to England in custody when he fell ill at Bayonne in 1333; he was given medical treatment, but died there. See R.M. Haines, 'Sir Thomas Gurney of Englishcombe in the county of Somerset, Regicide?', *Somerset Archaeology and Natural History* cxlvii 2004, 45-65.
[3]   Brother-in-law of Thomas Berkeley, lord of Berkeley castle. He was involved in the plot to bring down the earl of Kent in 1330, and fled abroad to escape arrest. He was condemned to be executed in the parliament of November 1330 and a reward of 1000 marks offered for his capture (*PROME* iv.106). However, he was in touch with the English government in 1335 and in 1339 was granted an annuity of £100. He was then in Flanders, but was not allowed to return to England until 1347. Four years later he was restored to his lands, and spent the last decade of his life in England. Edward III clearly did not believe that he was one of his father's murderers. He is named as such by Adam Murimuth and the Anglo-Norman *Brut*.

and whenever they liked, no matter where they went in the kingdom, while every man in the kingdom was forbidden to contravene these orders on pain of forfeiture of his lands and his life.[1]

Edward was taken at night by his enemies from Kenilworth, and, with no escape now from a life full of suffering, he was brought first to Corfe castle and then to Bristol.[2] There he was for some time kept shut up in the castle, until some townspeople got to know of it and made plans to set him free and take him overseas, just as he wished. But as soon as Edward's keepers learned of their plans, they took Edward in the dark silence of the night from that place to Berkeley.

The inhumanity of his tormentors towards him was worse than that of wild beasts. He was not allowed to ride except at night, or to see anyone, or to be seen by any friend. When he did go riding, they compelled him to go thinly clad and bareheaded. When he wished to sleep, they would not let him. They prepared for him not food which he liked but food which he loathed. They contradicted his every word. They falsely declared that he was mad. In short, they opposed his wishes in everything, so that he might soon die of cold or lack of sleep or uncooked and uneatable food or at least of melancholy when he caught some common illness.

But Edward had the best of natural constitutions for brave resistance to these hardships, and as he also by the grace of God endured his weaknesses, he overcame all the devices of his evil keepers by nature or by grace. Often these servants of Belial gave the servant of God poison to drink, but either Edward by his physical strength emptied himself of the poison, as Galen in his third book about simple medicine[3] says that men of a balanced constitution can do, or, as I more truly believe, the Almighty on high kept his confessor for a more public martyrdom.

Respected sir,[4] I am writing about well attested happenings, which would crash their thunders over the world in a brighter light, if fear of the pious king's enemies still alive did not stop men from making clear that truth which cannot be hidden for ever.

Then, as I have said, Edward was led away toward Berkeley on horseback, with those satraps [31] of Satan packed closely around him. They led the exemplar of endurance through the granges belonging to the castle of Bristol, and there that villain Gournay made a crown out of hay and, daring to touch the Lord's anointed, put it on the head which once had been consecrated with

---

[1]   There is a vast literature on the death of Edward II, for which see Phillips, *Edward II*, 543, n.128. The basic reference point is T. F. Tout, 'The captivity and death of Edward of Caernarvon' in *Collected Papers of Thomas Frederick Tout*, Manchester 1933-4, iii 145-90. For the idea that he escaped and survived into the 1330s see Ian Mortimer, 'The death of Edward II in Berkeley Castle', *EHR* cxx 2004 45-65, and for a reaffirmation of the traditional view, W. Mark Ormrod, *Edward III*, London 2011, 122-4.

[2]   Corfe is also named by Adam Murimuth and the *Brut*, but not by other writers.

[3]   Galen's substantial work on medicines was known under the Latin title *De simplicium medicamentorum facultate* in the middle ages.

[4]   This is probably Thomas de la More (p.xvi above).

holy oil, while the knights mocked him and said in bitter irony, 'Avaunt, sir king,' which is to say 'Proceed, my lord king.' These criminals were afraid that, if they continued to go straight ahead, they might be met by some friend of Edward or by some band which in pity was coming to set him free. And so they went downhill towards the left and rode through the marshes which end at the river Severn.

The enemies of God cast about for a means of disguising Edward so that he might not be easily recognised by anybody. They hit upon the idea of both cutting his hair and shaving his beard. So, when on their journey they came to a ditch in which water was running, they commanded Edward to dismount for a shave. They sat him on a molehill and the barber brought a basin of cold water which he had taken from the ditch. When the barber and the others said that cold water should be quite good enough for the occasion, Edward said, 'Willy-nilly, we'll have some hot water for my beard,' and, that his promise might come true, he began to weep copiously. This story was told me by William Bishop who was still alive after the great plague. He had been in charge of Edward's escort, but in hope of the divine mercy he confessed his sin and in contrition repented of it.

At length they came to Berkeley castle where the noble Edward was shut up to exercise the virtue of patience like an anchorite. Like the blessed Job he had been robbed of his temporal kingdom, though not by foreigners but by his own wife, servants and maidservants, and he had been deprived of the control exercised through honours and advantages. Now he waited for the heavenly kingdom to replace the earthly.

His wife Isabella found it hard to bear that the life of the husband she hated so deeply had been prolonged all this time and she complained about it to her master the bishop of Hereford. She pretended that she had had some extremely ominous dreams, so that, supposing they were true, she had a real fear that her husband, if he was one day restored to his former position, might condemn herself as a traitor to the fire or to perpetual bondage. The bishop also had the same fears as Isabella, for he knew that he had committed lèse-majesté. Others, whom the devil had joined to this alliance [32] against God and his anointed, were seen to be afraid for the same reason. So many important people, both ecclesiastics and laymen and of both sexes, resolved that the cause of their great dread should be put to sleep together with Edward, whom they all out of fear wished to be dead.[1]

So they sent letters of blame to Edward's keepers, falsely accusing them of guarding him more negligently than they should have done and of looking after him too kindly. They also half hinted to the keepers that Edward's death would be pleasing to them, and that it did not matter whether it was natural or violent. Also the keepers were influenced by a sophistical ambiguity thought up by the bishop, who wrote, 'To kill Edward do not fear is good.' This sophism can be divided into two statements, the first of them being the first four words, namely

---

[1]   An echo of Ovid, *Amores* II.i.10.

'do not kill Edward,' and the second being the remaining three words, namely 'fear is good,' and, if this is done, the sophism does not seem to be suggesting any treason. But the receivers of the letter, who were well aware of what was in the bishop's mind, altered the sense of the sophism so that they read the first part as, 'to kill Edward do not fear,' and then added on to that 'it is good.' In this way they evilly emphasised the evil in the message sent by one who was aware of the evil in the message but did not spell it out.

That cunning sophist used this sophism because he knew that unless he gave his consent in writing, those who were to execute the cruel command would not dare to kill Edward, fearing that they might one day be accused of having done this without the consent of the great men in the kingdom. So because the bishop had finally decided on Edward's death and perhaps because he accused himself of consenting to it, he carefully devised that the command in his letter of authority should be capable of two interpretations. On one interpretation or reading it encouraged foolish men to kill an innocent man. But on the other interpretation he himself would be thought to have had no part in this horrific crime.

And it actually happened just as he had thought. For in the end those who murdered Edward and who had assumed that the letter confirmed their friendship with Isabella and with the sophistical, deceiving bishop, discovered that both she and the bishop were zealous superintendents of the person given to them for safekeeping, namely lord Edward, and that they themselves for their faults were being threatened with an ignominious death as the pay for traitors. And then these fools were at a loss and did not know what to do except to display the letter from Isabella and the bishop, confirmed by the seals of the other conspirators, [33] as evidence of their giving their consent to the murderers. The bishop did not disown the letter. He admitted it was written by himself and the others, but interpreted it as being a fervent expression of innocence and loyalty. As for those who had mis-read his letter and had foully treated an innocent man on their own authority, the bishop did not cease to hound them with terrible threats which would compel them to take to flight. So much for the sophistical letter.

When he had been brought to Berkeley castle, lord Edward had been civilly and kindly received and treated by Thomas Berkeley, the lord of that feof, but after Edward's torturers received the letter, they exercised the power entrusted to them for the control of the castle. At once they gave orders that Thomas Berkeley should have no communication with Edward. Thomas was not only sorry but also ashamed that he was now forbidden to do what he wished to do and what he had previously been allowed to do. With a heavy heart he said farewell to lord Edward and departed to his other dwelling places.[1]

---

[1]   Berkeley claimed in 1331 that he was lying sick at Bradley, some miles to the north, and was ignorant of what was going on at Berkeley Castle. There is a detailed analysis of the evidence by Phillips, *Edward II*, 579, 581, which leads him to the conclusion that Berkeley was probably lying and that he 'was clearly close to the scene, but was either negligent or given a hint that he should stay out of the way'.

Then began the final persecution of Edward, which continued until his death. First they shut him in the closest of chambers, and for many days they tortured him almost to suffocation by the stench of corpses placed in a cellar underneath his chamber. Indeed one day the servant of God at the window of his room lamented to some carpenters working outside that that unbearable stench was the heaviest punishment he had ever endured. But those tyrants saw that the stench could not of itself cause the death of a very strong man. And so on 22 September[1] they suddenly seized him as he lay on his bed, and smothered and suffocated him with great, heavy mattresses, in weight more than that of fifteen strong men. Then, with a plumber's soldering iron, made red hot, and thrust through the tube leading to the secret parts of his bowels, they burnt out his inner parts and then his breath of life. For they were afraid that if a wound was found on the body of the king, where friends of justice are accustomed to look for wounds, his torturers might be compelled to answer for an obvious injury and suffer punishment for it.[2]

In this way the knight, for all his strength, was overpowered. His loud cries were heard by men inside and outside the castle, who knew well enough that someone was suffering a violent death. Many people in Berkeley and some in the castle, [34] as they themselves asserted, were awoken by his dying shouts and took compassion on the sufferer, making prayers for the holy soul of one emigrating from this world. Thus the kingdom of the angels in heaven received one hated by the world, just as it had hated his master Jesus Christ before him[3]. First it received the teacher, rejected by the kingdom of the Jews, and then the disciple, stripped of the kingdom of the English.

The traitors who brought about the glorious and noble end of Edward were Thomas Gournay and John Maltravers. But they were outlawed and, as I have said, driven into exile by Isabella and the bishop of Hereford, who turned against them just so that their own hands and intentions might be seen to be clear of guilt. Gourney fled secretly to Marseilles, but was discovered and captured there three years later. He was being brought back to England to pay the penalty for his crimes when he was beheaded at sea. There was a fear that he might have accused the magnates and great prelates and several others of the kingdom of having suggested his crime to him and of having showed him that they assented to it. The other, Maltravers, lay hidden for a long time in Germany, doing penance for his sins.

---

[1]   The usual date of the murder is given as 21 September, and this is the date Edward III commemorated: TNA E 101/383/1.
[2]   See introduction, pp. xvi-xviii for a full discussion of Baker's account of Edward's death.
[3]   John 15:24.

The reign of Edward III [1]

As I have written earlier, the glorious king Edward had handed over his crown to his firstborn son, Edward of Windsor. When the news of this had been established as certain, the magnates and prelates of the kingdom in a parliament at London immediately gave their consent to Edward, the firstborn of Edward, as his father's successor, and had him crowned by Walter Reynolds, the archbishop of Canterbury, at Westminster on 1 February. He was a youth of about fifteen, and one who found favour with God and the whole world. At the great ceremony of his coronation there were present as many foreigners as Englishmen, particularly the mercenaries of queen Isabella his mother, whom, as I have said, she herself had invited from Hainault and Germany. The new king was crowned with the crown which his predecessor, the holy and blessed Edward [35] the Confessor, was once accustomed to wear. Although the crown was large and of considerable weight, the new king wore it in so manly a fashion that those, who knew from experience how young the boy was and how large and heavy the crown, marvelled at it. On the same day the three sons of Roger Mortimer and many others were decorated with the belt of knighthood.

On the eve of the feast of St Nicholas in this year master James Berkeley was unanimously elected bishop of Exeter and consecrated in Canterbury on the middle Sunday in Lent.

After his coronation the new king Edward, the third of this name after the Norman conquest, together with his mother and those mercenaries of hers marched towards Scotland. He had collected a huge army of soldiers, the majority of whom went willingly rather than under compulsion. When the army arrived at York, there was a serious conflict between the citizens and the mercenaries from Hainault, in which many citizens were killed by night and part of the city burnt.[2] After peace had been restored on terms too favourable to the men of Hainault, the army moved forward towards Scotland. The Scots were waiting for them at Stanhope park. Although the English army was three times bigger than the Scottish and, as all knew, of a much stronger composition, the Scots, who were in league with some perfidious English nobles, were allowed to return home unharmed by these traitors, with the friends of the king of England knowing nothing about it.[3] The king returned to England. It was a weak beginning, but the prelude to happier and better

---

[1] There may have been separate chronicles for the two reigns (see introduction, p.xxv). See appendix for the alternative version of the text from 1327 to 1329.

[2] Le Bel, 36-8 [43–7], gives a full eyewitness account of this; he was with the Hainault contingent under John of Beaumont.

[3] The Scots simply decamped on the night of 6-7 August and went home. Edward is said to have wept in frustration at his failure to engage them in battle: *Brut*, i.251

things. He sent back home the men of Hainault and the other mercenaries, who took with them as presents large sums of money and many choice jewels.

In this year lord James Berkeley, the bishop of Exeter, [36] entered upon the way of all flesh and lord John Grandison was consecrated bishop of Exeter as the pope's appointment in the Roman curia on the feast of St Lucy.

In this same year lord Edward, the father of the king, crossed over to heaven, as I have said earlier.

In this year Charles de Valois, the uncle of Charles king of France and of Isabella the mother of the English king, was accused of treason. He had always hated the English, and, as I have said, had led a French army against the earl of Kent in Gascony, but now he was accused of inviting the French king his nephew, that is the son of Philip the Fair his brother, to hunt and dine with him in a desire to murder him, and for this unworthy act he was handed over to his executioners. The story goes that after the hunting some mace-bearers of the king entered the room where the banquet was to be held and discovered that a treacherous scheme was afoot. For armed men, who had a palisade in a wood full of troops, murdered those of the king's inner household sent in advance to the banquet by putting nooses of silken cords around the necks of these nobles and hanging them from beams. It was only with difficulty that the mace-bearers escaped from a struggle and told the king of the danger devised against his person. So the king took himself off to other safer parts and Charles de Valois was taken prisoner. Although he was guilty of lèse-majesté, out of reverence for his royal blood he was not hung or beheaded but was made to sit without under-garments on bare marble, which was continually sprinkled with cold water until de Valois ended the length of his evil days through the cold.[1]

This Charles was the brother of Philip the Fair the former king of France. [37] Philip had three sons, Louis king of Navarre, Philip count of Poitiers and Charles, once count of the March near Gascony but then the current king of France, and also one daughter, Isabella queen of England of whom I have spoken, whose son was that glorious and magnificent triumphal king, Edward III king of England. Now the son of that Charles de Valois was Philip de Valois, father of the John of whom I will speak later.

After the death of Philip the Fair, king of France, his son Louis took his father's crown, urged on by the advice of his uncle Charles, but in the first year of his reign he sentenced to death by hanging Enguerrand de Marigny, who had been the principal counsellor of his father Philip. Also his queen, the daughter of the count of Burgundy, was accused of adultery with the knight Philip d'Aunay and put to death by suffocation.[2] Then Louis married

---

1   This curious story, which sounds more like the sudden executions of high-ranking nobles under Charles de Valois' son and grandson, Philip VI and John II, is not found in any other chronicle, English or French. Charles de Valois died on 16 December 1325.

2   For the affair of the Tour de Nesle, in which the wives of Philip's three sons were all accused of adultery with Philippe and Gautier d'Aunay, see E. A. R. Brown, 'Diplomacy, adultery and domestic politics at the court of Philip the Fair', in *Documenting the Past*, ed. J. S. Hamilton and P. J. Bradley, Woodbridge & Wolfeboro, NH, 1989 62-77. One of the consequences of the episode was the lack of heirs to the French throne.

Clementia, the daughter of the king of Hungary. She bore him a son, who lived for just seven days. When later the baby's father died and left this world, Philip succeeded to his brother's kingdom. But when Philip without having produced an heir of his body met his father and brother on death's journey, he was succeeded as king by Charles, the third of the brothers.

When his uncle, Charles de Valois, a man of extreme cunning, saw that his nephew's queen, once a countess, had for a long time failed to get pregnant and that the king was despairing of fathering a child, he began to hope, and not in vain, that the kingly crown might fall into the hands of himself or his heirs. And so he took steps to accelerate this desired good fortune by hastening to shorten the life of his nephew Charles, who was then king. He was also goaded to such an act of madness by his fear of the king of England. For he knew that the young Edward was lawfully by reason of his mother the next heir to the kingdom of France of his uncle Charles, and he was afraid that he himself and his heirs might be justly set aside and that Edward, who was already successfully ruling over England, Ireland, Gascony and other western lands, might also follow his grandfather and three uncles and become king of France. That sad old traitor thought that it was possible that his nephew king Charles might live for a very long time without producing an heir. If that happened, then king Charles' nephew, the king of England, whose continually increasing royal power was detestable to him, might either through his own greatness or through his just adoption [38] by the nobles of France, frustrate the hopes for rule of himself, who would then be an old man, and of his heirs and justly deprive them of the French kingdom. What he thought might happen did actually happen, as by the grace of God will become clear later.

Robert Bruce also died in this year.[1] He left behind a son David who was seven or eight years old, and the Scots made him their king. His right of succession was as follows. Alexander, king of the Scots, had three daughters but no sons. The first was married to John Balliol, the second to John Comyn and the third to Robert Bruce, an Englishman born in Essex. After the death of king Alexander, with the consent of Edward king of England the Scots had appointed as their king John Balliol, the husband of king Alexander's eldest daughter, and Balliol on behalf of the kingdom of Scotland did homage to the king of England and swore fealty to him. But later, at the instigation of the disturbers of the peace of the kingdom of Scotland, John Balliol renounced by royal letter and by noble envoys the fealty and homage which he been forced to give and promised various other forms of subjection which he was willing to demand from king Edward. Despite this, he nevertheless kept the kingship of Scotland, but not for long. For the king of England extended a long arm from Winchester and put to flight from Scotland John Balliol king of the Scots[39] and his son Edward.

While the two of them were journeying to France, the English king seized the castles and fortifications of the Scots, and the Scots, in an act of nothing

---

[1]   7 June 1329

other than witless rashness, took for their king the husband of the second daughter of king Alexander, namely Robert Bruce. For he was a warrior to his fingertips, except that, failing in his ambition of becoming king, he abandoned the loyalty without which no warrior wins praise and dared to rebel against his natural lord.

Well, as I have already described, that Robert died and the Scots planned to have his son as the next heir to the kingdom and as their king. But their plans were to be scattered to the four winds by Edward Balliol, the son of king John Balliol and the eldest daughter of king Alexander, who returned from France to make peace with the English, with the help of God and Edward III king of England, whose famous deeds I am intending to describe.

In AD 1327, in the twelfth year of pope John and the first year of king Edward III, Charles king of France entered upon the way of all flesh.[1] He was the uncle of the king of England and the brother of Isabella, the mother of our king, and also the third of those three brothers who ruled one after another after the death of their father Philip the Fair. He was succeeded as king by Philip de Valois, the son of his uncle, that traitor Charles de Valois, whom I have written about earlier.[40]

In the fifteen days of Easter of this year, in a parliament held at Northampton in the name of the king but not by his contrivance, a shameful peace was made between the English and the Scots. It was agreed between them that David son of Robert Bruce, who, as I have said, had been chosen as king of the Scots, should marry Joan the sister of the English king and should rule peacefully together with her as the rightful king of the Scots.[2] This afterwards came to pass. Also in the same year the young king of England, who was neither ruling himself nor being well ruled by others but being led astray by traitors, granted a new charter to the Scots, although there was a general ignorance of the details of its conditions and contents. In the old charter the people of Scotland together with their king John Balliol had made a perpetual submission to the English both of themselves and their heirs, and, as a witness of this, the seal of the king of Scotland, together with the seals of the leading men and prelates of that kingdom, had been affixed to this same charter. But now, before the eyes of the councillors of both kingdoms, the old charter was brought in on a long spear, read out, and then completely revoked and burnt in the presence of all at Berwick. It was at Berwick that David, having married the sister of the king of England,[3] was crowned king. When the little lad was brought to the altar, he stained it because of the diarrhoea from which he was suffering, so that one of the Scots, James Douglas, said to his friends, 'I am afraid that he may

---

[1]   1 February 1328
[2]   The treaty was accepted by the English on 4 May 1328. The Scots accepted it separately, and referred to it as the treaty of Edinburgh. For analysis of the negotiations, the treaty itself and the consequences, see Sonja Cameron and Alisdair Ross, 'The Treaty of Edinburgh and the Disinherited (1328-1332)', *History* 84 (1999), 237-56. David was four and Joan seven when they were married on July 17.
[3]   17 July 1328.

stain the whole kingdom of Scotland.' Because of this mishap he was called by blasphemers, 'David altar-shitter.'[1]

David was the first of all the kings of Scotland to be anointed at his coronation with the holy oil. At a parliament held in York the Scots made a petition about the great stone, which was known as the throne of the Scots, because the kings of Scotland had been customarily enthroned upon it. This stone was now fixed by iron chains to the floor of Westminster abbey under the royal throne next to the high altar.[41] The Scots asked that the stone should be released and given back to them so that they could consecrate their king upon it as they had done of old. The council of the king gave its assent to this petition and high-ranking envoys were sent to get the stone. But when the abbot of Westminster heard the request of the envoys, he wrote to the king and his council, saying that this stone had once been brought from Scotland with immense effort by Edward, the king's grandfather, and devoutly offered by him to the abbey, so that now it could not and should not be carried off from that church. After this response the envoys returned to Scotland without the stone.[2]

This marriage and all the good things that now happened to the Scots came about as a result of the schemes and efforts of Isabella mother of the king, Adam bishop of Hereford[3] and Roger Mortimer on the English side, and of James Douglas on the Scottish side. Isabella, Adam and Roger favoured the Scots because they were afraid that they might be driven to seek Scottish help when attacks were justly hurled against them as a result of the death of Edward the father of the king. Or, as some said, if the king of England should die through some misfortune, Roger Mortimer through Scottish help could then get his hands on the kingdom and on Isabella the mother of the king. It was also said the reason why the earl of Kent, the king's uncle and his closest ally by blood, was later beheaded was so that the young king Edward should be deprived of all the help of his friends, just as once his father had been.[4]

When David's coronation and marriage had been thus celebrated at Berwick, James Douglas journeyed to the Spanish frontier near Granada. Here this stout knight showed his worth in praiseworthy efforts against the Moors and Saracens. After many victories which God gave to the Christians under his leadership, James fought on his own against five Saracens all at once. He received five fatal wounds and was killed by the Saracens. But he also killed all of them, a feat which was witnessed by the Carmelite brother Thomas

1   The nickname is recorded by the *Brut* chronicle, i.255; the *Chronicon de Lanercost*, ed. J. Stephenson, Edinburgh, 1839, 349, mentions it in connection with his capture at Neville's Cross in 1356.
2   A writ to the abbot requiring him to surrender it was issued on 1 July 1329, but was successfully resisted by him: see Joseph Ayloffe, *Calendars of the Ancient Charters, and of the Welsh and Scottish Rolls, Now Remaining in the Tower of London*, London 1774, lviii..
3   There is no evidence to support Orleton's involvement; on the attempts to blame individuals for unpopular policies at this time see Haines, *Church and Politics*, 39.
4   For a discussion of Mortimer's attempts to infiltrate Edward's closest circle see Ormrod, *Edward III*, 80..

Lavington, who was then as a secular doing all he could in the army of the Christians under the leadership of James Douglas. The incident was doubly pious for Douglas. For Robert Bruce on his death bed had honoured him by saying, [42] 'I made a vow to God that I would fight abroad in person against the enemies of Christ. I shall not be able to do this now in my lifetime. Of all my dearest Scottish friends you are the most experienced soldier, and so I beseech you to carry my heart to the frontier at Granada and fight against the enemies of the name of Christ.' James said in reply to him, 'I call upon the heart of Christ Jesus and swear by it that I will both carry your heart, as you have asked, and will die fighting against those accursed enemies.'[1]

After this marriage of his sister, the king of England, soon after the feast of the holy Trinity, travelled to Hereford for the solemn nuptials of the daughters of Roger Mortimer with two nobles, the son of the earl marshal and the heir of lord John Hastings. There also took place there an important tournament, at which the mother of the king was present.[2]

In the month of November of this year came the death of Walter, archbishop of Canterbury.[3] He was succeeded after a canonical election by master Simon Meopham, doctor of theology. Also in this year died master Thomas Cobham, bishop of Worcester.[4] He was succeeded by Adam Orleton as a papal appointment. Adam had previously been bishop of Hereford, but he had gone to the curia on his own business and on that of the mother of the king. The pope also appointed master Thomas Charlton, who was then present in the curia, as bishop of Hereford.

In AD 1328, the second year of the reign of the third Edward after the conquest, after the fifteen days of St Michael the king held a parliament at Salisbury,[5] at which he made three men earls. Lord John of Eltham, his brother, was made earl of Cornwall, Roger Mortimer was made earl of the March of Wales, and Butler of Ireland was made earl of Ormond.[6] The earl of Lancaster, lord de Wake and some other nobles absented themselves from this parliament, and lord Henry Beaumont and the earl marshal were in their company. But they came under arms to the vicinity of the parliament. This angered the king, but later on during the summer, at the instigation of the archbishop of Canterbury, they made their submission to the king's grace at Bedford.[43] Soon afterwards the earl of Lancaster went blind and devoted himself completely to the patient service of God.[7]

1   This story is also told by Le Bel, 53-4 [86–9], from whom it was copied by Froissart.
2   31 May 1327: J. Smyth, *The Lives of the Berkeleys*, Gloucester 1883, I, 325
3   9 November.
4   27 August 1327.
5   16 October – 31 October 1328.
6   James Butler.
7   This is not entirely accurate: he was active in government service in the early 1330s, after Mortimer's fall from power, and as late as 1339 he was party to a treaty between England and Brabant. He died on 22 September 1345.

In the same year around Ascension time the king crossed the sea,[1] leaving his brother the earl of Cornwall in charge of the kingdom, and did homage with certain qualifications for the whole duchy of Aquitaine and the countship of Ponthieu to the king of France, Philip de Valois, the son of Charles the traitor. But Philip, king of France, accepted the homage with different qualifications, namely that he was not accepting homage for the lands which his father Charles had ridden across against the earl of Kent, as I have described earlier, but was keeping these for himself and intended to keep them until he should be recompensed for the losses and expenses which his father had sustained and incurred while fighting there[2].

In the same year Simon, archbishop of Canterbury, held a provincial council in London.[3] Some weighty measures were passed: on Good Friday and on the commemoration of all faithful souls there should be a complete cessation from work done in service, and on the feast of the glorious conception of the virgin the mother of God praises should be paid to God in celebration. Also the archbishop and the other bishops present excommunicated and published as excommunicated all those who in any way had laid violent hands on Walter Stapleton, bishop of Exeter, when he was so dreadfully murdered, and also all those who had given them their help or consent or advice.[4]

In AD 1329 certain men wished to find out which people were still friends of Edward II, the recently murdered king of England. So they made up the story that he was living a life of great ease in Corfe castle, but was never willing to be seen in the daylight. To back up this story, on many nights they danced over the walls and towers of the castle, carrying before them candles and lit torches, so that the country bumpkins who witnessed it should imagine that they were honouring some great king whom they were guarding in the castle. The news [44] spread through the whole of England that the father of the king was still alive.

So the earl of Kent sent a Dominican friar there to find out the truth of the matter. He thought that he had bribed the porter of the castle and would find out the truth, but he was himself tricked. For he was taken into the castle so that he might lie hid in the daytime in the porter's lodge, but at night time might see whom he wished to see. When night came, he was told to put on ordinary clothes to conceal his identity and was led into the hall. There he seemed to see Edward the father of the king in person sitting royally at supper. Believing this to be true, he reported what he had seen to the earl of Kent. So the earl, in the presence of some men whom he should not have trusted, swore

---

[1]   He arrived in France on 26 May 1329: Ormrod, *Edward III*, 82.
[2]   The issue was in effect that Philip was refusing to give back the Agenais, which Charles had conquered in 1324.
[3]   27 January 1329: *Annales Paulini*, i.344
[4]   The duplication in MS Bodley 761 ends here.

that he would work for the deliverance of his brother from the prison where he was being kept.[1]

In the same year, the third year of his reign, the king held a parliament at Winchester at the prompting of those who hated his father.[2] As a result of the strings pulled by the king's mother and Roger Mortimer at this parliament, the earl of Kent the king's uncle, many other nobles and men of religion (provincials of the Dominicans and the Carmelites of the blessed Mary) and brother Richard Bliton were accused of conspiracy. For it was claimed that they had plotted to release the king's father from prison and to restore him to his kingship, even though this whole matter was a fabrication and a fantasy.

Then the earl, on account of some confessions he made and some letters which were found about him, was beheaded, although none of these confessions or letters, even if they had been true, should have made this great earl deserving of punishment. As for the others, the provincials of the Dominicans and the Carmelites of the blessed Mary were exiled, the bishop of London was released and the priest Robert Taunton and some Carmelite and Dominican brothers were put in prison. The earl's death was not particularly displeasing to the people of England, seeing that the wicked men of his household had roamed the land, picking up things belonging to the people at the 'royal' price, that is paying little or nothing for their purchases.

In this year about the middle of Lent the church at Salisbury [45] became vacant through the death of master Roger Martival,[3] and by papal provision lord Robert Wyvil, the secretary of the king's mother, was appointed to this church.

Also in this year lord John bishop of Bath died.[4] The canons elected in his place master Ralph of Shrewsbury, doctor of law and theology. He was consecrated by Simon, archbishop of Canterbury.

Also in this year the pope repeatedly brought weighty processes of law against the duke of Bavaria who was tyrannically usurping the Roman empire.

In this year of 1329, on 15 June the feast day of St Vitus and St Modestus, queen Philippa gave birth to a son at Woodstock, Edward prince of Wales, the firstborn of the king.[5]

---

[1]   The rumours of Edward II's survival appear to have been spread by Roger Mortimer with a view to entrapping men like the earl of Kent and archbishop Melton of York who were ready to believe that he was still alive, and to use the former king as a means of overthrowing Mortimer and Isabella: see Ormrod, *Edward III*, 85-6, and R.M. Haines, 'Sumptuous Apparel for a Royal Prisoner: Archbishop Melton's Letter, 14 January 1330', *EHR* cxxiv (2009), 885-94; Kathryn Warner, 'The Adherents of Edmund of Woodstock, Earl of Kent, in March 1330', *EHR* cxxvi (2011), 779-805.

[2]   11 March to 23 March 1330: *PROME* iv. 97-8.

[3]   14 March 1330.

[4]   9 May 1329.

[5]   Information repeated (correctly) under 1330 below.

In AD 1330, the fourth year of king Edward III, on the first Friday after the feast of St Luke, a parliament was held at Nottingham,[1] at which Roger Mortimer the earl of March, glittered in all his transient glory as the principal adviser of queen Isabella, at whose nod everything was arranged. Nobody dared call him by any other name than earl of March. A bigger, noisier crowd waited on him than waited on the king's person. He awarded honours to those he loved. He allowed the king to stand up out of respect for him. When he went out with the king, he would arrogantly walk side by side with him, never letting the king go in front though sometimes doing that himself. An official, who had been assigned to the lord king to arrange lodgings for his nobles and had secured a lodging inside the town for the earl of Lancaster, the kinsman of the king, was roundly rebuked by the earl of March, wanting to know who had lodged a bold enemy so near to queen Isabella. The terrified constable gave his master a lodging for the earl of Lancaster a mile outside the town, and placed in the other lodging the earl of Hereford and John de Bohun of Essex, the constable of England.

Murmurs of criticism, which flew to the ears of the people, now arose among the nobles from those who said in secret that Mortimer, the lover of the queen and the king's master, [46] was panting to overthrow the royal blood and usurp his royal majesty. Such murmurings brought terror to the king's ears and to such friends of the king as William Montagu, Edward de Bohun and others. These now formed a conspiracy to save the king. They considered, and justly, that they would be saving their country and doing it a service, if they were to put that Mortimer to death. The conspirators were joined by Robert Holland[2] who had been keeper of the castle for many years and who knew well all its most secret winding ways. They discussed with him how the king and his friends without the knowledge of the doorkeepers might get access from outside the castle to the queen's bedroom.

With lighted torches the keeper led his master the king into the castle by a secret underground passage, which began from far outside the castle and ended in the middle of the kitchen or of the hall of the main tower where the queen was lodged. Springing from the depths of the underground pathway, the friends of the king armed with drawn swords made for the queen's bedroom, which by the grace of God they found open. They left the king outside the door so that his mother should not see him and entered the room. They killed the knight Hugh Turpington who tried to stop them, the blow being dealt by lord John de Neville of Hornby. Then they found the queen mother apparently prepared for bed and sleep and the earl of March, the man they wanted. They seized him and took him away into the hall, with the queen crying aloud, 'Dear boy, dear boy, have pity on gentle Mortimer.' For she suspected that her son was there, even if she could not see him. The conspirators speedily sent

---

[1]   19 October 1330. This was not a parliament but a council of state, in that writs of summons were not issued in the normal form.

[2]   He was in fact William Eland; Robert Holland was constable of Chester Castle.

for the keys of the castle so that the complete control of the castle had now passed into the king's hands. But they did this so secretly that no one outside the castle knew of it, except the friends of the king.[1]

At dawn the next day, amid a terrifying hue and cry, with the earl of Lancaster who was now blind himself joining in the shouting, they took Roger Mortimer and some other friends of his, who had been seized with him, through Loughborough and Leicester to London. Here he was committed to prison in the tower, as had happened to him once before,[47] and, by the verdict of the parliament of the realm sitting at Westminster, on the following eve of the feast of St Andrew[2] he was drawn and hung on the common gallows of thieves at the Elms, and thus by his death brought to an end the civil wars which throughout his whole life had been frequently started by him. He was judged worthy of death by his peers in this parliament, yet he did not appear in person before them and he was not given the right of a reply, for ever since the deaths of the earls of Lancaster, Winchester, Gloucester and Kent, nobles were not given the chance to state their case but perished without reply and without lawful conviction. Hence this earl came under the law which he had appointed for others, and he justly had the same measure meted out to him which he had meted out to others[3].

The causes for the death of the earl of March which were placed upon him were as follows.[4] Firstly, that he had consented to the suffocation of the father of the king. Secondly, that in return for a large sum of money he had stopped the king from winning honour at Stanhope Park. For it was he who had given the Scots the signal to flee, at a time when it was thought that the English army would probably have won the battle, if Mortimer himself, who was to all intents and purposes the leader of the boy king and of the army, had not been jealous of the king having a glorious start to his reign. Thirdly, that it was he who had brought about the marriage arranged between the sister of the king and the son of Robert Bruce, of which the friends of the king had already repented, and who had advised, or rather ordered, the abolition of the submission, which the Scots of old owed to the king of England, by means of the burning of charters and the generous grant of complete liberty, as I have already described in detail. Fourthly, that he had used up to no purpose in superfluous expenditure on himself and the queen mother the moneys found in the treasuries of the king and the earls of Winchester and Gloucester,

---

[1]   Other accounts of this event are given by Sir Thomas Gray, *Scalacronica*, ed. and tr.Andy King, Surtees Society ccix, Newcastle 2005, 104-7 (Gray served with Montagu in Flanders in 1337, and this may be his source) and the *Brut* chronicle (i.270-1). Gray says that a postern gate was left open, but this does not preclude the use of the tunnel mentioned in the *Brut* and Baker, since such a gate was used for a concealed exit. Baker builds on the fairly brief exchanges in the *Brut* to construct a conversation which incriminates Isabella and Mortimer as lovers. See intro-duction, p. xix

[2]   29 November 1330.

[3]   Matthew 8:2.

[4]   This is a summary of the case put forward against him in parliament: see *PROME* iv.103-106.

while he had never shown any concern for the needy state in which the king found himself at the beginning of his reign. Fifthly, that he had appropriated to himself wardships and rich marriage dowries at no small loss for the king. Sixthly, that he had deliberately been a bad councillor of the king, and that he had shown this trait particularly when, in order to confirm the friendship of the French king to himself, he had instructed the easily persuaded boy king to go to France as king and by a demonstration of homage and fealty to acknowledge Philip de Valois as the true king of France. This deed also was properly regretted [48] by all the friends of the king. Public opinion does not allow me to uncover the other causes of his death. We must leave these to the secrets of his conscience and to the examination of the eternal Judge. Also put to death with him were his friends the knight Simon Bereford and John Deverel his squire. As a remission for his sins Deverel would have willingly made a public confession about the cruel death of the king's father and the manner in which he was murdered, if he had not been denied the time for this by the enemies of justice and of truth.

In this year the lord king with the bishop of Winchester and lord William Montagu and just a few others crossed the channel. Just like a merchant, the king travelled with knapsacks but without armour and had barely fifteen horsemen with him. He gave out that he was travelling to fulfil a vow and left his brother, John of Eltham, in charge of the kingdom.[1] Before the end of the month of April he returned, and there was an impressive tournament at Dartford. And a little before the feast of St Michael there were the most handsome tournaments at Cheapside in London, attended by the lady queen Philippa and a large retinue of her maidservants. The canopied tents, which had been newly set up for the spectators of the tournament, collapsed, though without doing any harm. The pious queen did not allow the carpenters to be punished, but by her prayers and genuflexions so recalled the king and his friends from their anger that by this act of mercy she caused everyone to love her, as they thought about her goodness.[2]

In this year the lord pope John XXII, in the fifteenth year of his papacy, allowed the king tithes for four years on the goods of the English church, keeping a half of them for himself.

In this year, that is 1330, the fourth year of the king, on 15 June there was born at Woodstock the firstborn son of the king, lord Edward of Woodstock. I hope that the divine mercy will allow me to write in their places of the praises and the proud triumphs he enjoyed in his capture of the French king and on other occasions.

---

[1]   The real reason was to negotiate with Philip VI over outstanding matters concerning his homage.

[2]   The tournaments were on 2 May and 23-25 September 1331. There is a fuller account in *Annales Paulini*, 352-5.

In AD 1331, the sixteenth year of pope John and the fifth year of Edward III the king solemnly celebrated the feast of Christmas right up to Epiphany at Wells. Many expensive marvels took place there.

Around the time of the next following feast of St Laurence[1] there arrived in England Edward Balliol, the son and heir of John, king of the Scots. As I have said, he had formerly been exiled, but now he was declaring his right to the kingdom of Scotland. At his side came also lord Henry Beaumont, David earl of Atholl, Richard Talbot, the baron lord Ralph Stafford, Fulk FitzWarin and many other nobles, all asserting claims to lands and possessions in the kingdom of Scotland, which belonged to them by right of inheritance or as dowries from their wives but which had been unjustly seized by the magnates of Scotland. So they asked the English king that he would allow them to recover their kingdom and the estates which belonged to them and that he would help them to do so. But the king of England thought of the peace recently made between the kingdoms and the fact that his sister was queen of Scotland, and so did not allow them to march with an army through his land to attack Scotland.[2]

So these nobles acquired a fleet and, starting from English waters, they made for Scotland under sail. When they tried to land on the shore at Kinghorn near Dunfermline abbey, they met with stouter resistance than they had expected. But the few English infantry quickly landed and drove into flight all the Scots that met them together with their leaders, the earl of Fife and Robert Bruce, the son of Robert who had once been king; and, before the army of armed men could march down to the shore in proper array, many Scots had been killed, and the standards of Edward Balliol and the other lords had been peacefully set up at Dupplin Moor. Then on the day of St Lawrence there was a major battle at Gaskmoor. Two thousand English defeated forty thousand Scots, who because of their numbers even crushed one another in the mêlée. Five earls and many other men were killed or overwhelmed. The next day the English took the town of Perth, which was stocked with food and well fortified. They held on to it for a long time afterwards,[50] though by divine rather than human means, as the Englishmen then present told the tale.[3]

In this year the archbishop of Canterbury visited the diocese of Bath and celebrated Christmas at Wiveliscombe, while the king, as I have said, was at Wells. The archbishop gave instructions that he wished to begin his visitation of the church of Exeter on the Monday after the feast of the Ascension. The bishop of Exeter appealed against this happening. But, despite this, the archbishop arrived at the town of Exeter on the said Monday, but was not

---

1   Probably the feast of St Lawrence martyr, 10 August 1331, rather than St Lawrence archbishop (3 February).

2   'Edward III clearly knew about Beaumont's plans for a war of private enterprise, and there can be little doubt that he gave it his unofficial blessing.' Ormrod, *Edward III*, 149-50.

3   On the action at Dupplin Moor, see R. Nicolson, *Edward III and the Scots*, Oxford 1965, 85-90.

allowed to enter the closed church by the crowd of armed men who prevented it.

In AD 1332, the sixth year of the king, now that the Scottish war had begun, many English nobles and soldiers were invited with promise of payment to join lord Edward Balliol and his companions. Together with many others who were eager for praise and who joined them at their own expense, they set out for Scotland around the feast of the nativity of St John Baptist, and laid siege to the town and castle of Berwick.[1] Now the king of England gave thought to the many insults which he and his predecessors had suffered at the hands of the Scots. He also considered that the cause of lord Edward Balliol, king of Scotland by conquest, was a just one, and that the concord existing between himself and the Scots had been brought about by treachery, when he himself was publicly treated as a minor in the custody of his mother, who herself was ruled in all things by the counsel of Roger Mortimer, that traitor to him. And so, like the apostle Paul, when he became a man, he put away childish things.[2] Against the wishes of his mother he collected an army. He alleged, not the defence or the establishment of his own rights, but his advancement and support of the just claim of his friend Edward to be king of the Scots, and a little before the feast of St Margaret, he made a strong attack on Berwick.[3] Those being besieged had many treacherous discussions with the king of England and the conqueror of Scotland, just so that they might keep their town free from assault, while waiting for the help promised from outside. This help did come, but in vain. [51]

In AD 1333, the seventh year of king Edward III, on the feast of St Margaret the virgin, a huge army, gathered from all Scotland and divided into three forces, challenged the king's army to battle, intending, if possible, to lift the siege of the town. An agreement was made between the two sides:[4] if on that day the besieged Scots succeeded in receiving food from outside, they could continue with their rebellion, but if they were not comforted by such food getting through, they would surrender the town and castle to the king of England the next day. So four hundred armed Scots with supplies of small bread rolls were appointed to go round the flanks of the English army and to throw their rolls inside the walls so that technically at any rate it could be claimed the town was filled with food. But the men appointed to rescue the town in this way were killed by the mass of besiegers and by the rearguard of the English army and robbed of their bread rolls.

---

[1]   Edward arrived at Berwick about May 17 1333. Ormrod, *Edward III*, 615.
[2]   1 Corinthians 13:11.
[3]   27 June 1333: Nicolson, *Edward III and the Scots*, 123
[4]   The agreement had been made on 15 July, and specified that the town must be relieved by vespers on 19 July. It also set out the terms on which the town would be considered to have been relieved. The requirement that the town should be filled with food is not among them. Nicolson, *Edward III and the Scots*, 127

The English now divided their army. One half was told to continue with the siege, while the other, further divided into two squadrons, was prepared for meeting those Scots who had come to relieve the town. In this battle the English nobles learned from the Scots to keep their warhorses in reserve for hunting down the fugitives, and, contrary to the ancient custom of their fathers, to fight on foot. At the beginning of this battle between the armies fought on Halidon Hill a Scottish champion of enormous size took his stand in the middle between the armies, and, trusting more in his great physical strength than in God[1], this second Goliath challenged any Englishman to fight with him in single combat. This champion was called 'Bull turner,' in English 'Turnbull,' because this is what he could do. From the opposition ranks, Sir Robert Benhale, a knight from Norfolk,[2] on bended knee sought a blessing of the king and attacked the giant with sword and shield. A black mastiff accompanied and helped the Scottish champion. Sir Robert, with one stroke of his sword, cut the dog's loins and back into two halves. At this the dog's master came on more fiercely but also more rashly, and the knight cut off first his left fist and then his head.

At once the two sides engaged in battle, with the English king encouraging his men with wise and suitably cheerful words, but, because of the fierceness of the fighting on both sides, the day in its course had scarcely passed [52] its midway point when the Scots, with quite a few killed and with their three divisions now massed into one army, were finally forced to seek refuge in flight. The English king and his nobles mounted their horses and in hot pursuit drove the Scots into their wells and their very lakes, killing some and taking others prisoner, and scattering them over a five mile area. The number of Scottish dead was estimated at more than sixty thousand men. After that battle the false opinion was put abroad that the war with Scotland had finally ended, seeing that there was hardly a Scot remaining who had the ability, knowledge and wish to assemble an army and command it when assembled. The prelates of almost the whole kingdom of Scotland fled to France, and the more powerful of them went to the high pontiff and in tears begged him for help and assistance in their trouble.

After this victory the king returned to the siege of Berwick, and received the surrender of both castle and town from its governor earl Patrick. In the next following parliament at York this same earl Patrick swore fealty and homage to the king and received many honours from him. But he again broke faith, returned to his rebellious ways and found himself besieged once more, this time at Dunbar by William Montagu, earl of Salisbury.

The king carried out his will on the men of the town and castle of Berwick, and left behind a garrison for his loyal subjects of the town and castle, saying that the town belonged to his dominions by hereditary right after its conquest by his predecessors. He left behind in control of the whole Scottish kingdom

---

[1]   1 Samuel 17:45.
[2]   He was one of Edward's household knights in 1334-5.

Edward Balliol, the king of Scotland, and the others who wished to stay with him. He himself, on his return to England, went on holy pilgrimage to various places and in deep devotion gave the thanks due to God.

In the same year, around the festival of St Calixtus (the pope), the church of Canterbury became vacant because of the death of master Simon Meopham.[1] At the request of [53] the king the pope appointed to Canterbury master John Stratford, bishop of Winchester.

In AD 1333, the seventh year of the king, immediately after the festival of St Michael, lord Edward Balliol, king of Scotland, held a parliament in Galloway. It was attended by some English nobles who claimed lands and possessions in Scotland. After the parliament they returned peacefully to their native soil.

In the same year the king together with his pregnant queen celebrated the feast of Christ's nativity at Wallingford. The queen later gave birth to her daughter Isabella at Woodstock.[2] The king then went to York where he held a parliament which began on the Monday of the second week in Lent.[3] The king who had conquered Scotland was invited to the parliament, but did not come in person. Instead he sent some great men to make his excuses, namely the earls Henry Beaumont[4] and William Montagu and various other barons and knights. These announced to the English king that Edward, conqueror of Scotland, could not come into his presence without great risk to the resistance which was being made against the Scots who were lying hid in the islands. But the king did receive homage from this conqueror at Newcastle-upon-Tyne on the feast of St John following.[5] Also soon afterwards he received homage from the duke of Brittany for the earldom of Richmond.

He then summoned his prelates and magnates to come to him at Nottingham within six days after the feast of the translation of St Thomas, and there he arranged a parliament to be held in London. The prelates of the province were again summoned to this parliament, which was held on the Monday after the feast of the exaltation of the holy Cross,[6] and they made the grant of a tenth to the king. The people indeed made the grant of a fifteenth on lands and a tenth on merchandise throughout the whole kingdom, so that the evil Scots could be reined in. It was also reported to this assembly that the Scots had risen in rebellion and had taken captive Richard Talbot and six other knights and killed many foot-soldiers. Also in the same parliament the lord king acceded to the requests of some religious people and promised that he [54] would go to the Holy Land at his own expense. But he did not set a definite time for this. However he did command the archbishop of Canterbury to go to go to

---

[1]   12 October 1333.
[2]   Isabella was in fact born in June 1332.
[3]   21 February 1334.
[4]   Earl of Buchan in right of his wife. Montagu was not made an earl until 1337.
[5]   19 June 1334.
[6]   19 September 1334

the pope and the king of France, so that the kings I have mentioned, who had not yet been stirred to fight, could unanimously take up such a holy crusade together.

On 1 December in the same year the lord pope translated to the church at Winchester master Adam Orleton, who had previously been bishop of Hereford and then bishop of Worcester. Someone wrote these verses about his appointment:

> Thomas he left behind.
> Wulfstan he did not rule well.
> Why did he want Swithun next?
> Because its value was more.[1]

That is, it was a richer church. It was Philip of Valois, the pseudo-king of France, who ensured that this translation took place, for he poured out a stream of prayers on the subject to the high pontiff. But the lord king of England for a long time postponed the acceptance of it. He pointed out to the bishop that he had already been translated on other occasions. Also he said that at the time of Orleton's embassy to the king of France (for he had been the envoy when the king was crowned) he had pleased king Philip more than a loyal envoy could have done on that occasion. Indeed this was why his attempts to attend to the business of his lord, the king of England, had been useless and treacherous. And it was why Orleton had now found favour in the sight of this pseudo-king[2], who otherwise would never have bothered about the promotion of one Englishman, seeing that both he and his father had never loved an Englishman, as has already been shown and will be shown later. King Edward further argued against Orleton's translation that a nominee of the king of France could easily become a traitor to himself while working for his nominator, especially as that nominator had ignored the justice of God and men and had falsely and forcibly seized the crown of France, which belonged to king Edward by hereditary right, and the possessions of Edward's forefathers in Gascony.[3]

Nor was the king happy that the Roman curia was responsible for Orleton's translation. For, so it was alleged, the lord king of England had written to the lord pope, asking that another cleric should be promoted to that see and so took it badly that the pope should listen more attentively to the prayers of the king of France than his own concerning the appointment of bishops in

---

[1]   Thomas Cantilupe was bishop of Hereford, canonised in 1320:. Wulfstan was bishop of Worcester in the eleventh century, canonised in 1203. and Swithun was bishop of Winchester from 852 to 862, who was revered as a saint after his death. The contrast is between the supposedly venal Adam Orleton and his holy predecessors.

[2]   Esther 5:2 and 8.

[3]   The English administration was firmly opposed to Orleton's translation, and drew up a document making a series of charges against him concerning his behaviour at the time of Edward II's deposition, which form in part the basis for Baker's hostility towards him; Haines, *Church and Politics*, 61-63, 189-90. However, the support of Philip VI claimed by Baker seems to be entirely mythical.

his own kingdom.[55] For these reasons the king ordered the confiscation of the temporalities of the see of Winchester. However, on the Friday after the next following exaltation of the holy Cross, the king listened to the prayers of his bishops at a parliament in London and graciously refunded these temporalities.

Very soon after the feast of the Nativity in this year, Richard Bury was consecrated bishop of Durham in Chertsey monastery by the bishop of Winchester.[1] This was a papal appointment.

In AD 1334, the eighth year of king Edward, soon after the feast of St Dionysius,[2] John the archbishop of Canterbury crossed the sea to visit Philip of Valois, the so called king of France. In fact I prefer from now on to call him the tyrant of France, seeing that he was an enemy of the common justice and a usurper of the holy kingdom of France. The archbishop of Canterbury, a man of great wisdom and a leading exponent of both codes of law, went to this tyrant and asked for a happy continuance of the friendship between their kingdoms, based on the mutual love existing between the so-called king of France himself and his lord the king of England. Secondly he asked the tyrant that the towns and castles seized in Aquitaine by the tyrant's father, the traitor Charles, and kept by the tyrant himself should be restored to his lord the king of England. Thirdly he asked that the tyrant should recall his forces from helping the Scots who had no connections with him, and that instead he should help his relative, the king of England, against the Scots, either by troops or advice or just by being on his side. He added finally that on these conditions his lord the king was willing and ready to march at his own expense to the Holy Land with the so-called king of France against the enemies of the cross of Christ.

The tyrant's reply was that he judged the king of England to be unworthy of his friendship, so long as he kept up an unjust war against his friends the Scots, who were just men and ready, so he asserted, to comply with all just demands: he could not feel kindly disposed towards anyone who so savagely harassed those Scots by his invasions. As for the archbishop's second request, he could only agree to it if the king of England made good the expenses and losses incurred and sustained in the wars in Gascony by his father Charles de Valois. [56] To the third request he replied that he was a friend of the law and the common justice, and that he would never swerve from the justice which he loved because of kinship or a friendship based on the family. Instead his aim was, by all the ways and means in his power that he could devise, to increase the weight of the yoke of his persecution of all disturbers of the kingdom of the Scots. 'For peace,' said the tyrant in conclusion, ' will never be established among Christians until the king of France sits on the judgment seat in the middle of England and is judge and ruler over the kingdoms of

---

[1]   9 December 1333.
[2]   9 October 1334.

France, England and Scotland.' To that prophecy, which Philip de Valois made as the French king of that year, the archbishop made no further reply, but wrathfully withdrew to journey elsewhere.[1]

In the same year king Edward advanced to the marches of Scotland and wintered in those parts.[2] But when he heard that the earl of Atholl had treacherously gone over to the Scots and that Sir Henry Beaumont was besieged by the Scots, he invaded Scotland and got the siege lifted. He kept Christmas at Roxburgh.

Shortly after Epiphany the tyrant of the French sent the bishop of Avranches and a certain baron as his envoys to the king of England for the purpose of making peace with the Scots. The envoys waited around in England until the Monday in the middle of Lent. Then at Nottingham a truce was granted, which was to last until the next feast of St John, so that in the meantime a parliament might be held to discuss relations and peace between the kingdoms. In this parliament, held at York,[3] it was determined that the king with an army should ride across Scotland to beyond the Scottish sea, and this was soon afterwards done.[4] But the Scots had no wish to wait for a pitched battle, and pretended that they wanted to make peace. Many of them, but especially the earl of Athol, assembled for that purpose around the feast of St Michael, although others would have nothing to do with it.

As a result, the earl of Moray was afterwards taken prisoner near Edinburgh and committed to prison in England, while Sir Richard Talbot was ransomed for two thousand five hundred marks. Then the earl of Athol, wishing to show the genuineness of his return to the English side, rode [57] against the Scots in order to besiege one castle. But while he was riding with only a few followers, he fell among great numbers of the enemy. Unwilling to surrender he fought hard but was killed together with fourteen of his squires just after the feast of St Michael.[5] All this time the king remained on the Scottish border. The envoys of the king of France never left his side. They were waiting for a peace or a lengthy truce, which would not be just useless to the English but actively harmful.

In this year around the feast of St Martin Sir Edward Bohun,[6] a man of fine character, was drowned in the marches of Scotland. A page of his was trying to drive a herd of stolen cattle across a river. Sir Edward saw that he was in danger, and rode his warhorse into the stream to come to his aid. But the huge stones and boulders over which the waters were flowing were so smooth that

1   Haines, *Archbishop John Stratford*, 237-8.
2   He left Newcastle with a smaller army than he had hoped on 14 November 1334, planning to campaign through the winter. The project was abandoned in January, and Edward began his journey south on 2 February 1335. Nicolson, *Edward III and the Scots*, 181-8.
3   26 May 1335. PROME iv. 206
4   Edward mounted a major campaign from July to September 1335, with one of his largest armies.
5   At Culblean on 30 November 1335. Nicolson, *Edward III and the Scots*, 233.
6   Edward III's cousin, and twin brother of Humphrey Bohun, later earl of Hereford.

the horse was unable to keep its footing and fell, and its heavily armed master was drowned in deep water before anyone could help him.

Also on 4 December in this year pope John XXII died in his palace at Avignon. On 20 December pope Benedict XII was elected. He was crowned on the Sunday after the following Epiphany.

In AD 1335, the first year of pope Benedict XII and the ninth of king Edward, the king continued to remain in the marches against the Scots. Envoys from the pope and the French acted as mediators, but the many peace discussions were unsuccessful, and although many truces were granted at the urging of the crafty Scots, nothing concrete was achieved because the Scots had killed the earl of Atholl while a truce was pending, as I described in my record for the previous year.

In this year the king received a tenth from the burgesses, a fifteenth from other laymen, and a tenth from the clergy. Around Pentecost he held a parliament at Northampton.[1] He left the prelates and the others discussing matters, while he himself with a few men rode secretly to Berwick. From there he took a few armed men with him and came to the town of Perth, where his people were amazed at his arrival, especially with so small a company. He fortified Perth with ditches and ramparts and then sent his company together with the king of Scotland the conqueror to ride across his fatherland and to search out those Scots who were still resisting. But none [58] dared to wait for their coming, but hid themselves in the mountains, marshes and forests.

After the Northampton parliament the envoys of the French tyrant went back to France. They could see how the king of England and his parliament took very little notice of the letter of their lord Philip de Valois with its threats that he would be the enemy of the king of England, if Edward did not agree to peace with the Scots. Back in France they reported how at their urging the king of England had frequently made truces and peace agreements with the Scots to his own disadvantage, but also how he intended to ignore Philip's threatening letter and to resume war against the Scots, even though they were the tyrant's friends.

The tyrant congratulated them on their report. For he put out of his mind the truces which to please him the king of England had made with the Scots to his own disadvantage. Instead he ruminated on the lack of attention paid to his threatening letter, and rejoiced that he had found a pretext for unfurling his fleur-de-lys banner against his kinsman and the true heir to the kingdom of France which he himself had usurped. So, puffed up by anger and pride, the tyrant roused the French to war against the English. This was the beginning of that terrible war, which the tyrant himself could not bring to an end, even when he had been often routed in battles on sea and on land, and when the kings of Bohemia, Scotland and France had been killed or captured and much blood had been spilt by those who were redeemed by the blood of Christ.

---

[1]   A royal council, not a parliament, held in the king's absence at the end of July.

In AD 1336 around the time of Epiphany the king and the archbishop of Scotland returned to London for the burial of lord John of Eltham earl of Cornwall, the brother of the king. He had suffered the common fate of death at Berwick in the previous October. They buried him at Westminster.[1]

The king called a parliament at London for the Monday after the feast of St Matthias the bishop and the first Sunday in Lent.[2] At it he made his firstborn son Edward duke of Cornwall; Henry of Lancaster, the son, earl of Derby; William Bohun earl of Northampton; William Montagu earl of Salisbury; [59] Sir Robert Ufford earl of Suffolk; Sir Hugh Audley earl of Gloucester, and Sir William Clinton earl of Huntingdon. Together with these he made twenty-four new knights.

It was also decreed at the same parliament that no wool produced in England should be exported but should all be made into cloth by the English, and that all fullers and weavers who had been properly taught how to make cloth should be welcomed in England and enjoy certain privileges, of whatever grade they were and wherever they came from. Also, they were to live free of taxes to the king and to make whatever livelihood they could that was appropriate to their skill. Although, at the start, this regulation seemed devoid of profit, the kingdom's manufacture of cloth subsequently increased by more than twenty times its previous estimate.

It was also decreed at this parliament that no one in future should buy cloth brought to the country from overseas manufacturers and that no one should wear fur, unless he had an income of £100.

In AD 1337, the eleventh year of the king, soon after the feast of St Michael, the lord king held a parliament in London and the archbishop a convocation of the clergy.[3] The clergy granted a tenth to the king every three years, and at the same time the towns of burgesses and non-burgesses granted a fifteenth, both of them for help in the Scottish war which was then boiling up and for resistance to the French tyrant who was displaying the savagery of his nature by his threats and cruel deeds. For he even outlawed or killed or imprisoned with confiscation of property all Englishmen found in France, menacingly claiming that he was wanting to avenge his friends the Scots. Moreover he did not leave for king Edward any town or castle in the dukedom of Aquitaine or the countship of Ponthieu which he was able to take into his own hands. And so the English king, to get the money as soon as possible for wool sold for an agreed price to merchants of the kingdom, sent the thirty thousand sacks of wool to Brabant under the escort of a fleet, commanded by the earl of Northampton. As the earl had in his forces a huge contingent of archers and

---

[1]   In January 1337.
[2]   3 March 1337; much of the business had been prepared at a great council at Nottingham the previous September. *PROME* iv.208–227. See Ormrod, *Edward III*, for the political background to this decree, designed to promote the cloth industry in England.
[3]   26 September 1337.

Welshmen, [60] he persuaded the count of Brabant to change his mind and to stand as a friend of the king of England against all his enemies.

Also in the same year the English king wrote letters explaining how hostilities had arisen between himself and the tyrant of France. He gave these letters to his faithful knight from Burgundy, Sir Walter Mauny, to be taken by him to the counts of Hainault, Guelders and Juliers. All these counts in letters patent to the king promised him their loyal friendship against all his unjust enemies. While he was on this embassy Sir Walter Mauny wished to avenge the blood of two Englishmen, who had been killed by the inhabitants of an island near Flanders when they were in search of fresh water for their ships, and he gave orders for all the men found in this island to be put to death at the mouth of the sword. These orders were put into effect, with Sir Walter himself standing by.[1] He also took prisoner the brother of the count of Flanders. But when the brother was brought before the English king, he was honoured with beautiful presents, with horses and with jewels and sent back to Flanders a free man.

So this is how the war against the French began. When news of it reached the Roman curia, the lord pope sent two cardinals to restore peace between the two kings.[2] The two cardinals in the king's presence at Westminster explained the reason for their coming. A king's council was summoned for the day after the purification of the glorious Virgin.[3] After consulting with his leading men king gave this final reply to the cardinals. He said that he had been distressed beyond measure by two things, the denial of his generally acknowledged right to succeed to the kingdom of his ancestors, and the cruel way in which his enemy Philip de Valois had behaved towards the English. For not only had he driven out the English from the kingdom of France as if they were Jews or enemies of Christ, and killed, robbed and imprisoned them. He had also unjustly and without cause taken away from himself the duchy of Aquitaine and the countship of Ponthieu, and in addition had encouraged the Scots in rebellion against him by his support, advice and actual aid. But, despite all this, the king said that he gladly agreed to the peace between the nations asked for by the church. He made an offer to the cardinals, [61] as if to the king of France, for the pardoning of these injuries; in return for peace and the peaceful possession of Aquitaine and the other feofs which had belonged to his ancestors and which he himself ought to possess by right, and also in return for the recall of the French troops helping the Scottish rebels, he, the king of England, would give a sum of money to be agreed upon by discussion between themselves or the marriage-portion of his firstborn son, and he

---

[1]   Sir Walter Mauny was not from Burgundy, but from Masny in Hainault, and had been a page of queen Philippa's; in the Scottish campaigns Jean le Bel noted (61 [110]) that 'of all the army he was one of those who exerted himself the most and risked the most, and it earned him the king's great favour.' In this case, he seems to have overstepped the mark, and endangered the very alliances Edward was seeking.

[2]   They arrived in December 1337: Ormrod, *Edward III*, 197.

[3]   3 February 1338.

would also renounce his right to the crown of France and provide help against the Saracens.

Having received this reply, the cardinals left the council with light hearts, thinking the war was now over.[1] On the next feast of the translation of St Benedict, accompanied by John archbishop of Canterbury, Richard of Durham and the knight Sir Geoffrey Scrope, they set sail to carry the reply of the English king to the French tyrant, and with the authority to treat for peace.[2] But all king Edward's very reasonable offers were never able to soften the mind of a tyrant who was confident that with the help of the Scots he could forcibly remove the king from the kingdom of England and all his other possessions.

In AD 1338, the fourth year of pope Benedict, the twelfth of this name, Edward king of England soon received a reply from the French tyrant rejecting the terms offered to him (which I described in my account of the previous year) and rejecting the help of the king of England against the Saracens. The king also realised from clear signs reliably reported to him by his loyal subjects that the French tyrant had hired pirates and also had organised his own army for the destruction of England. And as he thought it safer to meet his adversary boldly in the kingdom of France to which he laid claim than feebly to wait for his cruel appearance in England, he crossed the sea with a fleet of armed men on Friday 16 July in the twelfth year of his reign. Accompanied by his pregnant queen and her two daughters in his fleet of five hundred ships he landed at Antwerp. They were given an honourable and peaceful welcome and had meetings with the marquis of Juliers, the duke of Brabant, the counts of Guelders [62] and Hainault and other magnates of those parts. These all promised him their loyal support against all his enemies with the sworn proviso that they would be fighting at the king's expense.

After this the king went to Cologne, where he had discussions with Louis, duke of Bavaria, who said that he was the king of Germany and the Roman emperor. He then returned to Brabant, and stayed in the town of Antwerp for a time. After further discussions with the king of Germany and the establishment of friendship between the two of them, the king of England returned to Malines in Brabant. The cardinals and the bishops of Canterbury and Durham returned from their audience with the tyrant of the French, and waited for the king at Arras.

In a council of that year called by the duke of Cornwall as guardian of the land and by the prelates and the barons, a grant of wool to the king from the people was made by those who were present.[3] In a further meeting on 1 October of the clergy, who had been absent at the previous council, the clergy

---

1   This was hardly likely, unless they were extremely optimistic; it is possible that the re-mark is connected with Archbishop Stratford's efforts to promote a peace in opposition to the king's determination to go to war: Haines, *Archbishop Stratford*, 255
2   The English envoys were appointed on 21 June 1338: *Foedera*, II.ii.1043
3   At the parliament of 26 July 1338 at Northampton.

granted a tenth for the third year after then, but unanimously refused the payment of wool made by the people.

In AD 1339 the king of England was making arrangements, as I said before, with the dukes of Bavaria and Brabant and his other friends for the pursuit of his right to the kingdom of France. Meanwhile the French tyrant, in his wish to vomit forth his evil intent, long ago conceived, to clean out the kingdom of England, hired ruthless Genoese pirates and sent them to damage the shipping and harbours of England. In the harbour of Sluys in Flanders they captured and took to Normandy five large ships of the king, the ships however being empty of men and merchandise, as the sailors had gone ashore for some carefree amusement.[1]

Also, at about 3 pm on the next Saturday after the feast of St Michael,[2] fifty galleys well packed with armed men landed at Southampton. The troops sacked the unprotected town and spent the night there, as the townspeople had run away in a panic flight. But the next day the people round about came to the help of the townspeople and three hundred of the [63] pirates were killed, including their captain, a young knight who was the son of the king of Sicily. The French tyrant had granted to this knight whatever he could obtain in the kingdom of England. But he was knocked flat by some English rustic, and although he shouted out, 'Ransom,' he was beaten and clubbed to death by this same rustic who shouted back, 'Yes, I know that you are a Frenchman';[3] for he did not understand his victim's speech, and he had never learned about preserving well-born prisoners for ransom. So those Genoese left alive, after burning just Southampton, fled to their galleys with some of them being drowned. Afterwards the inhabitants built a strong wall all around their town.

In this year the king of England spent the whole winter at Antwerp, where the queen bore him a son, lord Lionel, the earl of Ulster.[4]

Also the king was made a vicar of the empire by the duke of Bavaria, who claimed to be the emperor. On this matter the pope sent the duke of Bavaria a quite strongly worded letter of remonstrance and advice, dated the thirteenth of November in the fourth year of his pontificate. While this was going on, the king was still as before overseas, for the moment suspending the war undertaken for his rights.

On the eve of the feast of the Annunciation[5] eleven galleys set fire to the town of Harwich, but a contrary wind stopped the blaze from spreading and

---

[1]   These were the *Edward*, *Christopher*, *Black Cog*, *Catharine* and *Rose*; the *Edward* and *Christopher* were recaptured at Sluys in 1340. For this and the raids on England in 1338-9 , see Graham Cushway, *Edward III and the War at Sea*, Woodbridge & Rochester NY 2011, 74-79. Baker says that four ships were retaken: the *Christopher*, the *Black Cog*, *Dionysus* and *George* (p.61 below).

[2]   3 October 1338.

[3]   In the original, 'ransom' and 'Frenchman' are nearly identical: 'rancoun' and 'Francoun'.

[4]   Born at Antwerp on 29 November 1338.

[5]   24 March 1339.

doing harm. Later on in the year about the time of Pentecost, Norman and Genoese pirate galleys and pinnaces again showed themselves on the sea off the port of Southampton. Their envoys, whom they told to spy out the resources of the town, said threateningly that they were intending to land. But because the pirates found the townspeople prepared to resist, they turned instead to the isle of Wight. However they did not land here either, giving way before the inhabitants who prevented it. Next they moved to other less well fortified places along the coast, where, behaving like robbers, they did much damage. Afterwards on the feast of Corpus Christi[1] they burnt some fishermen's huts and boats at Hastings and killed their owners.

Next they many times showed themselves off the isle of Thanet, Dover and Folkestone, but did little harm in those places except to some poor fishermen. Then in the harbours of Cornwall and Devon [64] they did much harm to the fishermen and burnt the vessels which they found unmanned. Finally in the week of Pentecost[2] they suddenly entered Plymouth Hoe, where they destroyed by fire some large ships and a great part of the town. They were met by Sir Hugh Courtenay earl of Devon, an octogenarian knight, together with some other knights of that county. These men of Devon lost a few of their men, who were disarmed and killed by the crossbow bolts of the enemy archers, but they then attacked the pirates at close quarters. They killed many of them on dry land and drove the remainder down to their ships. Many of these could not reach their ships and some five hundred, according to the estimate of those present, were drowned in the sea.

The king was still in Brabant when he heard the grim news from messengers that the ruthless pirates of the French tyrant had completely destroyed Southampton and other ports of England together with their ships. In the presence of his friends, the marquis of Juliers and the cardinals, the king pointed out that he was now bound to take his revenge on his enemy the tyrant of the French. But the cardinals said in reply to this, 'The kingdom of France is surrounded by a silken thread, which all the power of England is not strong enough to break. And so, my lord king, you must wait for the Germans and your other allies, most of whom have still not arrived, so that with their help you may at least seem able to do damage to the French, and can then make an honourable peace with the powerful French king, with ourselves by the grace of God as mediators.'

The king and his earls were furious at these words. They had no thought of waiting for the Germans or for money from England to arrive, for the king realised that by waiting he would lose more of the time which was suitable for war. Finally he declared that he would ride into the land of France with his banner unfurled. There he would wait for the threat of the French power and either overthrow its onset or die honourably in the battle.

---

[1]   17 June 1339.
[2]   After 16 June 1339.

On the eve of the feast of St Matthew in AD 1339,[1] the thirteenth year of his reign, the king of England with twelve thousand armed men began to ride against the tyrant with banner unfurled, burning and destroying towns and castles wherever he went. [65] On the first night, when darkness had filled the sky, Sir Geoffrey Scrope, the justiciar of the lord king, took one of the cardinals, Bertrand de Montfaves, deacon of Santa Maria in Aquiro, to a large, lofty tower and showed him that the whole land towards France for a space of fifteen miles was everywhere on fire. He said to him, 'My lord, does the silken thread surrounding France seem to you to have been broken?' Without making any reply to this, the cardinal fell down as though dead, stretched out on the floor of the tower in sorrow and fear.

For five weeks the king continued his advance into the kingdom of France. On each day's march he went as far as his army could manage, and, as the people fled in fear before him, his soldiers laid waste the whole district of Cambrai, Tournai, Vermandois and Laon, except for the walled cities with their churches and castles. Never did anyone dare to block his path as he marched, even though the French tyrant in person had gathered his men in huge armies inside his walled towns and himself lay hid in St Quentin, the strongest town. Nor did the tyrant ever dare to go outside the walls of the towns to defend the land, which he said was his, against the king of England at the head of the English army in the open field. As a result, among the other insults hurled by the whole world against the tyrant, someone shot the following verses, on a piece of paper tied to an arrow, into the town of St Quentin:

> If, Valois, you're a fighter of valour, away with your fear.
> Don't stay lurking in hiding, make your strength clear.
> A flower without dew, in the fields you wither and dry.
> MENE, TEKEL, PERES;[2] no lion, but a hare or a lynx. [3]

And, because he was called Philip de Valois, someone else used his name in these lines:

---

[1]   20 September 1339.

[2]   Daniel 6:25-7; like Belshazzar, Philip is found wanting and is condemned.

[3]   *Political Poems and Songs relating to English History,* ed. Thomas Wright, Rolls Series, London 1859, I, 40:
>   Si paleas valeas, Valoyes, dimitte timorem;
>   In campis maneas, pareas, ostende vigorem.
>   Flos es, flore cares, in campis viribus ares,
>   Mane techel phares, lepus es, lynx, non leo, pares.

Geoffrey's version reads:
>   Si paleas, valeas, Valoys, dimitte timorem;
>   Non lateas, pateas, maneas, ostende vigorem.
>   Flos es, rore cares, campis marcescis et ares;
>   Mane techel phares; lepus et linx, non leo, pares.

There is a further variant in the poem on the battle of Crécy printed by Wright (I, 28) from which the next couplet comes. See Rigg, *A History of Anglo-Latin Literature 1066-1422,* 261, 263 for both verses.

'Phi' denotes filth, 'lippus' sore eyes, which all hours are harmful.
Both filth and sore eyes are bad. So in all ways 'Phi-lippus' is bad.[1]

The men from Brabant now decided to go home, as their food had run out
and the keen cold of winter was at hand. While they were on their journey,
the French king [66] noticed their absence and moved his men towards the
army of the English king, who awaited the coming of the tyrant with pleasure,
and recalled the men of Brabant. When he received a letter from the tyrant
saying that he wished to join battle with the English king, the king replied
that he was willing to wait for him on the plain for three days. But although
the king waited for him for four days on the chosen field, the tyrant refused to
come any nearer than two miles from him. Instead he broke down bridges, cut
down trees and covered open paths with their lopped off branches to prevent
the king from following him.[2] He himself returned to Paris in disgrace. When
the king of England learned of this, he followed the advice of his friends and,
owing to a lack of provisions, returned through Hainault to Brabant, where he
spent almost the whole winter.

During this time he formed a close alliance with the Flemings. They
were ready to swear complete obedience to him and to do him homage and
fealty, provided that he called himself the king of France, and from then on
wore armour decorated with the fleur-de-lys as a sign of that kingship. For
otherwise they dared not obey him because of an interdict of the pope which
had been placed upon them if ever they rebelled against the king of France.
So on the advice of his nobles and friends the king came to an agreement with
the Flemings, took up the name and arms of the king of France and received
Flanders into his dominions. From that moment the Flemings over a long
period obeyed him in all things as being the king and conqueror of France.[3]

On this matter of the title and the arms the French tyrant once spoke as
follows to some Englishmen who had been sent to him. 'We are not displeased,'
he said, 'that our cousin wears arms quartered with the arms of France and
England joined together. For we would gladly allow him to bear part of our
royal arms, seeing that he is a mere bachelor from the weaker side of our
parentage.[4] But what does annoy us is that in his seal and letters he names
himself king of England before king of France, and that he puts that quarter of
his arms with leopards as the first quarter before the quarter with the fleur-de-

---

[1]   *Political Poems and Songs*, I, 27:
       Phy foetet, lippus occulis nocet, ergo Philippus
       Dux nocet et foetet, sordida fata metet.
      Geoffrey's version reads:
       Phi nota fetoris, lippus nocet omnibus horis,
       Phi nocet et lippus; nocet omnibus ergo Philippus.
      'Lippus' is sore-eyed in classical Latin.
[2]   The French were encamped at Buironfosse and the English at La Flamengrie; the abor-
      tive encounter is known by either name.
[3]   The formal proclamation took place in the marketplace at Ghent on 26 January 1340:
      Ormrod, *Edward III*, 212.
[4]   Philip is pretending that Edward is only a simple knight bachelor, not even a banneret.

lys. For we can see from this that he judges the small island of England to be more worthy of honour than the great kingdom of France.'[1]

Sir John Shoreditch, a knight and envoy of the English king, said in reply that his lord the king of England had only been following contemporary [67] custom and had quite reasonably put on his arms the title and badge of his forefathers above the title and badge which had come down to him on his mother's side.

While the king was busy with the matters I have just described, some sailors from the Cinque Ports just after the feast of St Hilary[2] embarked in well-armed pinnaces and light boats and landed on the coast at Boulogne. In the misty weather they were hardly noticed in the harbour, and in the lower town they burnt 19 small galleys, 4 large vessels and 20 light boats with their equipment as well as the houses on the waterfront. One such house was very large and crammed with oars, sails and the crossbows needed by the sailors and marines of the nineteen small galleys. Finally a fight started between the townsmen and the English, and several of the inhabitants were killed and fell.

Not much later, at the beginning of February, the king left his pregnant wife behind in Ghent and returned to England.[3] He held a parliament at Westminster,[4] during which the laity granted him a ninth fleece of wool, a ninth lamb and a ninth sheaf of every sort of corn, and the clergy granted a nineteenth. The king at this parliament also decreed and had it proclaimed that no Englishman should bear arms for the French king, just because of Edward's title and arms as king of France.

Soon after Easter[5] the earls of Salisbury and Suffolk with just a few men made an attack on the town of Lille in Flanders which was on the side of the king of France. In pursuing the fleeing Frenchmen they came too close, in fact inside the gates. The portcullis fell. The Englishmen were suddenly surrounded on all sides by a crowd of armed men, taken prisoner and conveyed into France. The two most experienced knights (unless that rash attack should stop them being called experienced), were callously treated by the arrogant and angry Frenchmen. Although they had given their word not to escape when they surrendered, they were actually shackled in irons and carried, not on horseback, but in a cart like robbers.[6] And in the middle of each small town or village an order was given for the cart to halt so that the prisoners could be cursed and shouted at by the populace. Like this they were brought into the presence of the French tyrant, who would have starved them

---

[1]   See W. M. Ormrod, 'A Problem of Precedence: Edward III, the Double Monarchy, and the Royal Style', in *The Age of Edward III*, ed. J. S. Bothwell, Woodbridge and Rochester NY 2001, 133-153 for a full discussion of the question.

[2]   Mid-January 1340.

[3]   20 February 1340.

[4]   29 March to 17 May 1340: *PROME*, iv.261–76

[5]   16 April 1340.

[6]   The shame of a knight appearing in a cart is the central theme of the Arthurian romance by Chrétien de Troyes known as *Lancelot or the Knight of the Cart*.

in a squalid [68] prison and then shamefully put them to death, if he had not followed the advice of the king of Bohemia and abstained from his blood lust.

In AD 1340, the fourteenth year of his reign in England, the lord king kept the feast of Pentecost at Ipswich while preparing for his crossing to Flanders. He had intended to travel with just a small company, but when he heard a rumour that the French tyrant had sent a great Spanish fleet and practically the whole French navy to block his passage, he himself summoned from the Cinque Ports and elsewhere his own navy of two hundred and sixty ships both great and small. On the Thursday before the feast of the nativity of St John Baptist,[1] with a favourable wind blowing, the king began an easy crossing and on the Friday, which was the eve of that nativity, he caught sight of the French fleet in the harbour at Sluys, ready for battle and drawn up like lines of castles. He anchored out at sea and all that day considered what was the best thing to do.[2]

But very early next morning on the feast of St John the French fleet divided into three squadrons and moved a mile nearer the king's fleet. When he saw this, the king said that they should wait no longer, and he and his men ran to arm themselves and were soon ready. After 3 pm, when he had the wind and the sun behind him and the tide with him, he divided his fleet into three squadrons and made his long desired attack on the enemy. Blood-curdling cries ascended to the heavens above the wooden horses, just as Merlin had prophesied.[3] An iron rain of bolts from crossbows and arrows from bows sent down thousands to their deaths. Those who wished or were brave enough to do so fought at close quarters with spears, axes and swords. Many had their brains knocked out by stones thrown down from the tops of masts. With no word of a lie, there was fought a sea-battle so massive and so dreadful that a faint-heart would not have dared to look upon it even from a distance.

The size and height of the Spanish ships nullified many of the English attacks. But in the end the French were defeated, and the English took possession of their first squadron, having driven the men from the ships. The French ships were then chained together so that they could not be parted the one from the other. With just a few English guarding that first squadron which was now empty of Frenchmen, the other English ships turned their attention to dealing with the second French squadron, and with great [69] difficulty made an assault on it. But the men were driven out of it more easily than from the first squadron, for the French for the most part now left their ships of their own accord and drowned in the sea. By the time that the first and second naval squadrons had been defeated, it was getting dusk and the English decided to wait until the morning, both because of the darkness

---

¹   23 June 1340
²   See Cushway, *Edward III and the War at Sea*, 90-100, for a full account of the battle and its consequences: also Ormrod 222-4.
³   Not traced; 'the prophecies of Merlin' was often a generic term for political prophecies, and was not restricted to Geoffrey of Monmouth's *Prophetia Merlini*.

of the night and their own extreme weariness. As a result the thirty ships of the third squadron escaped during the night. One of these ships, a huge vessel called *James of Dieppe*, wanted to tow away with it a ship of Sandwich, which belonged to the prior of Christchurch at Canterbury. But its sailors with the help of the earl of Huntingdon put up such a stout resistance that the struggle lasted the whole night. On the next day, when the Normans were eventually defeated, the English found in the captured ship more than four hundred men slain.

When at daybreak the king discovered that thirty ships had escaped, he sent forty well armed ships in further pursuit. In command of them was John Crabbe, who was thought by the English to have experience in naval matters and knowledge of French harbours. But what his experience achieved is unknown.

In the first squadron of captured ships the victorious English found the four ships, which, as I described earlier, were originally stolen and taken away from Sluys harbour by the French. The names of these ships were firstly *Dionysius*, secondly *George*, thirdly *Christopher* and fourthly *The Black Cog*.[1] The number of warships captured in that battle was as many as 200 and the number of barges as many as 30. The enemy lost more than 25,000 men killed and drowned. The English lost 4,000 men killed, including four knights, Sir Thomas Monthermer a kinsman of the king, Sir Thomas Latimer the son, Sir William le Boteler of Southborne and, so it was said, a fourth knight, whose name I have not heard.

About the same time the Scots refused to keep the truce made between themselves and the king and advanced into England in great numbers. Almost the whole march suffered from the killings and burnings of these plunderers. Even when they were about to take their loot back home, the marcher lords of the area took no steps [70] to meet them in a battle, or rather kept putting it off, although they had been given much money by the king to guard the marches. It was the common people who bravely attacked the Scots as they returned homewards. They recovered the captured booty, killed many of the enemy and imprisoned for ransom more than eighty of the more important Scots.

Afterwards, around the time of the feast of St Peter ad Vincula, some French pirates with Spanish help made an attack on the Isle of Wight.[2] Their unexpected landing was met by the knight Sir Peter Russell and the people of the area. They powerfully drove off the pirates and killed many, but the knight was fatally wounded and died in the struggle. The pirates then moved on to Devon and burnt the town of Teignmouth. Then they sailed round to Plymouth but did no damage to the well-defended town, although they did burn some manors outside the town and took with them wherever they pleased a certain knight whom they had taken prisoner.

---

[1]   See n. 130 above.
[2]   30 July 1340. See Cushway, *Edward III and the War at Sea*, 107-8

After the naval battle described earlier, the king led back to England the forces which he had taken out.[1] He divided the spoils among his earls, and visited the holy places of England, where he humbly gave thanks to the Giver of victories. Later, with the agreement of the important men of his council, he crossed the sea to Flanders, as he had previously planned. He took with him Robert count of Artois, who had lived for a long time in England at the expense of the king. He had fled for refuge to the king of England because, of course, he had been looking for help against the French tyrant who was unjustly occupying the lands of his fathers in Artois and Brabant. The king, in return for his homage, had pledged help and now provided it. He led his army through Flanders and Brabant and through the dominions of France and his own inheritance, and he again spent a long time firing the towns, putting the French to flight, and burning their cornfields or trampling them under his horses' feet. Finally he sent back to England the earls of Gloucester, Arundel and Huntingdon to watch over the kingdom and laid strong siege to the city of Tournai.[2] He had with him the marquis of Juliers, the duke of Burgundy and the counts of Hainault and Guelders[3] and with a few Englishmen he kept up a very strong blockade of the town, as the Flemings [71] sold him abundant stocks of the food which he needed. Of course agreements of mutual support had just been confirmed between themselves and the king of England, and in all matters they behaved towards king Edward, as if he were really the king of France.

Now that the siege had in this way been firmly established, the king wrote to Philip of Valois, tyrant of the French, saying that he would wait for him on the field of battle, so that the issue between them might be decided on a day to be fixed. The tyrant replied, appointing the day on which he threatened to lift the siege. But he never kept his word, although during the whole period he was lurking in his army not more than four miles from the siege.

The count of Hainault was given leave to lead his own men and three hundred archers and a few armed men from England against the town of St Amand, which was about fifteen miles away from the siege. These troops captured and killed fifty knights and many others and in their destruction of the town and all the nearby countryside they found almost boundless riches. The result was the provision of plentiful supplies of food for the army.

The siege of Tournai lasted right up until the feast of SS. Cosmo and Damian, which is the day before the eve of St Michael.[4] On this day, after repeated discussions about the possibility of a truce, the French did secure one. At their request it was agreed that the truce would last from then right up to the next

---

1 Baker is confused here. Edward did not return to England, but stayed in Flanders, while his fleet returned. Pilgrimages after a campaign occur in autumn 1333 after Halidon Hill, and in March 1343 after the Breton campaign (Ormrod, *Edward III*, 162, 224). On the latter pilgrimage he presented gold ships to commemorate Sluys to Walsingham, and to St Paul's, Canterbury and Gloucester .

2 The siege formally began on 1 August 1340.

3 'count of Celrie' in the Latin original.

4 27 September 1340. The truce was in fact agreed two days earlier:*Foedera* ii.ii, 1127.

feast of St John Baptist, so that in the interval peace might be discussed. Also prisoners were given back on both sides, but with an agreement under oath that they would be returned again on the feast of St John Baptist, if a final peace had not been arranged by then.

So ended the siege of Tournai. To tell the truth, the king of England was not best pleased. The trouble was that, although he only had a few Englishmen with him, they were all mercenaries, and for fifteen days they had not been paid, as the expected money had not come from England. Also the duke of Brabant and the count of Hainault had only been giving powerful military help to the king so that he might assist them to regain the towns and castles which the French king had taken from them and was unjustly holding. But now that they had actually regained them and the reason for their efforts no longer existed, they had no further wish to fight the wars of another. So with one accord they called upon the king, and almost compelled him, to make a truce, [72] since he was obliged at that time to do as they wished. The only people who were not pleased by the making of the truce and the lifting of the siege were the English, the Flemish and the other few mercenaries.

So the king departed for Flanders and returned to Ghent on the feast of St Michael. There he stayed for a long time, waiting for the confirmation of the truce and the arrival of the money, which never came.[1] All the Englishmen waiting with the king in Ghent thought that he was staying there for the feast of the nativity of Christ. But one day the king, with no previous word of warning to his household and on the pretence of wanting to go for a walk, rode off in secret with eight of his men and came to Zeeland. Here he obtained a ship and after a voyage of three days and three nights he entered the Tower of London by water in the darkness about cock-crow on the feast of St Andrew. He was accompanied by the knights Sir Nicholas Cantilupe, Reginald Cobham, Giles Beauchamp, John Beauchamp, and by the clerks William Kildesby and Philip Weston.

At dawn the king immediately sent for the chancellor, the treasurer and the justices who were then in London. He at once removed the bishop of Chichester[2] from his position of chancellor and the bishop of Coventry[3] from his office of treasurer, as it was his intention to have sent them to Flanders to act as pledges for the money. But the bishop of Chichester pointed out to the king and his councillors the danger of the canon law which loomed over those who imprisoned bishops, and so they were allowed to leave the tower. But the king gave orders for the following people to be sent to different prisons: the senior justices, that is Sir John Stonore, Sir Richard Willoughby, Sir William Shareshull, and especially Sir Nicholas de la Beche, who previously had been

---

[1]   The income from the taxes intended to pay for the war had fallen drastically short of expectations: of an estimated yield of at least £80,000, only £15,000 had been collected, and only 5% of the revenue from forced sales of wool had been realised. The problems encountered are analysed in Ormrod, *Edward III*, 228-9.

[2]   Robert Stratford.

[3]   Roger Northburgh.

the keeper of the Tower of London, and Sir John Molines knight; also the merchants Sir John Pulteney, Sir William de la Pole and his brother Richard; and the senior clerks of the treasury, that is Sir John of St Paul, Sir Michael Wath and Sir Henry Stratford, and from the exchequer Sir John Thorpe and very many others. Nor did he release them from prison until the abatement of his anger at the withholding of the money which they should have sent for the siege of Tournai.

In this year about the time of the nativity of our Lord, came the deaths in Ghent of two of the principal councillors of the king, namely Henry bishop of [73] Lincoln and Sir Geoffrey Scrope, justice of the peace.

In AD 1341, in the fifteenth year of his reign in England, the king celebrated Christmas at Guildford, and afterwards held a tournament at Reading. Also on the feast of the Purification he held a great tournament at Childs Langley[1] in honour of the nobles of Gascony upon whom he had placed the belt of knighthood while he was there. Also in this year he made the knight Robert Bourchier chancellor of England, and he appointed the knights Robert Sadington and Robert Parning one after another to the office of treasurer. Also the king sent out justices to sit in every county and to inquire about the collectors of the tenths and the fifteenths and the wool, and about various other officials.

Because the people of London refused to allow justices to sit within their city to make inquiries of this kind, as this was contrary to the liberties of the city, the king gave orders that the travelling justices, when about to inquire about the deeds of Londoners, should begin their sessions in the Tower of London. But the Londoners refused to make answer there until their liberties were confirmed. And as no such confirmation could be got through briefs or charters of the king from the royal chancery, there arose such a tumult in the tower, fomented by persons unknown, that the justices made out that they were unwilling to hold their sessions there until after Easter. Meanwhile the king, who was deeply disturbed by the riot, went to great lengths to find out the names of those who had caused it, but could only discover that the authors of the tumult that had arisen were some middle-class citizens protecting their liberties. When he had calmed down, the lord king forgave the Londoners for this offence, and the justices gave up their sessions in that place.

In the fifteen days of Easter of that year a parliament was held in London.[2] The earls and great men of the realm, that is the peers and the commons, among other petitions asked that both the great charter and the charter about forest land together with other liberties of the church and kingdom should be observed to the letter, and that mayors should be chosen in the parliament by the peers of the realm to act as officials of the lord king. But on the advice of his

---

[1]   Correctly King's Langley, 2 February 1341.
[2]   8 April 1341.

private council the king refused to listen to these petitions.[74] The parliament as a result was prolonged right up to Pentecost, when the king did finally make the following concessions. From now on his chief officials would swear in parliament to act justly by every man as they carried out their duties. If they failed to do this, on the third day after the beginning of all parliaments they would resign their offices, make reply to the individuals complaining about them and, if necessary, be punished by the judgment of their peers. A decree on these and other matters was sealed with the seal of the king, and then the prelates and the other magnates were permitted to go home.[1]

About the beginning of July in this year the lord king received a letter from Louis, duke of Bavaria and the usurper of the Roman empire. Using as an excuse the alliance recently begun between himself and Philip king of France, Louis said that he was displeased with the war against the French started by the king of England and that he advised the re-establishing of peace and concord between the kings. He offered himself as a peace-maker, and promised that he would be glad and willing to spend time on this matter and to undertake the hard work involved in such a burdensome business. To make more sure of gaining his ends, he made this request of the king: 'May it please you to give us in a letter of yours a pre-arranged permission to negotiate an agreement and to set up a truce for one year or two.' Also later in the letter Louis excused himself for the friendship which, as I have said, he had begun with the king of France, by saying that he had been able to accept this friendship without dishonour, seeing that the king of England without the knowledge of the emperor had made a truce with king Philip with a fixed terms for peace discussions. For this reason the king of England should not be upset by his friendship with the king of France. He added as a coda to the letter, 'We have reasons for cancelling the office of vicar which we offered to you. Given at Frankfurt 14 June, in our twenty-seventh year as king and our fourteenth year as emperor.'

The king replied to what was called an imperial letter as follows: To the most serene prince, lord Louis, by the grace of God ever the august emperor of the Romans, greetings from Edward, by the same grace of God king of France and of England and lord of Ireland' – [2]

In AD 1342, in his sixteenth year as king of England and his third year as king of France, the king gave the earldom of Cambridge to John of Hainault,[3] the uncle of [75] queen Philippa. He then celebrated the feast of St Katherine and the solemn feast of the nativity of our Lord at Newcastle. Because David, king

---

[1]   Baker's account passes over the major confrontation between archbishop Stratford and Edward III during this parliament. He summarises very briefly the crisis between the king and a parliament trying to restrain his autocratic behaviour, which resulted in the major concessions made by the king.

[2]   The point is that Edward used the title of king of France in his reply, thus refusing Louis' offer of mediation.

[3]   Baker is wrong: William, marquis of Juliers, Philippa's brother-in-law, was made earl of Cambridge on 7 May 1340.

of the Scots, threatened to join him for this festival, the king gathered an army and invaded Scotland. He pursued the fleeing David to beyond the Scottish sea, destroying everything except the castles and marshes in which the Scots and their king David were hiding.

William Montagu, earl of Salisbury, assembled a fleet of small boats and invaded one of the islands (and that the best) of those belonging to Scotland which are called the 'outer isles.' He was victorious and conquered the whole of this island, which is known as the Isle of Man. The lord king generously gave possession of the island to the earl as its conqueror, and had him named and crowned as king of that land.[1]

Then the king returned to southern parts. He celebrated an outstanding tournament at Dunstable involving two hundred and thirty knights,[2] and in the same year allowed one tournament to be held in Northampton.

Also in a parliament held at Westminster[3] lord John, archbishop of Canterbury, was reconciled to the king. In the presence of the king in the parliament, though not regarding him as his disciplinary judge, he swore that, although it was with his advice and agreement that the king had done homage to the French tyrant for the dukedom of Aquitaine and the countship of Ponthieu, he had never agreed to this with the intent of harming the king or of currying favour with the French tyrant by giving advice of this kind. Rather it was because at the time he thought it was the best thing to do for peace and the advantage of the king and the kingdom.[4]

After this parliament the king had a gold coinage struck of three values, a noble of 6 shillings and 8 pence, a half-noble piece of 40 pence, and a quarter-noble of 20 pence.[5]

In AD 1343, the seventeenth year of the reign of the king, at the prayers of the king's friends, the landowning churchmen freely granted him as help in his just war precious jewels both gold and silver, and even horses and two-horse and four-horse chariots. As a result his treasury was noticeably enriched.

In the same year the king's appropriators were commissioned to find out which citizens, on their own account or on another's, held feof lands worth a hundred shillings or more, [76] and to report their findings to the king's council, giving the names of the landholders in writing. Also other men were commissioned in every county to assemble archers for testing and also other

---

[1]   Apart from the capture of Stirling by Henry Percy, there was little military action; tournaments were held at Melrose, Roxburgh and Berwick in December 1341 and January 1342. The dates for these and the following tournaments are supplied from Edward III's itinerary in Ormrod, *Edward III*, 618-9.

[2]   11-12 February 1342, to mark the betrothal of prince Lionel to Elizabeth de Burgh, countess of Ulster. The Northampton tournament was on 14 April 1342.

[3]   28 April 1343. *PROME* iv. 325-353

[4]   See Haines, *Archbishop Stratford*, 219. This refers to the homage of 1331; unlike that at Amiens in 1329, there was no qualifying clause, and the homage was specified as 'liege homage'. The differences were slight but important; but it is interesting that Baker thinks that this was the key issue in the dispute between king and archbishop.

[5]   Baker describes the unfamiliar coins as a gold penny, half-penny and farthing.

men capable of bearing arms. They were to bring the weapons with which they knew best how to defend themselves or attack the enemy. When all these who were of a lawful age had been assembled and tested, they were told that they should be ready at the king's command to go with him to fight his enemies and those of his kingdom. In the same year many, who were called to help the king against the Scots, were not prepared to go, but instead contributed money, with which the king could pay wages to mercenaries so that they could stay at home.[1]

In AD 1344, the eighteenth year of the king of England, various nobles were sent to help Sir John Montfort, duke of Brittany, whose wife and sons remained in the care of the king. They were the earl of Northampton, the earl of Oxford, Sir Hugh Despenser and Sir Richard Talbot, knights, and Sir William Kildesby the king's clerk. Each of them was in charge of great forces of armed men and archers.[2] They set out for Brittany, managed to land against the wills of their enemies who tried to stop it happening and fought many bitter battles against them. Finally, having already captured walled and unwalled towns and forts, they took by assault the castles of Brest and Temple-le-Carentoir. Now they had got control of the whole country, part surrendered and part destroyed, as far as the town of Morlaix. But here they were met by lord Charles de Blois with a huge army.

At this meeting of the enemy armies on open ground near Morlaix, the courage of both nations, the Frenchmen from Brittany and the English, was put to the test. Both sides fought so bravely in that battle that we never heard of the like happening in the battles of Halidon Hill or Crécy or Poitiers. On the one side the commander was Charles de Blois, to whom the French tyrant had given that land as his dukedom, and on the other was William de Bohun earl of Northampton, whom the king of England had put in command of this army so that he might protect the rights of John Montfort, the natural duke of that land.[3] These two commanders showed all the courage of high-born heroes and would have preferred to lose everything rather than turn tail and leave the field and so show themselves shameful faint-hearts. Both sides fought with great courage. In fact no Englishman or Frenchman, unless he was a liar, would be able to say that the French had ever fought so bravely or for so long hand to hand on the field of battle, in all the wars in France up to the capture of John, the pseudo-king [77] of the French.[4] Three times that day both sides withdrew a little to get their breath back and take a rest as they leaned on their pikes, lances and swords. But in the end, as the French soldiers fled, the great-

---

[1]   See F.M. Powicke, *Military Obligation in Medieval England*, Oxford 1962, 195–8
[2]   Northampton sailed on 14 August 1342; he was preceded by Despenser's small force, which had originally been intended for Gascony. Cushway, *Edward III and the War at Sea*, 112.
[3]   This was the English view: John of Montfort and Charles de Blois were rivals with very similar claims to the duchy.
[4]   i.e. Poitiers in 1356.

hearted Charles was forced to take to flight as well, while the English were left alone in peace and safety.[1]

In AD 1345, the nineteenth year of his reign, the king sent to Gascony Henry, earl of Derby and later duke of Lancaster, the earl of Devon, the earl of Pembroke, Sir Ralph Stafford who was not yet earl of Stafford but a baron, and Sir Walter Mauny.[2] These nobles conquered walled towns and castles, and bravely won many glorious victories. They took by storm the town of Aiguillon and assigned it to the custody of Ralph Stafford. Later they turned aside to other towns such as Bergerac, called 'the strong room of France' because of its fortifications, Saint-Jean d'Angély, La Réole and many other large, strong, well fortified places, all of which they captured after hard toil and dangerous assaults.

On this campaign the duke of Lancaster was often fighting in underground mines, dug to overthrow towers and walls. He met strong counter attacks from the brave defenders and fought hand to hand against the besieged, and in these same mines he made both Gascons and Englishmen knights, a thing unheard of before.[3] Indeed the duke of Lancaster rode across a great part of Gascony, and captured in the process two hundred and fifty towns, cities, castles and forts, Finally he got as far as Toulouse. Here he sent letters, inviting the ladies and high-born maidens of Toulouse to dine with himself and his earls and with Bernard, sire d'Albret, an Aquitanian loyal to the English. But God was protecting the city, for the earl of Lancaster did no harm to the inhabitants, except to make them shiver in their shoes, as the besieged afterwards told me.[4] Indeed the mendicant friars of the town had been forced to take up arms, as the prior of the Carmelites of the blessed Mary of Toulouse was in command of the citizens from his quarter of the town. He had a silver banner with a picture in gold of the blessed virgin on it, and, amid a hail of missiles, he displayed the picture on his banner at the walls of the town and he caused the duke of Lancaster and many of his army to kneel [78] in devotion to it, though among some he aroused only derision.

Later, around the Lent of the second year, the duke of Lancaster and the earls returned to Bordeaux, Bergerac and their other fortresses, taking with them the booty, the captives for ransom and the great quantities of gold and silver which they had amassed. When they had done this, John of Valois, the firstborn heir of the French tyrant and duke of Normandy, laid siege to the town of Aiguillon and its governor the baron of Stafford with a great crowd of young knights and not a few German mercenaries. They so cleverly

[1]   The result of the battle was far from clearcut: Northampton was surrounded by French infantry afterwards, and the French siege of Morlaix continued. See Sumption, i.402.
[2]   The expedition left from Falmouth on 23 July 1345. For the subsequent campaign, see K. Fowler, *The King's Lieutenant: Henry of Grosmont, First Duke of Lancaster*, London 1969, 53-64.
[3]   Reference to status of these duels.
[4]   See introduction, p.xiv for the implications of this remark. However, Baker has confused the expedition of 1345-6 with that of 1349: see Fowler, *The King's Lieutenant*, 84-8.

surrounded Stafford's forces with trenches that there was no access for the English to the men in the town without great danger, at least while the French were opposed to it. But no less cleverly and bravely did the besieged guard and defend their town, and very often their troops fought hand to hand against the French outside the walls and the gates. Indeed Stafford and his men were by no means idle. They several times had skirmishes with the besiegers, and they frequently cheered the besieged with fresh supplies of food. But they were unable to lift the siege completely. It was impossible to make a proper attack on the besiegers, who were protected by their trenches and who refused to agree to fight a battle on open ground. They replied instead that they had not come there to fight a battle, but to lay siege to that town.

This siege which they had undertaken lasted until after the feast of the beheading of St John. But then John of Valois heard that the king of England was campaigning against his father at Crécy. As he was afraid that he might get to his father's presence and council too late, he lifted the siege on his own initiative, and, having burnt his tents and pavilions, began a concealed flight in the darkness of the night. The besieged nobles, that is the earl of Stafford and the son of the sire d'Albret, chased after the fugitives and made an attack on the rear of their force. They cut off the tail, and brought back to Aiguillon horses and prisoners. The townsmen were also considerably enriched by the tents they saved from the fire, and greatly heartened by the joyful news of the flight of their attackers.

During these happenings in Gascony and the earlier ones in Brittany (all of them more remarkable than my account of them), the lord king was making his plans for crossing the sea. Archers were selected, the tenths and fifteenths were collected from the townsmen and the countrymen, and twenty thousand sacks of wool were granted to him. Also,[79] Sir Godfrey Harcourt of Normandy came to the king and asked for his help against the tyrant of the French, who had unjustly robbed him of his lands and possessions and was keeping them for himself as his own. He made homage to the king and swore fealty to him. Afterwards he was sorry for what he had done, and turned traitor on the king of England to take the frown off the French tyrant's face. I shall touch on these matters later.

In AD 1346, the twentieth year of the king, the earl of Northampton and the other lords who had set out with him for Brittany, as I have described, handed over the castles they had won in the duchy of Brittany, now well supplied with food, to the care of loyal men and returned with glory and honour to England and the presence of the lord king.[1]

After this, the king, who had a fleet waiting for him at Portsmouth and Porchester, was in a hurry to cross to Normandy. The earls of Northampton, Arundel, Warwick, Huntingdon, Oxford and Suffolk were to sail with him,

---

[1]   Northampton left from Southampton for Brittany on 11 June 1345, and was recalled in January 1346.

as were Sir Godfrey Harcourt, the bishop of Durham and the king's clerk Sir William Kildesby. Each one of these was taking with him a great mass of armed men and archers. But from 1 June to 5 July the king waited at Portsmouth and Porchester for a favourable wind which was slow in coming. At long last, marvellous to relate, they began to make sail with a thousand ships, pinnaces and small boats. Then the king's council met in secret. For the ships' captains still did not know to where to steer their ships when they left harbour, but, as ordered, were following the admiral. But on this same day the king sent messengers from his ship to the other vessels, which were now a long way from the shore. They were to tell the helmsmen to follow the admiral and to direct their ships to the harbour of La Hogue in Normandy.[1]

At last on 13 July they reached the harbour they were making for, and, when they had landed, the king made his firstborn son a knight and prince of Wales on the shore there[2]. The prince immediately knighted lords Mortimer, Montagu and Roos and, together with these, various others were similarly promoted to the status of knights. For the rest of the day and the whole of the night the king lodged in the town of La Hogue. On the next day, a Thursday, after his army had set fire to the town, the king marched through the countryside of Cotentin [80] and lodged for the following night in Morsalines.[3] He stayed there for five days, and during this time he laid waste the town of Barfleur and all that sea coast, and set fire to the town and the whole country roundabout. Then the English came to the fine town of Valognes, which they likewise burnt. Then to St Côme du Mont, near the river Douve, and Carentan. Then they came to Serins[4] and the city of St Lô and the fine town of Torigny, all of which were burnt, and that night the king lodged at Cormolain. Then they came to Gerin, a cell of the monastery of Caen,[5] and there nothing was left unlooted.

On the Tuesday following they made an assault on Caen, and, after a hard struggle, they entered this noble city by the bridge where the resistance had been fiercest. There one hundred and forty three knights were captured or killed. These included those good knights, the count of Eu and the count of Tancarville, the chamberlain, who with other prisoners and also the abbess of Caen were sent to England. More than one thousand three hundred of the citizens who resisted the English were killed. The army stayed in Caen for six days, and the spoils which had been seized up to then from the towns and the countryside were sent or sold to or through the sailors, who had been following the king off shore and destroying all the naval defences` of the French.

---

[1]   The account of the Crécy campaign which follows, its source and the relationship to other chronicles and records is discussed in the introduction, pp.xxi-xxiii above. Place names have been modernised throughout, and doubtful identifications indicated.

[2]   Edward had in fact been prince of Wales since 1343.

[3]   Baker is the only source to mention *Marcelins*, a small hamlet inland from the beach at St Vaast-la Hogue.

[4]   Possibly Sept-Vents, near Caumont.

[5]   Le Cairon, four miles west of Caen.

Then they came to a strongly defended monastery and to the town of Troarn, which is situated in the marshes, and afterwards to the fine town of Argences. By night they came to Rumesnil, burning everything. Then in the city of Lisieux they found the cardinals of Clermont and Naples and one archbishop, who all offered a peace treaty to the king. But the king, who stayed there for three days, refused to discuss peace at that time.

Then they passed by Le Teil-Nollent and the town of Brionne and lodged at Le Neubourg, and afterwards at Elbeuf sur Seine. There the Welsh swam across the Seine and killed many of the local people who resisted them and tried to stop it happening. Then they advanced to near the castle and town of Pont de l'Arche, both strong places which were not captured. That night they lodged at Léry sur Seine, near to the fine town of Louviers, which they burnt. Afterwards they passed through the castle and town of Gaillon, which they captured and burnt, and lodged at Longueville, [81] which is near the good town and castle of Vernon. These were not captured or even touched, and there they entered into France.[1]

That night they burnt the castle of Rocheblance,[2] which is situated beyond the Seine, and lodged at Freneuse sur Seine.[3] After that they passed by the town of Mantes and spent the night at Epone. On the next day, a Friday, they marched to Fresnes, and on the Saturday they came to the fine town of Poissy. The bridge there had been broken down by the French to prevent the king from crossing the Seine by it, but the king himself, with the opposite intention, had it rebuilt. On the same day, a Sunday, three large battle squadrons came from Amiens and France to block the king's passage. But after a sharp encounter there, in which 300 French were killed, while the rest slipped away in flight, the English burnt 32 two-horse and four-horse chariots, full of cross bows and their bolts, other weapons and food supplies.

After their stay there was extended to two days, they marched to Grisy[4] near Pontoise, and, having lodged at Auteuil on the Wednesday, on the next day they left untouched the city of Beauvais on their flank and, passing through Troissereux, they were quartered by the king at Sommereux on the Friday. On the next day they attacked and took by storm the strongly defended town of Poix and burnt the castle. Then, having spent Monday and Tuesday on the march, they stayed at Airaines.

Then, having lodged at Acheux, on Thursday they came to Noyelle sur Mer, where there was a ford called Somme de Port across the tidal waters.[5] Frenchmen from the city of Abbeville and the country round about appeared on the other side of the ford, divided into three frightening battle arrays,

---

1   i.e. territory unequivocally French; Normandy was still claimed by the English kings.
2   Probably La Roche-Guyon, mentioned two days later in *Acts of War*; see Ricard Barber *Life and Campaigns of the Black Price*, Woodbridge and Rochester, 1979, 35
3   Baker has 'Frevile'.
4   Baker has 'Gersile'.
5   This could be Port-le-Grand, which is upstream of Noyelles, but it seems more likely that it is the name of the ford across the tidal mouth of the Somme: 'vadum aque de Summe de Port'.

shouting with great confidence and intending to stop the English crossing the ford. The English had a hard fight against them, with lord Hugh Despenser[1] being the first to engage with the enemy. But, by the grace of God, the English gained the opposite bank against the resistance of the French trying to stop them, and more than two thousand of the enemy were killed and fell in the struggle. The same night the English captured and burnt to ashes the town of Crotoy, where more than three hundred Genoese mercenaries were killed and fell in their perilous defence of the town.

On the evening of the Friday following, with the king in his quarters on the bank of the Somme, there appeared, on the bank already crossed by the English, Philip de Valois, the tyrant of the French, and with him the kings of Bohemia and Majorca, at[82] the head of an army beyond counting divided into eight great battle-arrays. The French shouted boastful cries against the king and his Englishmen, as knights on both sides jousted in the ford and on the banks, as was the custom in war[2]. The king sent an envoy to the tyrant, offering him a peaceful and unharmed passage across the ford so that he might make his own choice of a site suitable for a battle. But this Philip, who previously had threatened to pursue the king, was now full of fear and refused to fight then, but turned aside as if to cross the river at another place. On the next day, a Saturday, the king moved his army to the fields of Crécy, where he was met by the army of the tyrant. The king as always was ready for battle. He gave the command of the first array of his army to his son, the prince of Wales, command of the second array[3] [to the earls of Arundel and Northampton], and he kept the command of the third array for himself. When he had seen that all his men were awaiting the enemy's attack as infantrymen, with the warhorses and coursers and their food being kept in reserve for hunting down enemy fugitives, the king entrusted everything to God and to the blessed Virgin.

The French army was arranged in nine divisions. The first division was entrusted to the king of Bohemia, a man of great wisdom and experience in arms, who on the same day asked the tyrant for the first division to clear his name and prophesied that, contrary to the tyrant's judgement of him, he would die fighting against a nobler knight of the world; for the tyrant had reproached him for his faint-hearted remark that the king of England would not be the first to run away, and so he with great persistence obtained the command of the first division. The heroes in the tyrant's massive army were so sure of victory that they individually asked for individual Englishmen to be lodged in their gaols. The king of Majorca asked for the king of England to be given to him, others for the prince, others for the earl of Northampton and others for such Englishmen as appeared to be of noble birth. But the astute tyrant, in his fear that they would be too busy with capturing their nobles for ransom and so panting with less enthusiasm for the common victory, ordered

---

[1]   Son of Hugh Despenser the younger, reinstated in royal favour in 1332.
[2]   A skirmish rather than a joust.
[3]   Literally, 'the second line put [*missa*]'; there seems to be missing text here. The names of the commanders have been supplied from other sources.

his banner, called the Oriflamme, to be unfurled, for, once that was raised, it was not allowed on pain of death to take a prisoner for ransom. I should tell you that it was called the Oriflamme, as showing that when French mercy was set on fire, it was not able to spare the life of any man for ransom, just as oil, when set alight, cannot spare anything that is inflammable. [83] This banner, carried to the right of the royal standard of France, had on its sides the wide, golden lilies done in gold thread of the royal banner of the French, as if hanging in empty space. On the opposite side the king of England commanded his banner to be unfurled. On it was painted a dragon clad in his armour, and so the standard was called 'the Dragon,' and signified that the fierceness of the leopard and the softness of lilies were set to meet the cruelty of the dragon.

Drawn up in this way the battle-arrays remained stationary on the field from daybreak until evening, with the oppressively large French host increasing in number from continual fresh arrivals. At length, towards sunset, after the jousts of war between these very frightening armies, the trumpets blared, the drums and horns and clarions sounded, the French shouted at the English with the noise of thunder, and the French cross bow men started the battle. However, none of their bolts reached the English but fell a long way short of them. Our archers were roused into action by the deafening shouts of the French crossbow men, and, piercing and killing the enemy with their arrows, they brought to an end the shower of bolts with a hailstorm of arrows. When the Frenchmen in armour realised that their crossbow men had done no harm to the English, they mounted their young warhorses and nimble coursers, and, in their impetuous haste to display their martial virtues against the English, they crushed and trampled under the feet of their horses about seven thousand crossbow men standing between themselves and the English. From among these foot soldiers being trampled upon by the massive horses there arose pitiful cries of horror, which those at the rear of the French army thought came from dying Englishmen. In this way each Frenchman strove to keep up with his fellows in front. But it was mostly the novice volunteer troops making up a large part of the French army who were involved in this disorderly, rash attack, each of them eager for the great honour which they thought to gain from fighting against the king of England.

It was different on the English side. They said their prayers to the mother of Christ, and by fasting made that Saturday a holy day. Then in a short time they dug many holes in the ground in front of their first array, each hole being one foot deep and wide, so that if the French cavalry had pursued them too closely, (which, in fact, did not happen) their horses might have stumbled over the holes. Also they stationed their [84] archers with great care, so that they formed as it were the wings on the sides of the king's army and were not together with the men in armour. In this position they did not impede their own troops, and, instead of attacking the enemy head on, they sent the lightning flashes of their arrows into his flanks. Now loud screams of despair rose up to the stars, both from the French crossbow men, who, as I have said, were trampled on by huge horses and also from the warhorses which had been pierced by arrows, and the formation of the French array was thrown into terrible confusion by the stumbling horses. The French were cut down as they fought the English armed men with axes, spears and swords, and, in the middle of the French army, many were crushed to death by the pressure of the crowd without suffering any wound.

In this dread conflict between the armies the noble Edward of Woodstock, the firstborn son of the king, who was then sixteen, showed the Frenchmen his remarkable prowess as he fought in the front line. He pierced horses and laid low their riders, shook helmets and broke off lances, and skilfully avoided blows aimed at himself. He helped his men, defended himself and raised to their feet his prostrate friends. He gave an example to all his men of the right way to fight. Nor did he rest from his great efforts until the enemy had retreated behind the protection of a rampart of corpses.

It was from his experience of battle at Crécy that this prince with his reputation for warfare learned how to plan the battle of Poitiers, in which he later took the king of France prisoner. At Crécy those few men drawn up against the enemy in the front line remained in place throughout the battle with the young prince, while the Frenchmen kept changing and waves of fresh, new soldiers kept coming against the English as they replaced the killed or the weary or wounded who had withdrawn. Indeed their non-stop attacks kept the prince and his comrades so busy, that the prince was compelled to fight kneeling down against the masses of the enemy who poured around him. Then someone ran or rode to the king his father, explained the danger threatening his firstborn son, and asked for help. The bishop of Durham was sent with twenty knights to the help of the prince, but the bishop found the prince and his men leaning on their lances and swords, drawing breath and taking a moment's rest over long mountains of the dead, as they waited for the enemy to return from his retreat.

So the grim face of Mars showed itself again and again from the setting of the sun right up the third quarter of the night. In all this period the French three times raised the battle cry against our men and fifteen times made an attack on them, but in the end they were defeated and fled. [85]

The next day four battle arrays of fresh Frenchmen came up. As if they had suffered no defeat, they now for the fourth time raised their proud war cry against the English, and joined battle with them for the sixteenth time. On the other side the English, although weary from the labours of the day before, resisted them stoutly and after a sharp, fierce conflict, forced their foes to flee. The English pursued them as they fled, and during the chase and the battle from its beginning they killed three thousand Frenchmen on that Saturday and that Sunday.

The following people were killed at the battle of Crécy: the king of Bohemia, the archbishop of Sens, the bishop of Noyon, the duke of Lorraine, the count of Alençon and his brother, Philip count of Harcourt and his two sons, the count of Auxerre, the count of Aumale, the count of Salm, the count of Blois, the count of Flanders, the count of Montbéliard, the count of Sancerre, the count of Grandpré, and, so it was said, various other German counts whose names were unknown.

Among other lords killed were baron Robert Bertrand, marshal of the army, the count of Rosenberg, the highest in the council of the tyrant, the prior provincial of France of the hospital of St John, the abbot of Corbie, the lord of Moreuil, the lord of Cayeu, the lord of Saint-Venant, and several others, whose names the French captives did not know when questioned. The total of knights and men of higher ranks killed in that battle was more than four thousand. As for the men of other ranks killed there, no one took the trouble to count them. What brought those of noble birth to their deaths was each man's crazy presumption, mentioned earlier, that he could be the winner in the competition for the honour of capturing or defeating the king of England.

From 3 pm on the Sunday which saw the end of the two day battle, the English king and his army, now one mile distant from the dead, gave themselves up to thanking the Giver of victories[1] and resting their bodies. They also counted their numbers, and could not find that forty men from the whole army of the king had perished there. At length, at the hour of vespers, they took the body of the king of Bohemia, and had it washed in warm water, wrapped in linen cloths and placed on a knight's bier. Then, with the king and his earls standing there and with the clergy present, the bishop of Durham solemnly celebrated the exequies for the dead. [86]

On the next day a requiem mass and other private masses were celebrated on the travelling altar, and then, taking with them the body of the noble king of Bohemia, the English passed by the monastery of Maintenay. On the Tuesday following they had a difficult journey to the town of Maintenay, and from there they came to the abbey of Saint-Josse. Next they crossed a ford and came to Neufchatel. Having stayed there for two days, they next came to Calais, which they immediately besieged with a rampart all round it. This happened on 4 September in the twentieth year of the reign of the king of England and the seventh year since he had conquered France.

While Edward, by the grace of God king of England and conqueror of France, was besieging the unsackable town of Calais, the tyrant of the French sent a great number of Genoese and other mercenaries to David, the king of the Scots. In a letter to the Scottish king he urged him to be bold and invade England, now that, as he claimed, it had been emptied of its knighthood and men of war. Once he had looted it and had captured and reserved for his own use its castles and fortifications, the two of them, working together on some other occasion, could the more easily bring the whole of England under their control.

So, around the feast of St Dionysius,[2] David the king of the Scots invaded England with his Scottish army and the mercenaries who had been sent to him. The Scots passed by Berwick, which was defended by the English, and,

---

[1]   1 Corinthians xv.57.
[2]   9 October 1346

having passed through Alnwick forest and laid waste to the surrounding countryside, they finally captured a castle of lord Walter de Wake called Liddel. For some time this place was defended against the Scots by Sir Walter Selby, a fine, upstanding knight, but in the end Sir Walter was forced by the sheer numbers of the Scots to surrender himself for ransom to the victor, who granted this grace, just as any victor, proceeding according to the rights of war in battles with the Scottish and the French, was accustomed to do. But when the news of the capture of Sir Walter reached the ears of king David, the king gave orders for the captive, who was asking for his pity and seeking a ransom, to be put to death. Sir Walter begged to be brought alive into David's presence. He was granted the first part of his prayer, and then, kneeling before David, he asked that he might pay a ransom for his life. But he was a second time condemned to death.

Then the knight made his plea against the tyrant's cruel command. He claimed that, according to the ancient law of royal mercy valid as much in the kingdom of Scotland as in the kingdoms of England and France, any unfortunate man, even a prisoner of royal majesty, should enjoy the privilege of immunity, as long as he stood in the presence of a king, and that it never happened that anyone was thrust to the ultimate penalty, after he had humbly sought mercy from before the face of the king.

But the tyrant's malice was ingrained, and he tightened the evil rope by which Sir Walter was being dragged to the precipice. Forgetting the oil, the symbol of pity, with which he had once been anointed king, and acting as though he had been weaned on the milk of a lioness, he gave orders for the two sons of the unhappy knight to be strangled before the eyes of their father, and then for the father, who was now almost out of his mind with anguish, to be beheaded.

As God is my witness, I have enquired of many people, but I have never heard that Sir Walter committed any act of treachery against the king of Scotland or against any Scot.[1] I believe that it was this cruel and unjust murder of a father and his sons that was the major cause of the disasters befalling the king and his great Scottish army, which I shall now relate. As the unhappy Scots proceeded on their way, they showed no fear for St Cuthbert, although the ancient kings of Scotland had held him in great veneration and had enriched his monastery with generous gifts of alms. No, they showed no fear of Cuthbert or of laying waste his domain. For it was only after looting many of his estates that they came near to Durham, and, when they were not two miles away, they captured some monks of St Cuthbert and held them for ransom. They also made an agreement with the other monks about the fixed amounts of money and corn to be paid by the monks to stop further looting of their manors.

---

[1]   He had fought on the Scottish side in Edward II's reign, and was therefore regarded as a traitor by David II. See David Rollason and Michael Prestwich, *The Battle of Neville's Cross*, Studies in North-Eastern History 3, Stamford 1998, 3.

The news spread abroad of the sorrows of the Englishmen of the marches as they fled before the face of the enemy. So William de la Zouche, archbishop of York, who was then vice-regent to the king in the marches, called together at the head of their troops the bishop of Carlisle,[1] the earl of Angus, lord Mowbray, lord Percy, lord Neville and other nobles of the north, together with archers from the county of Lancashire. This force met the Scottish army at a place called Neville's Cross on the eve of the feast of St Luke the evangelist.[2] The Scots resisted stoutly, for the Scottish nation does not know how to flee. With their bent heads covered with iron, a dense [88] mass of Scots attacked the English forces, and in the first part of the battle frustrated the English archers by means of their polished helmets and the number of their shields joined strongly together. But the first array of the English in armour greeted the enemy with death-dealing blows. Both sides stood firm and fought, being more ready to die than to flee. You might have seen the Scots exhausted and sweating from the hard work of swinging their heavy-headed axes, but still holding their ground. For, where perhaps ten of them stood, shoulder to shoulder with each other, as one of them rushed forwards to deal a blow, you would have seen all ten rushing together with him. In this way these groups rescued those whom they saw falling in the battle.

The marshal of the Scots, earl Patrick, who had been put in command of the rearguard, turned to flee with some partners in his cowardice, as soon as he saw the English resisting and his own men falling. It was just as lord Percy had prophesied that same day. For he had said, 'The cowardice of that traitor, who has never even dared to meet us on an open field, will profit our army more than a thousand Scots could harm it.' So earl Patrick ran away, but the others loyally remained with their king, choosing a fair death before a shameful life[3]. They stood firm, closely banded together like a round tower, protecting their king in the middle, until there were barely forty of them left alive, of whom not one was able to escape. Finally their king David was taken prisoner by John Coupland, while all the others who had stood by the king were killed or kept for ransom. The English pursued the fleeing Scots, killing some and taking others prisoner, as far as Prudhoe and Corbridge.

In this great battle the following Scots were taken prisoner: David Bruce king of the Scots, the earl of Menteith, the earl of Fife, Sir Malcolm Fleming earl of Wigton; William Douglas, William Livingstone, Walter Haliburton, John Douglas, David Annand, John St Clair, William Mowbray, David fitz Robert fitz Kenneth,[4] William Ramsay, Adam Moigne, John Stewart, Roger

---

[1]   John Kirkby, bishop of Carlisle, 1332-53.
[2]   17 October 1346. Details of what actually happened are difficult to establish: 'the various accounts contradict each other too often to make a completely convincing reconstruction of the battle possible.' Rollason and Prestwich, *The Battle of Neville's Cross*, 9: table of differing accounts, 26-7.
[3]   An echo of Vergil, *Aeneid*, xi. 647.
[4]   The head of the Hamilton family; actually David fitz Walter fitz Gilbert.

Kirkpatrick, John Hume and William More, knights; James Sandelflome, James Lorein and Henry Ker, squires.

In the same battle the following men were killed: the earl of Moray and the earl of Strathearn; also Alexander Strachan, John Haliburton, Henry Ramsey, [89] Ness Ramsey, Adam Nicholson, Thomas Boyd, John Stewart, Alan Stewart, David de la Haye, Edward Keith, John Crawford, John Lindesay, Philip Meldrum, Henry Ramsey, Alexander More, Humphrey Boys, Gilbert Inchmartin, Robert Maitland and his brother Humphrey Kirkpatrick, John Strachan and Patrick Heron, knights.

Besides these, the pursuing English killed many of the fleeing Scots as they chased after them. But it was only the coats of arms of those I have named that were brought back from the main battle site and not those of the rest: otherwise we might have known from the number of the coats of arms the total number killed and all their names.

While this was happening in England, the king of England pressed on with the siege of Calais. The town was situated in the marshes of Artois and surrounded with a twin wall and a double ditch. It was right on the shore of the English Channel, looking across to the tower of Dover opposite. It had a harbour which afforded ships a safe enough anchorage and enabled the citizens to feel secure from the threat of the sea and scorn its dangers. The town and its well fortified castle had been built long ago by the mighty Romans. For after Julius Caesar had conquered the whole of France, he built Calais in Artois, and then, after conquering Britain, he built Chepstow castle in South Wales and the tower of Dover in Kent.[1]

King Edward surrounded his army with deep ditches to protect his men from assaults on them by the French, and stationed his fleet in front of the harbour of Calais so that food supplies could not be brought to the besieged by sea. Indeed the king kept a huge navy at sea to besiege the town and did not allow it to depart. Norman pirates at different times captured fifteen large ships together with some small vessels and took them off elsewhere for their own use. They also destroyed other ships by fire. Sir Edmund Hakluyt and Sir William Burton, knights, were captured at sea as they were sailing to England.

So the king put Calais under a strong siege, but refused to assault the town, for he realised that his army could not fight without danger because of its high walls and ditches.[2] Neither did he want to erect siege engines against the town, so that his catapults, as generally happened elsewhere, could batter and knock down the walls and thus allow a passage to his men, since there was an absence of firm ground on which to set up the machines. Besides, even if the walls [90] were knocked down, there were still the deep ditches, which were flooded every day with sea water and which could easily be defended against the whole world.

---

1   None of these are Roman constructions, though there was a Roman shore fort at Dover.
2   The best account of the siege of Calais is in Jonathan Sumption, *The Hundred Years' War: Trial by Battle*, London 1990, 535-571, 576-583.

Even so the besieged were afraid of the damage that siege engines could do to their walls, and so filled hurdles and sacks full of straw to lessen the force of stones hurled by the catapults, for they knew that less damage was done by those stones, which met with a softer target when hurled. The king refrained from assaulting the town and battering its walls, for he shrewdly realised that the famine which was making an entrance through the closed gates could and should tame the proud confidence of the besieged. Indeed in one place the people of Boulogne had been bringing in food for the people of Calais, not in ships through the deep water which was closed to them, but by bringing in boats filled with food when the sea had covered the sand with shallow water. But the earl of Northampton built a hedge or palisade of stakes from the dry land down to the deep water to stop boats of this kind from getting near. Later, when the French admiral wanted to attack the English ships with his war fleet, so that in the meantime the boats could bring food to the besieged town, the earl of Northampton met him and drove his ships away by his powerful attack.

In this way the siege tightened its grip. Beginning on the feast of the nativity of St Mary, it went on for the whole winter and a great part of the next summer, but then on the Monday after the feast of St James[1] the tyrant of the French arrived at the castle of Guines. He was accompanied by John his firstborn son and by the son of the king of Bohemia, later to be emperor of the Romans, and he promised with an oath that he would lift the siege by war or by peace, or bring food to the besieged despite the English. At length he came with his army to just within a mile from the English forces, and sent the duc d'Athènes, the duc de Bourbon and the count of Armagnac as envoys to ask for peace discussions. They did discuss a truce with the duke of Lancaster and the earls of Northampton and Huntingdon, but could not get the agreement of the English. So, after the jousts of war, both sides returned to their own tents. On the next day the tyrant offered a day for fighting a battle, and the king of England gladly accepted his offer.

Meanwhile the besieged made their state known to the French tyrant by signs. When the tyrant first arrived, they set up his banner on the main tower of the castle and also adorned the other towers with the banners of the dukes and counts [91] of France. Then a little after twilight, amid a great din of people shouting and of trumpets, drums and clarions, they sent skywards the very bright light of a fire from a high tower on the side of the city facing the French army. The flames lasted for a half hour. The second night they sent up a similar light, but rather weaker than the first, and the shouting was not so loud. The third night a flickering flame, barely visible to the French army and intended to last for about one hour, was allowed to fall into the castle's moat, and the cries were those of mourning and humble submission. By this the people showed that their strength for saving the town was finished, and the

---

[1] 30 July 1347; in fact the French arrived in sight of Calais three days earlier.

same night they collected in all the banners except the standard, as there was no prospect of any more such proud displays.[1]

At last the day of battle approached, preceded by the arrival of seventeen thousand men from England and the German league, who had come together to help the king. But when the tyrant of the French saw this increase in the king's power, at dawn on 2 August he fed his tents to the flames, thus sending the gloomy message to the besieged that he lacked the courage to help them, and in feeble fashion took flight. The duke of Lancaster and the earl of Northampton cut off his rearguard, and killed and captured many.

When the besieged people of Calais saw the shameful flight of the tyrant of the French, in great sorrow they took down his standard from the tower and threw it into the ditch. On the Saturday following they opened the gates and their captain, John of Vienne, a knight with much practice in the business of war, came into the presence of the king of England, sitting on a little nag as he could not go on foot because of the gout, and with a halter tied round his neck. He was followed by other knights and townspeople on foot, bare- headed and without shoes, and also with ropes around their necks. The captain offered a sword of war to the king, as a sign that he was the prime prince of battles among all Christians and one who had mightily taken that town with all knightly chivalry from the greatest king in Christendom. Secondly he handed over the keys of the town to the English king. Thirdly, calling upon the king's goodness and begging for mercy, he held out to him the sword of peace, so that with it he might make right judgements[2] and spare the humble and chasten the proud.[3] The king received what was offered and in his mercy sent the captain himself to England together with fifteen knights and fifteen townspeople, [92] enriching them with generous gifts and allowing them to go where they wished.[4] Also he ordered that the common people found in the town should be taken under safe conduct as far as the castle of Guines, once they had been refreshed with the king's alms.

After this capture of Calais, at the king's order his knights captured the manors of Marck and Oye. Then with great difficulty small fortresses were built in these manors. For, in the places where the walls which they built now stand, they set out one after another in a circle wine casks emptied of wine but filled with stones, to act as a wall against the enemy, while the castellans were busy with building the walls on the inside.

In AD 1347, the twenty first year of the reign of Edward king of England, while the king, as I have written above, was busy with the siege of Calais, robbers in England committed their crimes with more freedom than usual,

---

1   This story is not found elsewhere.
2   John 7:24.
3   Cf. Vergil, *Aeneid*, 6:853.
4   Le Bel, 202–3[165–8], has the famous account of the burghers of Calais, in which Ed-
     ward is only persuaded to show mercy by his knights, in particular Sir Walter Mauny,
     and by queen Philippa.

as they thought they had nothing to fear. So the justices punished robbers as much as other disturbers of the peace, on the grounds that they were being traitors to the king and the kingdom. The justices were as severe on clerics as on the laity and accused all such criminals of committing crimes, which by being against the king's majesty and for the destruction of his kingdom, were actually favouring the French.

After the capture of Calais there began in those parts that famous, widespread plague. Coming in a succession of waves from the east, it caused the deaths of large numbers of people in every part of the world, as I shall describe below.

The French used the opportunity given them by this terrible plague[1] and sent cardinals to ask for a truce lasting from the capture of Calais up to the next feast of St Barnabas. The king agreed to their request and a truce was drawn up by those cardinals and by the prisoners the count of Eu and the sire de Tancarville. The truce was written in French.[2] Here is my translation of it into Latin:

It is to be noted that this truce, entered upon by the two kings, applies to themselves and their subjects and their allies and their helpers and to the whole of the lands in their care, and that all the captains in the aforementioned war are in particular bound under oath to keep the truce.

On the side of the king of England this truce here entered upon is to include especially the whole of Flanders and the land of Avesnes and the town of Calais [93] and the domain of Marck and Oye together with the lands belonging to them, as defined by the cardinals and the lords of both councils.

Also, the truce is to include all the lands held by the king of England and his subjects and his allies and supporters in Gascony, Perigord, Limousin, Cahorsin, Agenais, Poitou, Saintonge and the lands which adjoin the duchy of Guines. Also included are all their possessions in Brittany and Burgundy, and all other lands wherever situated and all towns, estates, castles and movable goods, of which they have present possession.

Also to be protected under the said truce are the king of Castile, the duke of Brabant, the duke of Guelders, the marquis of Juliers, Jean de Chalon of Burgundy, the count of Neufchatel, lord Jean d'Aspremont, lord Robert of Namur, lord Henry of Flanders, and the people of Flanders and the country of La Bene and the people of Hainault. Also lord d'Albret in Gascony. Also the heir of sire Jean of Brittany, his relatives the count of Montfort and the duke of Brittany, the countess of Clisson, sire Ralph of Cours. Also the people of Genoa and all other subjects, relations, helpers and supporters of the lord king of England, of whatever condition or nation they may be.

And then on the other side, that of the king of France, there are to be included within the security of the truce all the Scots and the whole land of Scotland. Also the

---

[1]   Baker's chronology is wrong here; the resulting truce is dated 28 September 1347, a full year before the plague reached northern France.

[2]   The French original is in *Foedera*, ed. III.i 136-8

kings of Spain, Bohemia and Aragon. Also the dukes of Brabant and Guelders, and the duchess of Lorraine with her sons, and the countess of Bar with her boys. Also sire Jean de Hainault and the country of Hainault, the comte of Nemours, sire Louis of Nemours, the bishop of Liège, the people of Genoa, and all other helpers, relatives and supporters of the aforesaid king of France.

Moreover, the count of Flanders in particular is to be bound by his sacred oath to keep this truce and all its points, and neither he nor anyone else in his name is to stir up a war against Flanders or the Flemish for the time of the truce.

Also, all commanders and captains of war in Brittany on both sides are to be sworn to keep this truce.

Also, for the time of the truce neither king is to invade the land of the other, nor is the count of Flanders to invade the land of Flanders.

Also neither the king of France nor anyone else in his name is to have secret or open discussions with the Flemish or with anyone of them concerning the breaking or defiance or some dismissal of the submission and agreement [94] by which they surrendered to the king of England, nor are they to have such discussions with any other ally of the king of England.

Also this last mentioned article of the truce is to be observed on the part of the king of England, as far as all the friends of the king of France are concerned or those allied to him in any way.

Also neither party for the duration of the truce shall make any new moves or any harmful ventures.

Also the banished and the fugitives from Flanders and the country of Avesnes who have sided with the king of France are to abstain from entering the aforementioned lands, under danger of the penalties to be inflicted upon such transgressors.

Also no one in obedience to either of the two kings is to become obedient to the other of them, to whom he was not in obedience at the time of the conclusion of this truce.

Also no one who is subject to either of the two kings is to begin a war against a subject of the other king, but both kings are to be held responsible for restraining all their subjects from daring to stir up a war of this kind for whatever reason.

Also all merchants and also all subjects, helpers, relatives or people belonging for whatever reason to one side or the other of the two kings, and particularly included here are the English and the Flemish, are to be able freely and without any dispute to travel with their goods by sea or by land, or by lands and seas, to all the lands included in this truce, and to sojourn in those lands, just as they were accustomed to do in the times of other kings, when peace was kept between the two kingdoms. But that is provided that they make payment according to the customary dues of old and to such newly imposed dues as honest natives are bound to pay. But all people banished, for whatever reason, are exempt from this freedom. Persons of the same duchies, for whatever reason they were banished, are to enjoy the freedom and the immunity mentioned in this article of the truce.

Also all articles concerning merchants and their peace are to be read out in Paris and in the other good towns of France.

Also neither of the two kings shall bring it about by himself or through another or freely permit it to happen that the Roman curia makes some new trouble or ecclesiastical judgment upsetting the stability or peace of either of the two kings or of their friends, whether by reason of war or of some other cause. Rather the kings are to do all in their power, without evil contrivance, to prevent all such happenings. [95]

Also all sieges taking place through the power of any subject of the two kings in Gascony or Guines or Brittany or Ponthieu or in the islands in the sea or wherever, are to be abandoned immediately after the publication of this truce.

Also if a castle or town or fort, men or any other goods moveable or immovable were captured after the conclusion of this truce but before its publication, nevertheless they are to be returned completely to the state in which they were on the day of the conclusion of this truce.

Also, a just hearing is to be given to anyone wishing to complain about the escape or flight or breach of faith of any captive, and justices are to be specially appointed for this.

Also, anyone wishing to pay his ransom or to demand a debt owing to him from another or to lodge a complaint about someone is to be given a safe and secure conduct.

Also the truce is to be confirmed as applying to the Scots and their marches; but if the Scots were to wish or were to be able to break the truce, nonetheless the truce will be observed between the kings and the others included in the treaty.

Also, justices are to be specially appointed to ensure this truce remains unbroken. These justices or the kings are to make sure that, if anyone attempts anything contrary to this truce, the truce is to be renewed according to its proper state, nor is the truce itself to be broken on account of something done contrary to it, but the articles concerning the Scots will remain in force.

Also, if any renewal of this truce after a violation of it should become necessary, the justices appointed for this purpose should without delay attempt to patch up the truce in the places most suitable for this and chosen with the agreement of the parties. The justices to be appointed in cases concerning the validity of this truce are the constable and marshal of England and the duke of Lancaster and Bartholomew Burghersh on the part of the king of England; and the constable and marshal of France and the count of Athènes and lord Geoffroi de Charny on the part of the king of France.

Also it is decreed that this truce be publicly proclaimed in Gascony and Brittany within twenty days and in Scotland within thirty days from the date of the confirmation of the same truce, the truce itself to be valid at least until the next feast of the apostle St Barnabas.[96]

In this way a truce, which was essential while the plague was causing widespread havoc, was drawn up between the kingdoms. Then the king of England built a tower and a large wall between the sea and the harbour of Calais to stop naval attacks by the enemy, and he appointed John, lord Montgomery as captain of the city. Next the king took with him the queen and his firstborn and a large crowd of other nobles as well, and directed his fleet towards England. On this return voyage he met with such a violent gale that many of his ships were lost and the king himself only reached England after being in very great danger. He landed in London on 14 October.

In AD 1348, the twenty-second year of the king, after the lord king's return to England, both David king of the Scots and lord Charles de Blois were brought to the Tower of London. Charles de Blois had been captured recently at Easter in Brittany by lord Thomas Dagworth after many hard and dangerous battles.[1] The two of them subsequently remained for many years in England awaiting ransom. Also Sir John Douglas, who had been taken prisoner at the battle of Neville's Cross and had been brought with the king of the Scots to London, now made his peace again with the king of England and swore fealty to him. But when he later returned peacefully to the marches, he was invited to a hunt by Sir William Douglas, who treacherously rode him down from behind and killed him.[2]

After Easter in this year[3] the king held a council, at which regulations to control the officers of his household were put into force. If any of them took food from a person against his will and without paying him money for it, such officers were immediately to be punished with the ultimate penalty or to give up their position in the king's household. Sir Richard Talbot was appointed seneschal of the king's household and the executor of this measure.

The abbot of Dunfermline came to this council on a peaceful mission from Edward Balliol, king of Scotland by conquest. There also came with him the bishop of Moray and the bishop of Glasgow and two knights. They offered a ransom for David, the captured king of the Scots. But they were told that David did not qualify for a knight's ransom. For one who had no right to the kingdom of England had not been captured as one fighting for a just cause, but as a ferocious brigand who laid waste with fire and the sword everything that he touched. For this reason, as he was now held captive, he was required to submit to the grace of the king of England and to make reparation for all that he had destroyed. After that he might be able to find the grace of ransom in the king's sight. The envoys were also asked if they wished to discuss a final peace, but they replied that the powers entrusted to them did not go as far as peace discussions.

Also at this council, in the presence of Sir William Trussel, the earl of Menteith was put on trial and found guilty of being untrue to the homage and fealty he had sworn to the king of England, seeing that for a second time he had taken up arms and fought against this same king, his lord. For this he was hung, drawn and quartered.

There also arrived at the same meeting two counts and two clerics, sent from the inner councils of the electors of the king of Germany. They informed

---

[1] Charles de Blois was captured at the battle of La Roche-Derrien on 20 May 1347. Dagworth sold his prisoner to Edward III for 25,000 marks.

[2] Baker has the wrong Douglas: it was sir William Douglas who was murdered, by William, later earl Douglas, his kinsman.

[3] The four items attributed to this council appear to relate to separate occasions. The regulations for the household relates to January 1348 (*PROME*, iv. 420) ; the embassy from Scotland came in the latter part of the year; Menteith was executed in February 1347 (*Foedera*, iii.i, 108) and the answer to the electors of Germany was given on 10 May 1348 (*Foedera*, iii.i.161).

the king that he had been elected as the royal majesty of Germany in his absence. The envoys were received with fitting honour and thanks, and the king showed them kindness and lavish hospitality. He then said in reply to them that he was unwilling to shoulder so great a responsibility, until he should peacefully gain as his own the royal crown of France, which was owed to him by hereditary right.

In the same year after Easter the earl of Lancaster, later the duke, held an impressive tournament at Lincoln, attended by a great company of noble ladies.[1]

Also envoys came from the king of Spain to ask for the hand of lady Joan, the king's daughter, for the son of their master the king. But she entered upon the way of all flesh at Bordeaux, a victim of the great plague, which I shall describe later.[2] Her betrothed came to meet her there, but amid tears she was committed to a solemn burial. Her great beauty of body and the abundance of her virtues of character made her so appealing to everyone that the grief of her attendants at her death compelled them to follow their mistress on the pathway of death.

In this year master John Stratford, archbishop of Canterbury, died on 23 August, and was buried at Canterbury on 19 September.[98] Later master Thomas Bradwardine, a doctor of theology, was elected archbishop. But master John Ufford, the king's chancellor, was assigned to that position as the pope's appointment. However he died before being consecrated. Then, in the following year, master Thomas Bradwardine was elected for a second time and consecrated in the Roman curia, but he died in the same year.[3]

In this year, after the feast of St Martin, there was a meeting at Calais to renew the truce. Present on the English side were the bishop of Norwich, the earl of Lancaster, the earl of Suffolk and Sir Walter Mauny, and on the French side the bishop of Laon, the duke of Burgundy, the duke of Athènes, the count of Guines, the sire of Tancarville and the sire Geoffroi de Charny. The earl of Lancaster refused to come to an agreement with the French until two harmful forts at Calais, built in contravention of the articles of the former truce, had been destroyed. When this had been done, the truce was renewed, and was now to last until the first day of December of the following year.[4]

Also in the same year the lord king and his firstborn and the earl of Warwick and the bishop of Winchester went to Calais for the feast of St Andrew. From there the king sent the earl of Lancaster to Dunkirk[5], to receive there the fealty and homage due to him from the count of Flanders

---

[1]   He had been given permission to found a jousting fraternity, of which he was to be the captain, in 1344 (*Foedera*, iii.i. 5) to meet on the Monday after midsummer.

[2]   She died on 2 September 1348.

[3]   Stratford died in 1348. Offord died on 20 May 1349, Bradwardine on 25 August of the same year, both probably of the plague.

[4]   The negotiations began in October 1348 and were concluded on 13 November.

[5]   'Donemere'' in the Latin original.

accompanied by the sacrament of an oath. The count of Flanders did as he was asked.[1] Envoys were also sent to Boulogne to open negotiations there with the council of the French, which had withdrawn into France before their arrival. The king handed to his envoys, Sir Robert Herle[2] and Sir Thomas Verdon, a letter written and addressed to the tyrant of the French which was to be taken to that tyrant. In it the king asked to be assigned a day for battle, supposing that a new final peace could not be made between them. The tyrant did not allow these envoys of the king to come near him, but commanded them through his deputies to leave his kingdom, with the business they had come for uncompleted.

In AD 1349, the twenty-third year of the reign of the king, a wide spreading plague began among the Indians and the Turks in the east. It then affected the Saracens, Turks, Syrians and Palestinians, who live in the middle of our world. Next it wiped out so many of the population of Greece that men, now driven by terror, thought it worthwhile to receive the Christian faith and the sacraments, once they heard that on this side of the Greek sea death was not exercising its terror more frequently or more suddenly than usual. At length in wave after wave the grim slaughter reached the parts on this side of the Alps, and from there it spread to western France and Germany, and in the seventh year after its beginning it came to England.[3]

First it struck the ports on the sea coast in Dorset, and once again almost stripped the countryside of its inhabitants. From there it reached Devon and Somerset and got as far as Bristol, where it was so virulent that the men of Gloucester denied Bristolians any access to their town, since they all thought that the breaths of the living would be infected, if they were among those dying in this way. But at last the plague did get to Gloucester, and to Oxford and London as well, and in the end it so devastated the whole of England that scarcely one person in ten of either sex remained alive. There were not enough graveyards, and people chose places in the fields to bury their dead.

The bishop of London bought that piece of land in London called 'Nomansland,' and Sir Walter Mauny bought that which is called 'the new Charterhouse,' where they founded religious houses for the burial of the dead.[4]

---

1   This is incorrect: Edward and Louis de Mâle signed a treaty on 4 December 1348 in which Louis undertook to renounce his homage to Philip VI the following September if Philip did not agree to a list of demands to be put forward by Louis:. Ormrod, *Edward III*, 224.

2   Herle was captain of Calais after Sir John Montgomery. There is no record of this letter.

3   For the progress of the plague in the British Isles see Ole Benedictow, *The Black Death 1346-1353*, Woodbridge & Rochester, NY, 2004, 123-145.

4   Ralph Stratford, bishop of London, bought four acres of land in Smithfield in late 1348 as a cemetery, and when this was insufficient turned to Sir Walter Mauny, who persuaded the master of St Bartholomew's Hospital to rent him a further thirteen acres of adjacent land until such time as he could buy it. The new graveyard and chapel were consecrated on 25 March 1349. It did not become a Charterhouse, or Carthusian monastery, until the 1370s; initially there was only a small hermitage there. See David Knowles and W. F. Grimes, *Charterhouse*, London 1954, 5-7.

Cases heard at the King's Bench and the common courts necessarily ceased. A few nobles died, including lord John Montgomery, the captain of Calais, and lord Ghistel.[1] These two died at Calais and were buried at the house of the brothers of the blessed Carmelite Mary in London. A host of people beyond counting passed to the next world, and a multitude of monks and other clerics known only to God. The great plague struck down especially the young and the strong, while it generally spared the old and the feeble. Hardly any one was brave enough to touch a sick man, and the healthy fled from the possessions of the dead as being infected, however valuable they had once been and still were. People who one day were as cheerful as crickets, were on the next found dead. [100]

Victims were racked by abscesses suddenly breaking out on different parts of the body. So hard and dry were these abscesses that, when they were cut off, hardly any liquid trickled from them. Many got rid of them by incision or long patience. Others had small black pustules scattered over the whole surface of the body. Very, very few, in fact hardly anybody at all bounced back to life and health, once infected with these. This mighty pestilence, which began in Bristol on the feast of the assumption of the glorious Virgin, and in London around the time of the feast of St Michael, raged for a whole year and more in England, with such a devastating effect that it completely emptied many rural towns of every individual of the human species.

While the great plague was raging through England, the Scots rejoiced and thought that all their oaths against the English would now be answered; for at that time they were in the blasphemous habit of nastily swearing 'by the cheap death of the English.' But sorrow followed hard upon their extremes of joy. For the sword of God's anger[2] withdrew from England and in a furious outbreak of leprosy slaughtered as many Scots as it had killed Englishmen with abscesses and pustules.

But in the following year the plague raged in Wales as well as in England. Finally it sailed across the sea to Ireland, where it killed the English living there in great numbers but practically left untouched the native Irish living on the mountains and the higher ground. These Irish remained immune until 1357, but then they too unexpectedly suffered dreadful destruction on a wide scale.

In this year the bishop of Norwich,[3] the earl of Northampton, the earl of Stafford, Sir Richard Talbot and Sir Walter Mauny crossed the channel to renew the truce or to make a lasting peace. The French gave them a cordial welcome, but were not willing to agree to any lasting peace, unless Calais was given back to them. The envoys said this was impossible, and the truce was continued for the duration of a year.[4]

---

[1] Wulfard de Ghistels, an influential supporter of Edward III from western Flanders.
[2] Romans 13:4.
[3] William Bateman
[4] This is the 1348 truce, described on p. 85 above.

But the Flemings were now only willing to receive the count of Flanders if he agreed to renounce the French tyrant and to pay fealty and homage to the English king, with these promises being made under a solemn oath. So the count made a full submission to the king of England, so that he might hold the countship of Flanders from him, while showing faithful service to his legal lord. But never from that day on [101] did the count wholeheartedly keep the faith to which he had sworn. For not long afterwards he invaded Flanders with a French army, destroying, killing and feeding to the flames towns and everything which he could burn. But the people, together with a few Englishmen who had been assigned to the command of the castles, put up a fierce resistance to the count's tyranny. Very many Frenchmen were killed, and the count was compelled to turn tail and flee. Many were endowed with knighthood for their part in that battle. Among them was Sir John St-Philibert, an Englishman, who was decorated with military honour.[1]

Meanwhile on the feast of the nativity of St John Baptist and at the churching of the queen at Windsor impressive tournaments were held, attended by David king of the Scots, the count of Eu, the sire de Tancarville, lord Charles de Blois and many other foreign prisoners.[2] The king and his tournament masters allowed the foreign lords to take part, and the honour of the field was graciously adjudged to the count of Eu. Afterwards, as it was the time of full-grown beasts, the same prisoners, along with the king and other nobles of the kingdom, gave themselves up to the happy pleasures of the chase at Clarendon and in the other forests.

While the king was thus occupied, the French invaded the march of Brittany. Ignoring the general truce, they took up position in a wood near the castle of Phanes under the leadership of Raoul de Cahors, a knight but the son of a cobbler. A few of them by openly seizing booty stirred Sir Thomas Dagworth, the best of knights and the captain of the duchy, to go to the rescue of his country.[3] While he was engaged with at least sixteen of the armed robbers, he was suddenly surrounded by the rest from the wood, but, with his own men standing firmly beside him, he put to rout many of the enemy, in fact more than three hundred of them, according to the reports of those watching from the castle. Even after five crossbow bolts had lodged in his bare face and with all his men slain, he was still unwilling to surrender to the son of a cobbler; and, although deprived of his eyes by a huge spear, he killed or wounded the enemy, or for a long time did not allow them to come near him, until finally he was overwhelmed by a posse of armed men. His body was run through by a sword, [102] and his noble soul fled

---

[1]   This confused passage seems to refer to the battle at Cassel on 8 June 1347 when the Flemish defeated a French detachment under Charles d'Espagne, and to the Flemish revolt after the signature of the treaty of December 1348 (p.85-6 above) which was crushed by Louis de Mâle in January 1349.
[2]   24 June 1348.
[3]   Raoul de Caours ambushed Sir Thomas Dagworth between Auray and Vannes on 20 July 1350. It seems to have been a smaller engagement than Baker makes out.

from it, bewailing its fate,[1] but earning a nation's praise alongside her other defenders and champions. More than five hundred French men of arms and an unknown number of crossbow men had been involved in the encounter. The French had craftily cut off Thomas' archers from giving any help to their lord, so that the great hero, who had triumphed in various battles against hordes of Frenchmen, now himself passed through the gates of death.[2] To all Englishmen his death brought sorrow and grief, and to the French great joy, but not to all of them. For, although his deeds in war terrified the enemy, by the nobleness of his character he brought it about that both his prisoners and fugitives and free men felt love for him and compassion for a brave but undeserved death. But the cobbler's son, when he rejoiced in a triumph of which a great prince would scarcely have been worthy, merely heaped upon himself the envy of the French and the hatred of all good knights.

The French and the count of Flanders were still frightened to break the truce. But then the count and the duke of Brabant and very many others from the kingdom of France collected together an army and around the feast of St Michael again invaded Flanders. Some Flemish traitors who were on his side opened the gates of Bruges to him, and he slaughtered a great crowd of groups of citizens, who were loyal to the king of England their lord, in their homes and in their squares. He also sent envoys to the men of Ypres, Ghent and other towns, asking for or rather demanding the surrender of their towns. But their citizens, who had accepted the truce, wrote to the king of England, saying that, unless he helped them, they would be forced to surrender to the powers of the count and the tyrant of the French. So around the feast of All Saints, the king, accompanied by the earls of Lancaster and Suffolk and others, crossed the sea to Flanders and led his men towards the French. The truce between himself and the French was renewed, and the count of Flanders now for the third time submitted himself to the mercy and the power of the English king.[3]

The king returned to England for the solemn feast of the translation of St Thomas, confessor and bishop of Hereford.[4] The king celebrated this solemn occasion in honour of the bountiful confessor by giving a magnificent feast, piously attended by himself and other nobles of the kingdom. The huge expense involved was borne by Nicholas, baron Cantilupe, a kinsman of St Thomas himself.[103]

Just before this solemn feast, news was brought to the king by secretaries from Aimeric of Pavia, a mercenary knight, that on 14 January the knight

---

[1]   This is an echo of the Homeric tag for the death of a hero: cf. *Iliad* 16:587 and Vergil, *Aeneid* xi.831
[2]   Vergil, *Aeneid*, ii.661
[3]   This seems to be a further repetition of events of 1348. Edward was in Calais 30 November to 2 December 1348, and there is a gap of ten months before the translation of St Thomas Cantilupe.
[4]   Edward was at Hereford 24-28 October 1349 (Ormrod, *Edward III*, 622) Thomas Cantilupe had been canonised in 1320; a 'translation' of relics was a way of honouring the saint and the new tomb would have been designed to cater for large numbers of visiting pilgrims.

Geoffroi de Charny and great numbers of other Frenchmen would be admitted into Calais, for this Aimeric had himself sold Calais to him. But thankfully the town was saved by king Edward in the following manner.[1]

Aimeric of Pavia with other Genoese was stationed in Calais in the pay of the French tyrant, while Calais was under siege by the English king. But when, after the surrender of the town, the gift of life and limb and freedom as a knight had been given to him as to others, he became for the future a mercenary of the English king, and stayed on in Calais to help guard it.

At this time the belief was current that the knight Geoffroi de Charny, lord of Matas, was more practised in military matters than any other French knight, and that, besides his long experience of war, he was blessed with a quick and lively intelligence. Indeed it was for this reason that he was the principal adviser of the French tyrants right up to his own death and the capture of the crowned one of the French at the battle of Poitiers. This cunning schemer of crime brought himself to Aimeric's attention by a letter, and tried to overthrow Aimeric's loyalty to the English king by gifts of gold and specious promises. Finally the greedy one agreed with the false one that in return for twenty thousand écus d'or he would prepare an easy entrance for the French into the town through the tower of which he was in command, and do all he could to help in the complete capture of town and castle.

This treacherous pact had been confirmed as strongly as possible by oaths and the sharing of the sacrament of the altar by both parties. But, seeing that it was also full of cunning and craft and faith foresworn, it was steeped in evil from the outset. Indeed 'crimes are committed, without and within the walls'[2] not now 'of Troy,' but of Calais. For the existing truce and the laws of good conscience should have stopped the French from any trickery, public or private, which enabled them in time of peace to seize a town belonging to the king of England. And respect for his loyalty as a knight should have deterred Aimeric from betraying the English king and [104] from making a dishonourable agreement with the enemy which he was not even going to keep, although one ought to keep one's word even when given to an enemy. But Aimeric did not keep his word to the enemy, while his loyalty as a knight to his earthly king can only be regarded as doubtful. Also he served the Prince of Heaven in a most impious fashion, since he deceitfully called upon the body of our Saviour as a witness to his crafty agreement and then shared in the communion of the chalice. Nevertheless he wrote a letter to the English king about the whole matter, concealing nothing. In fact he was ready for friendship with the French, if they were successful, and for receiving the goodwill of the king if his plot with the French failed and they were convicted

---

[1]   This episode is also reported by Robert of Avesbury, 408-10; Gilles li Muisit, 260-3; and many later chronicles. The accounts by Baker and Le Bel (206-8 [176–82]) are written in a more flamboyant style, but agree in the major details; whether they are simply embellished, or rely on eyewitness accounts, is difficult to say. See Jonathan Sumption, *The Hundred Years War II: Trial by Fire,* London 1999, 60-2,

[2]   Horace, *Epistles*, i. 2. 16

of breaking the truce and also perhaps had many men taken captive who would need ransoming. This is what actually happened.

The king was anxious about the safety of a town which he had captured with very great difficulty and only after a siege lasting a year. Accompanied by his firstborn son the prince of Wales, the earl of March and a few others, he rapidly crossed the sea and arrived some few[1] days before the crucial day of the betrayal. On his arrival, he prepared a cunning reception for the French. He placed men at arms under the arches between the portcullis or closed gate and the doorways into the castle. In front of the men he placed a newly made, thin covering of wall. It was not a wall cemented together, but a wall of clay with its surface rubbed smooth and joining on to the existing wall. In fact it was so cunningly joined to the original wall that anyone who was unaware of the device would never have suspected that there were men hidden behind it. He also had the main timbers of the drawbridge almost sawn through, but in such a way that armed knights were still able to ride across. Next he craftily had a huge rock placed in an opening in the side of the tower overlooking the bridge, an opening originally made for the use of archers. Along with the rock he placed a concealed, reliable soldier who at the right moment could let it fall so that it broke in two the half sawn through bridge. The front of the opening was then cleverly filled up so that the new work looked like part of the old but so that the soldier stationed within could still look down and count the number of those entering.[2] While these [105]preparations were being made, very few were aware of the presence of the king or the prince of Wales, and, after their completion, the two of them secretly withdrew into the town.

On the day before the crucial day Geoffroi de Charny sent fifteen loyal men, carrying a great part of the gold which was the reward for the betrayal, to test Aimeric's reliability and to reconnoitre the layout of the castle. They visited every tower and covered corner, and found everything to their liking. So on the next day they raised the standard of the French king on the highest tower of the castle, and set the standards of Geoffroi and other lords also on the other towers. At this the people who were keeping watch over the town and knew nothing of the plot were so terrified that they flew to arms and prepared to make an immediate assault on the castle.

The fifteen French who had entered the castle the day before then quickly laid violent hands on Sir Thomas Kingston, who claimed that he knew nothing of the plot, and locked him in wooden stocks. Then some of the fifteen were dispatched to their French masters who were in ambush outside the fortifications. They pointed to the standard and the raised banners, and promised that all would go well if only their masters would hurry to the defence of the castle against the townsmen. So, rising from their hiding places,

---

[1]   Blank left in MS for number of days.
[2]   These elaborate details are only given by Baker. Le Bel (207[179]) says that the knights 'enclosed themselves in old walling', so some kind of artificial hiding place may have been created.

the French in large numbers broke through the gates of the castle with their usual native swagger.

The townsmen found it difficult to keep their hands from attacking the French,[1] but their leaders kept them back as if they were trying to avoid the danger of men springing upon them. Immediately the loyal friends of the king, who had been shut up like anchorites in their hiding places under the arches of the walls, made light of their long three day wait and prepared to attack. Also the man, who had recently been stationed in the opening with the huge rock, waited until he judged that there were still sufficient of his fellows to deal with the number of Frenchmen who had entered, and then let fall the massive stone entrusted to his charge. The drawbridge was smashed and the way barred by which a great enemy force had been about to enter the castle. Nor could those inside now get out by that way. This rock fulfilled as it were [106] the role of a portcullis which could be lowered. In the beginning it had been kept on high awaiting the moment to do its duty and had given the French safe entry and a false sense of security. But when the men at arms in hiding heard the crash of the rock breaking the bridge, they pushed aside the clay wall which hid them and, springing out from behind it, they gave a grim welcome to the French knights who had been invited in, by compelling them to engage with their ranks. A long and fierce conflict ensued, but in the end the enemy were overpowered and made humble submission to the will of their conquerors.

As soon as the French who had stayed outside the town realised their comrades had been tricked, they turned tail and fled. They were pursued by the lord king. He had with him fewer than sixteen men at arms and the same number of archers, who came at his call though they did not know who was calling them, and with these he harried the fleeing French, killed many of them and in a short time emerged successful from a dangerous piece of work. When the French at last realised how few English armed men were pursuing them, eighty of them banded together to fight the king. I do not dare to ascribe his successful attack on the enemy to his cleverness or to his remarkable skill as a fighter. I prefer to put it down to his courage. Anyway all are agreed that at this crisis he won the day, and, preserved by the grace of God, he gained the honour of putting the French to flight. For when he saw that the French had banded together, he threw away the scabbard of his sword, and, encouraging his men at arms and setting them at their stations, he challenged them to act like men.

Also the archers were placed in the marshes on the flanks of the men at arms, standing on dry hillocks and surrounded by muddy pools, so that heavily armed cavalry or infantry who came after them would instead be sucked down into the sticky mud. The king also encouraged his archers, and persuaded them to do their duty to him by these winning words, 'Do well, you archers, and know that I am Edward of Windsor.' Realising then for the first time that they had to do well as the king was present among them, the archers uncovered their heads, arms and chests, and, devoting all their skill

---

[1]   Calais was now largely inhabited by English settlers.

to making sure that no arrow missed its target, they greeted the approaching French with sharp arrows and gave them a very hot reception.

The men at arms of both armies stood on a long, narrow causeway, which was [107] hardly wide enough for twenty men at arms to be packed in a line across it. They had on either side of them a marsh which was impassable for men in armour, but in which the English archers stood secure, not getting in the way of their own knights, and piercing the Frenchmen with a hail of arrows from the flanks. So the king and his knights from the front and the archers from the sides killed and captured many Frenchmen, and those who manfully resisted for a long time were finally put to flight by the arrival of the prince of Wales.

After a long chase after the enemy, the English returned to Calais and counted up the numbers of the fugitives and the captives. They discovered from information given them by the prisoners that 1,000 men in armour and 600 men with weapons had come for the capture of the castle, and that the number of their servants was more than 3,000. The men of this force who were taken prisoner were the sire Geoffroi de Charny and his son, a fierce warrior, Oudart de Renty, who had once served the lord king in the office of mace-bearer, but who was then a knight and mercenary of the tyrant of the French; also Robert de Banquilo, Otto de Gule, baron de Martyngham, Baudouin Sailly, Henri de Prees, Gauvain de Bailleul, Pierre Rynel, Pierre d'Argemole, Eustache de Ribemont.

Many other knights and their squires were put to flight with their banners. These included the lord of Montmorency, also the lord of Landas who married the lady of Saint-Pol, the countess of Pembroke, in England, also Robert de Fiennes, the sire de Plancy, and another Eustache de Ribemont[1]. Those killed in the battle were Henri du Bois, the seigneur Archebaud and many others, of whom the victors took no notice.[2]

So a cunning plot which contravened the terms of the truce led its authors to disaster. Firstly Geoffroi brought about the capture of himself and his friends, the loss of much gold, the death of noble men, the flight of proud dukes, and in the end the failure of his whole base scheme. But neither did Aimeric escape the noose of misadventure, for he was later captured by the French and burnt alive with a red-hot iron, degraded from the order of knighthood by having his ankles cut off, [108] deprived of his tongue by amputation, and after all this hung and then beheaded and finally quartered. He certainly paid the penalty for his treachery and his false forswearing on the sacrament of the altar.[3]

---

[1]   Possibly Waleran de Ribemont, son of Eustache, mentioned in *Bourgeois de Valenciennes*, 266. Baker is the only author to give the names: Le Bel says simply that he does not know the names of ten of the captives (208 [180]).

[2]   Li Muisit comments that neither side in such an encounter can really tell what actually happened. *Chronique et Annales de Gilles li Muisis*, ed. Henri Lemaître, Société de l'Histoire de France, Paris 1906, 263

[3]   Le Bel says nothing of this, but Froissart has a long story of Charny's revenge. See *Froissart: Chroniques, Edition du manuscrit de Rome Reg. lat. 869*, ed. G. T. Diller, Geneva 1972, 892-3.

In the same year the earl of Lancaster and the barons of Stafford and Greystoke crossed the seas to Gascony about the time of the feast of All Saints. They were accompanied by the heirs of lord Percy and lord Nevill, by lord Furnival, Bartholomew Burghersh and many others. They were to put a stop to the rioting of John of Valois, the son of the tyrant of France, who had done too much damage in that dukedom.[1]

Also a royal council decreed that no justice of the king during the time of his office should receive fees or gifts from anyone except from the king.[2]

Also master Thomas Bradwardine, archbishop of Canterbury, died before being enthroned,[3] and master Simon Islip was elected as his successor.

Still in this year, in the county of Oxford near the town called Chipping Norton, a two-headed snake was found. It had two female faces, one decorated in the latest style, and the other copying the fashion of long ago. It also had large wings, like a bat.

In AD 1350, the twenty-fourth year of the king himself and the sixth year of the lord pope Clement, a year of Jubilee was celebrated.[4] In this year all Christians who went to the thresholds of the apostles and made a proper and sincere confession received a complete indulgence for all their sins.

In Gascony lord Furnival was taken prisoner during a rash and ill-advised attack on the enemy, and soon afterwards the king prepared to cross to France. But the earl of Lancaster, on his return from Gascony, told the king about a truce which he himself had made, and so the king postponed his sea crossing for the time being.

In that year on St George's day the king held a great feast in his castle at Windsor.[5]During it he instituted a chapel of twelve priests and founded an almshouse in which impoverished knights whose own resources were inadequate could obtain sufficient assistance from the perpetual alms of the founders of that college. The other people who contributed to the founding of that almshouse besides the king were of course the firstborn of the king, the earls of Northampton, Warwick, Suffolk and Salisbury, other barons and also some who were merely knights, namely Roger Mortimer now earl of March, Sir Walter Mauny, Sir William Fitzwarin, Sir John de Lisle, Sir John de Mohun, Sir John Beauchamp, Sir Walter Paveley, Sir Thomas Wale and Sir

---

[1]   Lancaster was apppointed king's captain and lieutenant in Poitou on 18 October; he returned to London on 10 May 1350: *Foedera*, iii.i.190 ; Fowler, *The King's Lieutenant*, 89.

[2]   This may be a reference to the trial of Sir William Thorpe for bribery by a tribunal which condemned him to death; but the peers objected to the proceedings, and Thorpe was pardoned: Ormrod, *Edward III*, 379.

[3]   Already mentioned on p. 85 above.

[4]   The first jubilee was instituted in 1300 by Boniface VIII, and was intended to be celebrated every hundred years; Clement VI changed this to every fifty years.

[5]   The date of the foundation of the Company (later Order) of the Garter has been much disputed, but it is possible that Baker is correct. His list of the founding knights is the oldest surviving evidence, as we only have fifteenth century copies of the statutes which include a list of founders, and the stallplates in St George's Chapel date for the most part from around 1420. See Barber, *The Triumph of England*, forthcoming.

Hugh Wrottesley. These men who were merely knights were linked with the richest earls because their worth had been tested and tried.

All these together with the king were clothed in russet gowns, spangled with gold, and with armbands of Indian blue. They also had similar garters on their right legs, and they wore a mantle of blue with the escutcheons of St George. Dressed like this and with bare heads they solemnly heard a ceremonial mass sung by the prelates of Canterbury, Winchester and Exeter, and then in due order seated themselves at a common table in honour of the holy martyr to whom they specially dedicated this noble fraternity, calling it the company of the knights of the Garter of St George.

In the following summer fighting broke out between the sailors of England and those of Spain. The Spanish blocked the seas off Brittany with forty-four huge warships and captured, looted and sank ten English ships which were sailing from Aquitaine to England. Having in this manner avenged injuries previously inflicted upon them, the Spaniards put in to the harbour of Sluys in Flanders. When the king of England heard of this, he assembled his fleet of fifty ships and pinnaces, intending to meet the Spaniards on their return home.[1] The king had with him the prince of Wales, the earls of Lancaster, Northampton, Warwick, Salisbury, Arundel, Huntingdon and Gloucester, [110] and other barons and knights together with servants carefully selected from their households and with archers.

Finally about the hour of vespers on the feast of the beheading of St John Baptist the two fleets clashed. The huge Spanish galleons towered above our own galleys and ships, like castles above cottages. They made a frightening attack on our men, repeatedly inflicting deep wounds on many of them by rocks which flew down from the mast turrets and by quivering bolts and arrows. None the less our men kept up the fight at close quarters with spears and swords and bravely defended themselves with the weapons the fleet possessed. Our men had never experienced anything much more dreadful than this frightening conflict, which grew more and more intense until finally our archers picked off their crossbow men, as their arrows had a longer range than the shorter distance of the bolts of the enemy, and so compelled them to desist from their duty. Also, fighting at close quarters with other Spaniards above the sides and the castles of their galleons, they forced the enemy to defend themselves with the tables from their ships as they prayed to heaven.

Moreover our men forced those Spaniards who were hurling the lightning bolts of the rocks from their turrets to turn to total self-protection. Now they did not dare to show their heads and shoulders as they had been doing. Only their hands were lifted above the turrets and even these were not safe from the piercing arrows. They no longer hurled the rocks but just let them fall, so that, as they fell, they were more likely to sink their own ships than our vessels.

---

[1]   This episode is usually known as the battle of Winchelsea, or of Espagnols-sur-Mer.

Then our men clambered up scaling ladders and burst into those ships from the West. They cut down with swords and axes the men who stood in their way, and in a short time were emptying ships which had been full of Spaniards and filling the empty ships with Englishmen, until envious night poured her darkness around them and they could no longer see the remaining twenty-seven Spanish ships. There you could have seen ships painted with blood and brains; arrows stuck in masts, sails, rudders and castles; archers collecting arrows from the wounds of the dead and praying, but in vain, for the fight to be renewed the next day. Our men cast anchor, thinking over the battle for which they had hoped, and imagining that nothing had been done while something remained to be done. They dressed the helpless wounded, threw the dead and dying Spanish into the sea, refreshed themselves with food and sleep, and did not forget to set armed men on guard throughout the night.

When dawn came up after the silence of the night, the English were prepared for new calls to battle, but in vain. For as they were rousing their men to arms with trumpets, clarions and bagpipes, they looked out over the sea under the fuller light of the rising sun and saw no sign of resistance. The twenty-seven Spanish ships not captured had made every effort and fled during the night, leaving for the king's pleasure the seventeen ships painted with drying blood and brains, which the English had looted late the day before.

The king unwillingly returned in triumph to England, but there were still dangers besetting himself and his men. For his troops brought home with them wounded heads, bound in bandages to hold them together, arms and legs pierced by bolts and weapons, torn out teeth and cut off noses, split lips and gouged out eyes. They rejoiced in these insignia of a glorious triumph and in their escape. Men who in the past had found pleasure in showing their cloaks stained with the blood of an enemy horse could raise a laugh in their present pain and weakness. The king now promoted to the honour of a knighthood eighty squires of noble birth. He also grieved for the loss of one man, Sir Richard Goldsmith, who, it was said, had sold his life very dearly – or, as the Spanish thought, too dearly.[1]

In this year Philip of Valois, who was called the king of the French, was summoned by an illness announcing his death to his examination before the Judge of consciences. He publicly confessed that he held the crown of France unjustly,[2] and he ordered his son John to agree to a final peace between the kingdoms. He also gave him the piece of advice that, when he should be the one to sit on the throne of the kingdom, he should never fight in armour

---

1   Honours in the battle were almost evenly divided; Gilles li Muisit, always doubtful about ascribing outright victory to one side or the other, is adamant that the English losses were probably greater than those of the Spanish, but admits that the Spanish fleet sailed away from the scene of the battle and did not return to English waters for some time: *Chronique et Annales*, 278. Baker and Li Muisit give the fullest accounts of the fight; Froissart has his usual romanticised version, but includes possibly authentic material about Sir John Chandos .

2   This is wishful thinking on Baker's part.

against the king of England to begin a battle. Philip then entered upon the way of all flesh and this John, his firstborn son, was crowned king of France. As he had no right to be king, from now on I shall be pleased to call him not king but the crowned one of the French.

After the much desired victory in the battle which I have described, the king wrote to the high pontiff, asking him to elevate to the office of cardinal a certain cleric of his realm. The king declared that he was very surprised that no Englishman for a long time now had been judged worthy by the Roman curia of being admitted to that holy office. After all, there were rich benefices reserved in the kingdom of England for the use of the reverend company of cardinals, and in the two universities of his [112] kingdom many outstanding clerics were elevated to the rank of master in any of the liberal sciences without any concern being felt, and then were no less praised and honoured for their goodness of character. The high pontiff wrote back, bidding the king choose the two clerics in his kingdom most fit for this great honour, and saying that the merciful father would then willingly grant the king's wishes for the two who were chosen, provided that in the judgment of the cardinals they were found worthy of the desired office, as being men who would bring honour to God and the universal church.

So the king presented with letters to the Roman curia his choices of master John Bateman,[1] bishop of Norwich, and Ralph Stratford, bishop of London. But they waited at the papal curia for a long time for the completion of their appointment, and in vain. For in the meantime John of Valois, the crowned head of France, came in person on a visit to the lord pope and presented many of his own clerics for promotion by the grace of the apostolic see. The pope made eleven of these Frenchmen cardinals, while the two English bishops, although outstanding doctors in both kinds of the law, were authorised to look after the sheep committed to their care.[2]

While these things were happening, two mercenary knights belonging to the king of Armenia arrived in England. They came before the king and showed him a letter from the king of Armenia. The letter stated that one of the two knights, a Cypriot called Giovanni Visconti, had brought an accusation against the other knight, a Frenchman called Thomas de la Marche, the bastard son of Philip the last king of France. The accusation was that Thomas had received a sum of gold from the Turks for betraying an army of the Christians to the emperor of the Turks, and to prove the truth of his accusation Giovanni had challenged Thomas to a duel, which ought to be decided by the judgment of Edward, king of England, as he was the most blessed of princes.[3]

So to settle their dispute the two knights fought in the lists of the king's palace at Westminster on the Monday after the feast of St Michael. [113] As

---

[1] Baker gives the wrong Christian name; the bishop was William Bateman.
[2] Baker's curious phrase means that they were not made cardinals, and that their jurisdiction was therefore limited to their own dioceses.
[3] Thomas de la Marche was actually accused of trying to betray the king of Sicily, Louis I, to the rebellious nobles whom he was besieging at Catania. (*Foedera*, iii.i 205)

proof of the justice of his case Thomas defeated his enemy, but he did not kill him, because Giovanni was so well protected by his armour that Thomas could nowhere make an attacking thrust with a weapon except on Giovanni's face, which was bare. And after the tilting and the fight on foot and while they were wrestling with each other sprawled on the ground, Thomas did cause wounds to Giovanni's bare face, inflicted by the short, sharp points of the steel-plated gauntlet covering the root knuckles of the fingers of his right hand, as he squeezed his hand together. (Nowadays such gauntlets are called 'gadelinges.') But Giovanni for his part had no similar short weapon enabling him to wound Thomas in the face. At this point, with Giovanni giving out terrifying screams, the king commanded the duel to come to an end and Thomas was adjudged the victor. Thomas gave the defeated Giovanni to the prince of Wales as his prisoner, and piously offered up his armour to St George in the church of St Paul.

After all this the Cypriot was set free and allowed to go, and Thomas went full of confidence to visit his brother, the crowned head of France. But he found that the crowned head and the nobles of France were very angry with him for agreeing to a single combat in the presence of the king of England. At this Thomas, who thought he could rely on the false friendship of his brother, wished to show that he had acted rightly and so among other things praised the nobleness of king Edward, his worldwide fame and the justice of his judgments. 'Although the Cypriot,' said Thomas, 'was a close friend of king Edward, the king did not allow him to be preferred to me, a Frenchman and the brother and friend of you, my lord king of France.' Also the count of Eu showered lavish praises on the English king, enumerating the comforts and kindnesses which he had received from the king at the time of his captivity in England. Amongst other things he recalled the extent to which that best of kings had banished envy from his heart. For at a tournament in which both he himself, a prisoner in England, and the English king were taking part, the king had not begrudged him being acclaimed the victor in the tournament.

But the crowned head of France was envious of such praises, [114] even though they were completely and fully deserved. Consumed with the wrath, which is the bastard offspring of envy, the stepmother of justice, he wickedly ordered the two speakers of these praises to be beheaded. He pretended that the count of Eu had enjoyed too close a familiarity with his wife, the queen, and that his brother had been guilty of lèse-majesté against France when he had entrusted his duelling dispute to the judgment of the king of England.[1] After thus killing his brother, he tortured his wife by starving her to death, although she was the daughter of the noble king of Bohemia, who had recently been killed in the battle of Crécy. Then he besmirched his royal honour by his

---

[1]   Baker is correct in recording the sudden execution of the count of Eu, in circumstances which still remain mysterious, but probably relate to John's suspicion that the count was about to go over to the English side. Thomas de la Marche was not executed, and the accusations against Bonne of Luxembourg are without foundation. Much of this passage reads like propaganda put about in England following the count of Eu's death.

filthy embracings and couplings with a nun, which lasted until he was taken prisoner at the battle of Poitiers, as I shall describe later.[1]

In AD 1351 and the twenty-fifth year of the king, in a parliament held in London after the octave of the purification of the glorious Virgin,[2] lord Henry, son of Henry earl of Lancaster and himself earl of Lincoln, Leicester, Derby, Grosmont and Ferrers, was made duke of Lancaster. By this generous act of the king he was given such liberties and privileges as no other earl had. Also Lionel, lord of Antwerp and the king's son, became earl of Ulster in Ireland,[3] lord John of Gaunt his brother became earl of Richmond, and Sir Ralph Stafford, formerly a baron, became an earl with the same title.

In the following Lent, Sir Walter Mauny and Robert Herle, the captain of Calais, rode into French territory. They looted a great swathe of it and brought back great numbers of cattle, oxen, sheep and pigs. With these they so restocked the larders at Calais that one fat cow was barely worth fifteen pence sterling.

After this around Easter time the duke of Lancaster proceeded from Calais to the coastlands of Artois and Picardy and burnt the suburbs of Boulogne. He then attacked the town, but was unsuccessful, just because his scaling-ladders were too short. So he laid waste the city and harbour of Thérouanne and also the towns of Fauquembergue and Etaples. In their harbours he set fire to more than one hundred and twenty ships of different sorts. [115] Then he set fire to the countryside round about and rode as far as Saint-Omer. Finally, having captured many forts he returned to Calais with great quantities of booty and very many captives.

Also around the time of the feast of St George there was an English success in Gascony. When the marshal of France with a large crowd of armed men devastated the country around the town of Saint-Jean-d'Angély, where Edmund Rose of Norfolk had been put in command, the people united with the garrison of the town and bravely went to meet the enemy. In the battle which ensued the townspeople, besides killing many and putting to flight more than four hundred knights, also took prisoner the marshal of France and many other French nobles.[4]

In the same year the English, led by Sir John Beauchamp, the brother of the earl of Warwick, began a campaign which started well but ended badly. Sir John, who was then captain of Calais, led out almost the whole garrison of three hundred armed men and three hundred archers and laid waste the surrounding countryside for three days. But, as he was taking back to Calais

---

1   Robert of Avesbury makes similar remarks about John's immorality
2   9 February 1351.
3   This is incorrect: Lionel was earl of Ulster through his marriage to Elizabeth de Burgh, countess of Ulster in her own right.
4   In fact the garrison took no part, as this was an attempt to relieve the town; despite the English victory in this skirmish, the town was taken on 31 August 1351: Sumption, *Trial by Fire*, 77–8.

booty beyond counting, he found the sire de Beaujeu and the sire de Fiennes with five hundred men of arms lying in ambush in three different places, awaiting the return of himself and his men. The English overpowered the men in the first and second places of ambush, but when they came near the road which leads to Calais they were met by fresh troops of the enemy. Sir John was a very vigorous knight and a man of amazing spirit. He thought it shameful to gather his men into some safe, defensible place, just as if he was running away from the French. He scorned to take to the nearby road as a refuge, although, if the English had taken it, the enemy would not have prevailed against them, if we can believe those who were there. So the English fought the French on the open plain. As they were already tired from two battles fought on the same day, with many of them seriously wounded and the archers with no arrows left, [116] it was extremely brave of them to meet the French, even if not very wise. Fierce fighting was renewed. This time the enemy leader, the sire de Beaujeu, was slain and fell, but, despite this, his men with great determination overcame our men and took them all prisoner except for a few. These few, who had been badly wounded in the other battles, got back to Calais, together with those who had been driving the captured livestock to the town before the third battle. No Englishman was killed in this third battle, at least no Englishman who was willing to surrender to an enemy. Just about all of these were later set free by ransom or in exchange for Frenchmen.[1]

In the same year Spanish ships authorised to discuss peace sailed to England, just as in the previous year it had been decided to do by means of these same ships which had been summoned and detained.[2] This time a truce to last for twenty years was made between the English and these ships. Also a truce to last for one year was begun between the kingdoms of England and France.[3] It was broken by the French when they took the castle of Guines, as I shall describe in my history of the next year.

Also at this time the best gold was changed for a new gold coinage.[4] For the old gold had been worth considerably more than the regulated price, and for that reason the Lombards and other foreign merchants had been buying up the gold and taking it out of the kingdom, to great loss for the king and the whole of England. A remedy for this was provided by the change I have described. Also new silver money was minted, the groat worth four pence and the half-groat worth two pence.

---

[1]   The battle took place on 8 June 1351, and was widely noticed in chronicles, because the loss of most of the Calais garrison laid the town open to attack; William Clinton, earl of Huntingdon was sent urgently at the end of June with no more than a couple of hundred men to hold Calais.

[2]   A truce was signed with the maritime towns of Castile and Biscay on 1 August 1351 (*Foedera*, III.i 228). Baker is perhaps trying to say that the ships from these towns had been arrested when they arrived the previous year, and were released on condition that a truce was arranged.

[3]   The truce with France was signed on 11 September. *Foedera*, iii.i.232

[4]   The order for minting the new coins was issued on 21 June 1351. *Foedera*, iii.i.224

About the beginning of January in AD 1352 the French were busy with repairing the walls of the town of Guines, which had previously been destroyed by the English. Some English knights, who were not pleased when they heard of this rebuilding, successfully devised the following scheme for its demolition.

There was an archer called John Dancaster who had previously been captured and imprisoned in the castle of Guines. As he did not have the means to pay his ransom, he was set free by the French on the condition that he served as an archer for them. This fellow became acquainted with the lewd embraces of a lewd washerwoman and learned from her of a wall that had been built across the bottom of the chief moat of the castle. It was two feet wide and extended from the rampart to the inner wall of the castle. It was so covered with water that it could not be seen, but it was not so submerged that a man crossing by it got wet further up than his knees. It had been made once upon a time for the use of fishermen and for that reason the wall was discontinued in the middle for the space of two feet.

Armed now with this information from his strumpet, John Dancaster measured the height of the wall with a thread, Having discovered it, he one day slipped down from the wall, entrusting himself to God, and crossed the moat by the hidden wall. He hid until evening in the marshes, came to the vicinity of Calais by night and waited for broad daylight before he entered the town, as he would definitely not have been let in at any other time.

He told those who were greedy for booty and keen to take the castle by stealth, where an entrance was lying open for them. These thirty conspirators made ladders of the length measured by him, and, wearing black armour without any brightness, they came to the castle of Guines by night, guided by John Dancaster. They climbed the wall with their ladders, knocked out the brains of a guard, who meeting them by chance was beginning cry out, and threw his body into the moat. In the hall they found and slaughtered many unarmed men who were playing at chequers or dice and who were as panic-stricken as sheep in the presence of wolves. Then, easily breaking into chambers and turrets where ladies and some knights were sleeping, they became masters of all that they wanted.

Finally, when all their prisoners stripped of all their weapons had been shut into one strong room, they set free those Englishmen who had been taken prisoner the previous year, fed and armed them, and put them in charge of their former masters. So in this way they seized all the defences of the castle, while the Frenchmen in the town who were superintending the rebuilding of the ruins knew nothing of what was happening to the French in the castle. The next day the thirty commanded the men working in the town to cease from their labours, and these quickly fled when they saw from this that the castle had been captured. The new kings of the castle allowed the ladies found there to depart on horseback, taking with them their dresses and the papers and charters which they needed to keep their feudal rights secure.

The same day there arrived to help them at their invitation other men from Calais, and with their loyal assistance they held the castle secure. About 9 am two knights arrived, sent by the count of Guines. Having asked for a truce, they asked the occupants of the castle who they were, [118] to whom they belonged and by whose authority they were holding a castle taken during a truce. To this they received the reply that the intruders were not willing to reveal their purpose to any man living, until they had been in possession of the place for rather longer.[1]

So, during a parliament being held by the English king on the feast of St Maurice the abbot, envoys arrived sent by the count of Guines. These declared in the presence of the king that the castle of Guines had been captured, and that, as this was an infringement of the truce, it should be handed back to them in its entirety according to the rights of the agreement between the two countries. The king prudently replied to the envoys that the crime had not been engineered with his agreement or knowledge. This being so, he handed to the envoys a letter of command to all his people, saying that no loyal subject of his should hold on to the castle of Guines which had been seized in this manner, but should deliver it to its lawful lords.

When the envoys returned home and reported the results of their embassy, the count of Guines went to the castle which had once been his, and asked the intruders yet again in whose name they were occupying the castle. When they kept replying that it was in the name of John Dancaster, the count asked if this John was a loyal subject of the king of England who would be likely to follow his orders. When John replied that he was not (for he knew what answer the envoys had been given in England), the count offered him for the castle, besides all the treasure found in it, many thousands of crowns or possessions in exchange and perpetual peace and the friendship of the king of the French. The occupants of the castle finally said in reply to this that before the capture of their castle they had been Englishmen by birth, but that because of their crimes they had been banished and exiled from living with the king of England in his kingdom and from peace and friendship with him. So they would willingly sell or give in exchange the castle which they now held, but they would do this to nobody sooner than to their natural king of England, their preordained sovereign. For, so they said, they would offer to sell him their castle in return for peace with him and a peaceful recall from exile. But, if he was unwilling to buy it, they would willingly take for the castle the price suggested by the king of France, or the price of anybody offering still more.

When the count had been got rid of by such talk, the king of England bought and occupied the castle which he had in truth long desired.[2]

---

1   See introduction, p.xxiii The castle was taken on 6 January 1352: Avesbury in *Murimuth*, 414.This piece of private enterprise put Edward in a serious quandary. It was a major breach of the truce agreed the previous September, but Guines was the nearest French fortress to Calais, and a place of the highest strategic importance.

2   In the course of the parliament of January 1352, during which the news of the capture of Guines arrived, Edward and his advisers decided to keep the castle, and therefore accused John II of serious breaches of the truce in order to justify their actions. *PROME* v. 34, 41.

The French had been accustomed to use this castle of Guines to block the English entry into the country lying beyond it. The castle had also offered great security [119] to the people of the area against foragers from Calais. So the French council wished either to regain the castle or to build another castle of similar usefulness to protect the country roundabout. To this end Geoffroi de Charny, who had been recently ransomed from an English prison, was sent to the area to carry out the following scheme.

Now for travellers from Guines to Calais, there was a place on the left which was strongly fortified, but which happened to be a monastery with a church in which consecrated virgins served God. This monastery, which was called La Bastide, was so near to the castle of Guines that Englishmen standing outside the gate of their castle could shoot an arrow into it. It could also be easily defended, for it had high walls like those of a castle and a large and lofty bell tower. Also, as it sat in the marshes, it could be surrounded by a moat with little effort.

The English had always been suspicious of this holy place, but, out of their devotion to Jesus Christ, they had always refrained from attacking it until Geoffroi de Charny, in violation of the truce, used it to set siege to Guines with a powerful armed force. For he removed the nuns from the church and tried to make a castle out of it, with a fence for its wall and a moat all round. He did this about the time of Pentecost in this year, when his men could work in the marshes without being hampered by the waters. The occupants of Guines castle were now under siege from in front. They could scarcely get out in their boats through the water-filled ditches or make their way over the pathless, watery marshes. Nor could the people of Calais supply them with any of the provisions they needed because of the besiegers posted in La Bastide. Several times the men in Guines sallied forth and fought with the men of La Bastide, but, although they killed some of the enemy, occasionally with arrows and sometimes with other weapons, these victims were too few in number. At last on an agreed day the men of Calais gathered together with the men of Oye and Marck and attacked La Bastide from the one side while the occupants of the castle did so from the other. They killed many, put several to flight and finally set fire to the whole of La Bastide, knocked down the walls and levelled everything down to the ground.[1]

In this year the lord duke of Lancaster travelled to Prussia. [120] While he was staying with the king of Krakow and Poland to fight against the Turks, his daughter in England on the orders of the king's council was married to William, count of Holland, the firstborn son of Louis, once duke of Bavaria and usurper of the Roman empire.[2]

In this year, on the eve of the feast of the assumption of the Virgin, the mother of God, Walter Bentley, the captain of Calais, Robert Knollys and other

---

[1]   Charny abandoned the siege of Guines in mid-July 1352.
[2]   Lancaster was in Prussia in early 1352; it seems unlikely that there was any fighting during his visit. Maud of Lancaster married William of Holland about this time.

men loyal to the king won an impressive victory over the enemy in the marches of Brittany. The contest was long and perilous, but the following Frenchmen were killed: the chief marshal of France, also the sires of Quintin, Tinténiac, Rochemont, Montauban, Raguenel, Lannoy, Montbouchier, Vielcastel and de la Marche, and 140 other knights together with the total of 500 squires. The coats of arms were found of all these, but the number of common people killed was not counted. The Frenchmen taken prisoner were the sire of Briquebecq the son of Bertrand the marshal, Tristan de Maignelais, the sire of Malestroit, the vicomte of Coëtmen, Geoffroi de Coeyghem, William de la Val, Charles d'Argeville, Jean de la Muce and more than another 130 knights together with their squires. The French army under the command of the marshal had been purposely drawn up by its leader with its rear blocked by the slope of a mountain, so that his men, in despair at their inability to run away, might fight as boldly as troops who were habitually brave. There were also present on the French side many knights from the company of the Star, who at their profession had sworn that they would never flee in fear from the English; forty five of this company were counted among the captured and the killed. Few got away from this battle without being wounded. Indeed the English captain Walter, who had suffered horrific wounds, ordered the execution of thirty archers who at the height of the struggle had run away in their terror at the size of the French.[1][121]

Also the earl of Stafford entered Gascony. He met a large army of Frenchmen who had come out from the fortification at Agen. In glorious fashion about the time of the nativity of the Virgin he routed the enemy, put them to flight and took prisoners. Among the captives was that famous knight called Boucicaut, a cautious commander with a great ability to anticipate what would happen. Also captured were seven knights of the company of the Star.[2] Soon afterwards in Gascony came the simultaneous deaths of Sir John Odingsells and Sir Thomas Wale, both knights of good repute.

Also in this year, when news came that pirates had infested the sea, seven warships with accompanying pinnaces and galleys were sent out against them, under the command of Sir Thomas Coke and Sir Richard Totesham. These stirred up the foam in the waters off the coasts of Picardy and Normandy, but before the feast of St George returned home saying their prayers.

During these happenings by land and sea, the duke of Lancaster, who had returned from Prussia, received a letter from Otto, the son of the German duke of Brunswick and a soldier in the service of the crowned one of the French.

---

[1]   The battle of Mauron, fought on 14 August 1352, was a major setback for the French in Brittany, who were trying to enforce the claim of Charles de Blois to the dukedom. Baker's account is a summary, with the names inaccurately copied, of the letter in Avesbury, *Murimuth*, 416. Le Bel (217[206-7]) claims that as many as 89 knights of the Star died, but the most serious losses were among the Breton supporters of Charles de Blois. The French imitated the English tactic of dismounting their knights and attacking on foot, and very nearly succeeded. See Sumption, *Trial by Fire*, 94-5.

[2]   The battle near Agen was in August 1352; Stafford was only in Gascony for three months.

In this letter Otto brought accusations against the duke of Lancaster, for he claimed that, as the duke was passing through Cologne on his way home from Prussia, he had maliciously told the citizens of the town that Otto was seeking to have him secretly seized so that he might be presented to the crowned one of the French as a prisoner. Otto added that, as he had never contemplated such an arrest, he was ready to clear his good name by a single combat, provided it was held in the court of the French king, and so prove the duke of Lancaster a liar on that matter.

The letter containing this challenge was not sealed. The duke did not wish to be seen to give foolish credence to a piece of paper, especially one handed to him by a lowly servant, and so he sent two knights to Otto to inquire into the reason for the accusation and to ask him for letters patent on the subject, properly signed and sealed. Having completed the business of their journey, the knights hurriedly returned from Germany, and the duke sent envoys to the crowned head of France, asking for a safe conduct for himself and his men. Having finally after much trouble obtained the permission from the king which he had sought, the duke of Lancaster came to Paris.

There, in the lists, [122] in the presence of the crowned head of France, the king of Navarre, the duke of Burgundy and very many peers and others of the kingdom of France, the duke of Lancaster mounted his warhorse in seemly fashion, giving every sign of having omitted nothing and being eager for the duel. So, completely ready, he waited for his opponent to finish his preparations and for the voice of the herald, cautioning them to remember their common oath that they would listen to his words and obey the rules. But, at the other end of the lists, Otto's recalcitrant horse was extremely unwilling to receive him, even when he was lifted on to it by helpers. And as Otto was carried off by his mount, he could not properly fix his helmet or his shield or lift his lance – or he feebly pretended that he could not. The crowned one of France, the king of Navarre and the others present immediately noticed Otto's lack of control, and the crowned head of the French at once took this single combat dispute into this own hands. First he commanded Otto to leave the place, while the duke waited in the area. Then on the order of the crowned one, Otto swore that he would never from then on bring accusations against the duke of Lancaster on this matter. The duke went back to his own country through Holland.[1]

Miscellaneous. In a parliament held at Westminster after Epiphany in this year it was decreed, after pressure from the citizens of London, that in future no known prostitute should wear a hood unless it was striped, or make use of furs or lined garments, on pain of forfeiture of the same.[2]

---

[1] Fowler, *The King's Lieutenant*, 106-110, has a full account of this episode. Henry Knighton, who had close links with Lancaster's household, provides considerable detail, which largely agrees with Baker (112-119). Both writers try to make Lancaster the victor, when in fact John II simply stopped the duel once the two parties had appeared in the lists.

[2] Not recorded in the documents printed for this parliament (13 January – 11 February) in *PROME* v. 33–63, but in the city letter-book for 1351 a proclamation to this effect is recorded: H. T. Riley, *Memorials of London and London Life*, London 1868, 122.

Also, to the great comfort of the people, the price of corn fell. This was caused by Dutch and Spanish merchants bringing corn for sale to the various ports of the kingdom.

Also in this year William de la Zouche of pious memory, the archbishop of York, migrated from this world. Master John Thoresby, bishop of Worcester and chancellor of the kingdom, was transferred to his position.[1]

In AD 1353, the twenty-seventh year of king Edward, in a parliament at Westminster on the day after the feast of St Matthew or St Mathias,[2] it was decreed that staples for wool (a staple being a meeting-place for merchants for buying wool), which formerly had been at Bruges in Flanders, should in future be in different parts of England, Wales and Ireland. As can be seen from the laws then passed, regulations against transgressors were drawn up and the privileges were given to all merchants, but especially to foreign ones.

After this parliament the earl of Northampton, throughout his life a famous hammer of the Scots, set out for Scotland with a great force of armed men, archers and Welsh brigands. The cunning tricks of the Scots had always done more harm to the English than the pompous posturings of the French, and now, when the earl rode across the march, he strengthened Lochmaben castle and other fortifications, and took prisoner some Scots who were waiting in ambush for him. These included the knight Sir James Ramsey who had inherited estates worth a thousand marks.[3] The earl also had peace discussions with the proud race of the Scots. They would willingly have ransomed their king and made a perpetual peace with the English, but only on condition that their king did not have his land from the king of England.

In this year on St Nicholas' day pope Clement VI died.[4] He was succeeded by pope Innocent, also VI. In his great desire for peace, pope Innocent sent the cardinal of Boulogne to Calais, in order that he might listen to the discussions about a final peace between England and France. For the councils of both kingdoms had come together at Calais with full powers to discuss and draw up the terms of such a peace.

In the end the councils came to the following agreement, that the king of England should resign all his rights which he had in the kingdom of France, give up his title as king of France and hold for himself and his successors as kings of England only the duchy of Aquitaine and the countships of Artois and Guines, but without holding them in any way whatsoever from the king of France. To these conditions the pious Edward, king of England and

---

[1]   Zouche died in July 1352.
[2]   St Mathias, 21 September 1353. *PROME*, v. 64-87
[3]   This expedition is not recorded elsewhere; there were unsuccessful peace negotiations during 1352 and 1353.
[4]   6 December 1352. As so often with Baker, the chronological sequence is erratic, as the peace mission of Guy, cardinal of Boulogne, belongs to April 1354.

France, in his devotion to the peace of Christendom, gave his pious and generous assent. Finally, so that agreements of such importance should be secure, high-ranking ambassadors [123] from both kingdoms were sent to the apostolic see. Representing the king of England on that embassy were the bishops of Norwich and London, the duke of Lancaster, the earl of Arundel and other knights. After their journey they were met at Avignon by the archbishop of Rouen, the duc de Bourbon, Geoffroi de Charny and others from the French council. All the ambassadors were received with great honour; indeed the duke of Lancaster was met by many cardinals and bishops, who escorted him for two miles to the city and palace of the lord pope.

At last in the very consistory of the high pontiff and in the presence of the cardinals and the ambassadors from both sides the ambassadors presented their cases. When these had been heard, the English asked for the confirmation of the agreements which had been recently made at Calais between themselves and the ambassadors of France there present. The French said in reply to the English that they would willingly welcome a peace, but that neither the French king nor they themselves could agree to the condition that the French king should lose Aquitaine and the two countships, as the English envoys had suggested; for they were part of the totality of the kingdom to which the king and themselves had sworn oaths at a time when they belonged with all rights to the kingdom of France. On the other hand they were ready to agree that the king of England should receive the use of the dominions of the duchy and the countships, just as his ancestors had received Aquitaine, but on condition that the kingship of the same should be reserved for the royal crown of France.

But the English envoys considered that such a kingship had often in the past caused the kings of England and France to decide matters by war, whenever the English had been slow in paying homage and swearing oaths of allegiance. And so they asked, for the sake of a perpetual peace, that these three dominions should be completely given up to their king without conditions, as had been arranged at Calais. But although the cardinal of Boulogne testified that such a demand had been recently agreed to at Calais and confirmed by men with authority, the French envoys now doggedly refused their assent.

There was even an answer to the French argument that the oaths sworn by their king and themselves meant that they were bound to preserve the totality of the honour of the kingdom and its possessions; for of course the lord pope, if he so wished, could absolve them from this oath for the sake of peace, [125] and would specifically do so for the particular issues which they had mentioned.

But the pope made no changes or innovations which had a marked effect on peace in the church and between the two kingdoms. So the ambassadors, who had been sent to Rome at great expense, returned without accomplishing anything, except that, when the bishop of Norwich, a man of great wisdom, died and was buried at Rome, the lord pope, at the urging of the ambassadors, appointed Sir Thomas Percy as his successor.[1]

In AD 1354 the king of Navarre killed Charles of Spain, the marshal of France, after a quarrel had sprung up between them.[2] To avoid being punished by the crowned head of France, the king of Navarre fled to his own lands. From there he sent his uncle with a letter of supplication to the duke of Lancaster, begging him to come to Normandy to his aid and defence, and to receive from him an oath of loyalty and friendship against all men living. So the duke obtained permission from the lord king and assembled a great fleet at Southampton. But when he was ready to sail, the knights returned whom he had sent on ahead as envoys to Normandy to find out the truth of this matter. They told the duke that his kinsman, the king of Navarre, had made his peace with the crowned head of France. So the duke's crossing of the sea was postponed for the time being.[3]

In AD 1355, the twenty-ninth year of the reign of Edward, the king himself and the prince of Wales, with everything else prepared, were waiting for a favourable wind for more then forty days. The king was at Sandwich, aiming for France, and the prince of Wales was at Sutton[4] in Devon, aiming for Aquitaine. During this time the crowned head of France divided his forces among the harbours of Normandy and other coastal places, to stop the king or the prince from landing. This operation was so extensive and so long lasting that the very French and their mercenaries did immense damage to their own country. Many thousands of crowns from the crowned one's treasury were spent to no purpose.[126] Finally, the crowned one, so penniless or so mean that he could not pay his own men, was deserted by them. When, later on,[5] the king of England was ravaging France, the crowned one did not have the troops for meeting his pursuer in battle, or, doubtless, he was a victim of feebleness and not brave enough to do so. He fled before the advance of the English, burning his own towns and destroying the food supplies, so that the king of England should not find food or lodging for his men. But the lord king pursued the crowned one himself for three days, staying each night in the place where the fugitive crowned one had lain in hiding the night before.

[1]   For a full account of the negotiations and the complicated political background, see Fowler, *The King's Lieutenant*, 122-144, and Ormrod, *Edward III*, 336-340. Baker's account of the proceedings at Avignon is the most detailed of an occasion which Ormrod calls 'one of the great diplomatic spectacles of the Hundred Years War'.
[2]   For the feud and ensuing murder, see Sumption, *Trial by Fire*, 108-9, 124-6; the basic cause was Charles de Navarre's anger at Charles d'Espagne's appointment as marshal, a post which he felt should have been his by right as a prince of the house of Valois.
[3]   The fleet was prepared in the early summer of 1355, but was delayed by contrary winds until September, when news of Charles de Navarre's double-cross reached England. Ormrod, *Edward III*, 343.
[4]   The central harbour in Plymouth Sound, now part of Plymouth.
[5]   This refers to Edward's brief campaign in November 1355, mentioned in the next paragraph but wrongly dated August, where John II adopted a scorched earth policy.

After August in this year the lord king and the duke of Lancaster with seven thousand armed men and their equipment entered France.[1] They marched southwards for nine days, burning everything and ravaging the country. On their return to Calais the king heard that the Scots had secretly entered and captured the town of Berwick.[2] Its governor, when it was captured, was baron William de Greystoke. He had not been invited to serve abroad with the king, but he had been given charge of Berwick. So the king hurried to Scotland, laid siege to Berwick and within fifteen days received the surrender of the town. Life and liberty were given to all found within the town.[3]

Then the king marched across Scotland as far as the Scottish sea. His army now ran out of food, for the Scots had carried all supplies to their islands and forts and across the Scottish sea before the expected arrival of the king. Also the ships appointed for the purpose had not victualled the army at Newcastle. So with the king's permission all his men marched back to England, with Sir Robert Herle, Sir Aymer de St Amand, Sir Robert Hildesley and others acting as a rearguard for twelve miles. But then the Scots found these gentlemen asleep at night and expecting no opposition. With loud shouts they burst in upon them. After a long resistance, Sir Robert Hildesley and Sir John Brancaster were taken prisoner, while Sir Robert Herle and Sir Aymer managed to get away. For the former two knights, when they saw the Scots prevailing, had reflected that the barons who were their own lords would ransom their [127] dependents, and would free them from Scottish captivity by bold or cautious means. And indeed their lords did just this. For, after some thought, they decided that the capture of a few, poor knights could be dealt with more easily than the capture of all the barons.

After this the lord duke of Lancaster, who had been appointed captain of Brittany,[4] set sail with a fleet for Normandy. He landed at La Hogue about the feast of the apostle St Barnabas,[5] and rode across the land with Philip, the brother of that king of Navarre who had invited the duke of Lancaster to help him.

In this year the crowned one of the French had his suspicions of the king of Navarre, the count of Harcourt and other nobles of his kingdom. So, having invited them to a banquet, he imprisoned the king and slew the rest.[6] The count of Harcourt was struck down with an axe, or, as some people say, was drowned tied up in a sack, while protesting that the only treachery he was

---

[1]   Edward embarked for Calais on 28 October 1355: Ormrod, *Edward III*, 624.
[2]   6 November 1355: Ormrod, *Edward III*, 345.
[3]   It was retaken on 13 January 1356: Ormrod, *Edward III*, 345.
[4]   He was appointed on 14 September 1355: *Foedera*, iii.i 312. The commission was renewed annually until 1358.
[5]   Actually on 18 June 1356. Fowler, *The King's Lieutenant*, 151.
[6]   The arbitrary arrest of Charles de Navarre and his supporters on 5 April 1356 drove Philip of Navarre and the Norman lords led by Godfrey d'Harcourt to rebel; by 12 May they had negotiated English support, and on 28 May issued letters of defiance to king John. Lancaster's fleet was already prepared, which implies that John II was correct in believing that Charles was already planning to go over to the English.

guilty of was that he had not stayed loyal to the king of England, but had unjustly rebelled against the one who was the true heir and in law if not in fact the king of the whole kingdom of France. After the king of Navarre had been imprisoned in this way, his brother Philip seized many forts in the Cotentin and in Normandy. With the help of the duke of Lancaster he gave them adequate provisions and strengthened them against the tyranny of the French by packing them with Englishmen and with his own countrymen.

At the same time as the lord king was crossing the seas to Calais and France, as I have mentioned, his firstborn son, lord Edward of Woodstock, the prince of Wales happily set sail from Sutton in Devon on the day after the nativity of St Mary. [1] He had with him the earls of Warwick, Suffolk, Salisbury and Oxford, and at the beginning of October he landed at Bordeaux. He was received with honour, being met by the bishop, clergy and monks all wearing their religious robes and by all the people. The lords and barons of Gascony had all come to Bordeaux to show their devotion and joy at this long awaited arrival of the prince. At a council of the nobles of Gascony and the lords who had come with the prince, a report was made about the count of Armagnac. [128] It was said that, as the deputy of the crowned head of the French, he had been appointed the general in chief and director of military operations against the English, and that by means of the universally rebellious Aquitaine[2] nation he had done more harm to the country and loyal supporters of the king of England than others of the kingdom of France. Having heard this report, the anger of the furious prince glowed white-hot against this pursuer of a war in Aquitaine, and with the agreement of the council of his lords he dispatched his troops to ravage the countship of Armagnac. They speedily set out and the prince first received the surrender of the forts of the county of Juliers, and then, by his ravaging of Armagnac, gave great comfort to the loyal lords of Gascony, who before the arrival of this noble prince had suffered similar treatment at the hands of those violent neighbours of theirs.

But at this point it will not be tedious to include a daily diary of the prince's march to Narbonne, so that the reader may have a clearer idea of what is now happening.[3]

Divine worship was piously performed on the first Sunday of that month, that is 4 October, and on the Monday following the prince set out against his

---

[1]   I.e.from Plymouth on 9 September.

[2]   Baker tries to invent an adjective, 'dexitane', 'the Dexitane nation'; he uses it again in the next sentence: in both instances he means Aquitaine.

[3]   This raid, like that of Edward III in Normandy in 1346, was designed to show the superiority of English power and to inflict economic damage on the French. For the detailed geography of the expedition and the Poitiers campaign of 1356, see Peter Hoskins, *In the Steps of the Black Prince*, Woodbridge and Rochester NY 2011, which is based on the author's personal retracing of the route on foot. Identifications of Baker's often garbled names in the following pages arederived from his account. Baker is the only source for the prince's detailed movements, and evidently had access to a document similar to the 'campaign diaries' for the Crécy campaign.

enemies from Bordeaux and lodged that night two miles from Bordeaux at the castle of Ornon.

On the next day [6 October] a long day of hard marching through woods, during which many horses were lost, took him through the middle of the walled town of Langon to the strong castle of Castets-en-Dorthe.

On Thursday [8 October] to the city of Bazas, which has a cathedral and Franciscan friary. At Bazas on Friday a proclamation was made to the army that each man should wear the arms of St George, and it was said that the enemy wore the same arms.

On Saturday [10 October] to Castelnau, where three castles of three lords look from a distance to be one castle.

On Sunday, 11 October, the army passed through the Landes of Bordeaux which are in possession of the count of Foix. That was a long, hard day's march through desolate country and many horses were lost. On that day in the empty stretch of land which I called the Landes, two miles from Arouille, the banners were unfurled and the army was divided into [129] three squadrons.

In the first squadron of 3,000 armed men there were at the banners the earl of Warwick the constable, Reginald lord Cobham the marshal, lord Beauchamp of Somerset, lord Clifford, Sir Thomas Hampton banneret, and with them seven barons of Gascony.

In the middle squadron of 7,000 armed men besides clerics and servants there were at the banners the lord prince with a double banner, the earl of Oxford, Bartholomew lord Burghersh, John lord Lisle, lord Willoughby, lord de la Warr, Sir Maurice Berkeley (the son of lord Thomas Berkeley who was then still alive but decrepit), lord John Bourchier, John lord Roos, the mayor of Bordeaux, the captal de Buch, the sire de Caumont, and the sire de Montferrand.

In the last squadron were another 4,000 armed men under the command of the earl of Suffolk, the earl of Salisbury and the sire de Pommiers, who led the men of Béarn. In the whole army thus arranged there were more than 60,000 men, counting the men in armour, the clerics, the servants, the archers, those with some armour and the lightly-armed troops.

Also on that day [11 October] Janekin de Berefort and some others were knighted, and the town of Arouille and three other towns, whose captain was William de Reymon, a loyal Englishman, were surrendered anew to the lord prince. The army were given quarters in these towns and stayed there for two days, while all who wished sallied forth, foraged for food and burnt the country of the enemy. They generally behaved like this until they returned to the land of peace.

On Tuesday [12 October] they lodged in the town of Monclar. The castle there was surrendered to them, and later back again to the French. Then, because of a fire which had broken out in the town and burnt it, the prince went out into the fields and spent the night under canvas, being unwilling to spend that night in the town for fear there might be similar fires during the night, and so that he might be always ready for the enemy. On that day three towns were attacked and burnt, and Gilot de Stratton [130] and various others were knighted. Also John lord Lisle, who had been wounded by a cross-bow bolt at the fort of Astanges, died on the following day, to the great sadness of the army.

On Wednesday and Thursday they remained at Monclar, and on Friday [16 October] they spent the night in tents outside the strong town of Nogaro.

On Saturday [17 October] they came to the fair town of Plaisance with its strong defences. All its inhabitants had fled, and the count of Molasin together with many knights and squires were taken prisoner in the castle by the captal de Buch, the sire de Montferrand and Adam de Louches, whose first day as a knight that was. They stayed there on Sunday, the day of St Luke evangelist and the third Sunday of the march. They took by storm the fort of Galiax and burnt it.

On Monday [19 October] they set fire to the town of Plaisance and, ignoring the town of Beaumarchés on their right, they lodged outside the town of the archbishop of Auch which is called Bassoues. On this day Sir Richard Stafford, the brother of the earl of Stafford, for the first time led his men under a banner. On the Tuesday this town was surrendered, and, because it belonged to holy church, the prince did not allow anybody to enter it other than certain persons who were ordered to bring out food.

On Wednesday [21 October] they left behind them on the left the fair town of Escamont, and arrived in front of the noble town of Mirande which is on the lands of the count of Comenge, and which was full of men of arms. The prince himself lodged in the imposing Cistercian monastery of Berdoues, in which no one living was found. On Thursday they stayed put, but did no damage to the monastery.

On Friday [23 October] they left behind the fair, noble province of Armagnac with its wealth and entered the province called Astarac. After a difficult journey through it by narrow tracks over mountains they lodged in the town of Seissan. They burnt this town, although the prince's herald had announced that this was banned. For that day's march and the following three marches they travelled near the lofty mountains of Aragon.

On the Saturday [24 October] they came to the town of Simorre, where the rearguard lodged in a large monastery which had been deserted by its black monks. The middle guard lodged at Villefranche, and the vanguard at [131] Tournan, both towns being rich and crammed with foodstuffs, but abandoned by their fleeing citizens.

On the fourth Sunday of the march [25 October], the day of St Crispin and St Crispian, they crossed a ford into the lands of the count of Comminges, which extended as far as Toulouse, but they were all laid waste by fire and the sword. Then they left behind on the left a town called Sauveterre in Astarac, and passed near to a strong city called Lombez. Pope John XXII had removed the black monks from Lombez and made it an episcopal see. They lodged in a large, rich town called Samatan, in the lands of the count of Comminges. There was a Franciscan friary there, but it was burnt together with the town.

On Monday [26 October] they passed through a wide, level, fair country, and marched on through the town of Sainte-Foy-de-Peyrolières until they came to Saint-Lys. On Tuesday they rested.

On the following Wednesday [28 October], the feast day of saints Simon and Jude, the army crossed the difficult, rock-strewn and completely terrifying waters of the Garonne. Later on the same day they also crossed the waters of the Ariège, which were even more dangerous than those of the Garonne, and marched downstream towards Toulouse. No one had ever these crossed these rivers on horseback, and so the terrified inhabitants of the district did not know what to do. They had always thought those waters made them safe, and now they were taken by surprise and unable to flee. Nor did they know how to fight back, as war's fury had never entered their land before then. That night the prince lodged at La-Croix-Falgarde, a small town one mile away from Toulouse. After this there was scarcely one day's riding on which our men did not take by storm towns, forts and castles, all of which they despoiled and consigned to the flames.

On Thursday [29 October] they came to the large, fair town of Montgiscard, part of the hereditary rights of Aimeric de la Fossade, but which the crowned one of the French had taken away from him because he was loyal to the king of England. Near this town were twelve windmills, which were all alike burnt by the English. Also two 'spies' or scouts were caught who said that the count of Armagnac was at Toulouse and the constable of France at [132] Montmaban, which was four miles from Toulouse, and that both of them were expecting the English army to come to besiege Toulouse.

On Friday [30 October] they took the straight king's highway through the good town of Bazière and through Villefranche to Avignonet. The whole army was lodged in this large town which belonged to the crowned one of the French. The middle-guard and the rearguard were lodged in a suburb of great quietness, the vanguard in another part of the suburbs and the Gascons and the men of Béarn inside the town, from which all the inhabitants had fled. Twenty windmills there were burnt to a cinder.

On Saturday, the last day of October, they lodged in the large town called Castelnaudary. The church of St Michael of the secular canons in this town, the Franciscan friary, the Carmelite convent of the blessed Mary and the hospital of St Antony were all consumed by fire, as the town called Mas-Saintes-Puelles with its Augustinian convent had been earlier in the day. On Sunday, the feast of All Saints, the army rested, though some of its members went out and captured a town, and received from the townsmen ten thousand gold florins for sparing the town and its possessions.

On Monday [2 November] they passed through Saint-Martin-Lalande and a large town called Villepinte and then entered the district of Carcassonne. The prince stayed the night at a village called Alzonne.

On Tuesday [3 November] they came to the fair city of Carcassonne. It was extremely wealthy, well-built, and larger inside its walls than London. Between the inner town or burgh and the outer town surrounded by a double wall ran a river under a fair stone bridge, at the foot of which stood a fair guest house. In the burgh were four houses for four groups of the religious poor. Their inhabitants, the friars, did not run away, although the townspeople and Poor Clares who also lived there did flee to the outer town. The whole army was well and comfortably lodged in the burgh, although barely taking up three quarters of it. They enjoyed an abundance of muscatel wine and other provisions which were both necessary and palatable. On that day the troops were drawn up in order before the burgh and the order of knighthood was bestowed on the sons of the sire d'Albret and on lord Basset of Drayton, who immediately [133] began serving under his own raised banner. Also Roland Daneys and many more were promoted to the ranks of the knights.

On the Wednesday and Thursday the army stayed in the burgh. A truce was declared and certain Englishmen, appointed for the task, discussed peace with envoys from the city: its citizens offered two hundred and fifty thousand gold crowns to save the burgh from being burnt. In reply to this offer of gold the prince said that he had not come there in search of gold but of justice, and not for the selling of cities but their capture. Then, as the citizens continued to be frightened of the crowned one of the French and were unwilling to obey their natural master, or in truth did not dare to for fear of being punished by the crowned one, the prince on the next day gave orders for the burgh to be burnt, though the religious houses were to be spared.

On Friday [6 November], the army set fire to the burgh and departed. Later, news came from the friars and others that the burgh had been burned to the ground. On that day, the feast of St Leonard, they left behind them on the left the castle of Bouilhonac untouched, and had a difficult march over rocks and water through the towns and district of Rustiques and a countryside which was totally burnt.

On Saturday [7 November] they had a wearisome journey, with the troops suffering from the wind and the dust. They left behind them on the left a freshwater lake called Esebon.[1] It is twenty miles in circumference, with no entrances or exits for any other sorts of water besides rainwater or water from springs. They then came to a town called Lezignan, which was surrendered to the prince but left intact, because the town belonged to the lady Yseult of Brittany, who was a friend of the prince. The prince lodged in a good town called Canet.

On Sunday, 8 November, they crossed the waters of the river Saude, partly by the ford called Chastel-de-terre, and partly by a new but unfinished bridge. After marching between lofty mountains for the whole of the rest of the day they came to the great city of Narbonne, which gives its name to that part of France. This strong, well-walled city contained the great cathedral church of St Justinian, an impressive castle for the bishop, and a strongly fortified tower for the vicomte of the town. Its district known as the burgh was actually larger and better built than the burgh of Carcassonne. In it were four houses

---

[1]   Marked on modern maps as Marseillette.

for the mendicant friars. [134] Between the large wealthy burgh and the very finely walled outer city ran the river Aude, which comes from Carcassonne and flows into the Greek sea, which is two miles from Narbonne. Between the outer city and the burgh are two stone bridges and a third one of wood, one of the stone bridges being a well-built one for the carriers of the different sorts of goods. The prince was lodged in the house of the Carmelite brothers of the blessed Mary. But for the whole of the night and the following day the citizens fought against the English army with cross-bows and other weapons. Many on both sides were wounded, and some were killed.

On Tuesday [10 November], after the burgh had been set on fire by means of burning carts, the army marched to the torrent of the Aude and crossed it in several places. During the crossing two of the lord prince's chariots were smashed and plundered by the citizens to his great loss. The prince lodged at the town and castle of Aubian.

On Wednesday [11 November], the feast of St Martin, the march was long and hard and especially damaging to the horses because of the many rocks. Also there was no water or even other food. The horses carried wine instead of water, the food was cooked in wine, and no liquid was found on the whole journey apart from wine or oil.

On Thursday [12 November] Theodoric Dale, a doorkeeper of the lord prince's chamber, became a knight. The army passed through the good town called Homps, where the officers of the count of Armagnac had lodged the previous night, and the middle-guard was lodged in the good town called Azille, which belonged to the count of Lisle. The prince spent the night in the house of the Franciscan friars, where a great store of muscatel wine in its cellars belonging to lady de Lisle was plundered. That day the English destroyed the good town of Pépieux and its castle called Redote. Captured enemy spies reported that the constable of France and the count of Armagnac had intended to have passed the night in the very towns where the English army did so.

On Friday [13 November] the army marched on a long, rocky and waterless journey to the town of Comigne. There they passed a bad night because of the lack of houses and water.

On Saturday [14 November] they turned back towards Gascony, leaving behind them on the right the lake of Esebon and Carcassonne and the whole of[1] their outward route. The rearguard lodged at a good town called Saint-Hilaire [135] and the middle-guard at Pennautier,[2] where a tower was captured from its defenders. But the prince lay that night beyond a bridge near to a fair stream of water. The country on both sides of this was laid waste by fire, together with the good town of Pezens, where the vanguard was lodged.

---

[1]   The army was a long way from its base, and a strategic withdrawal was now the most prudent course. The prince still hoped to entice the French to give battle, as appears below.

[2]   See Hoskins, *In the Steps of the Black Prince*, 77-82 for the problems of interpreting the prince's route from 13-15 November.

On Sunday [15 November], the feast of St Macutius, the English entered a fair, long and wide country and did a great march through it. The army speeded up because the prince was to lodge in the great abbey of the blessed Mary of Prouille, from the possessions of which there lived in separate cells 100 Dominican friars and 140 anchorite ladies, called Dominican sisters. The lord prince with many others was respectfully received into the holy confraternity of the house. On that day the army burnt among other places the town of Limoux, which had houses of various brothers and was bigger than Carcassonne, the fair town called Fanjeaux, which had twenty-one windmills, and the towns of Villar-St-Anselme and Lasserre-de-Prouille together with the whole country roundabout.

On Monday [16 November] the middle-guard lodged at a good town called Belpech. It was defended for a long time, but taken by an assault. The castle outside the town surrendered. The prince gave orders that neither castle nor town was to be damaged by fire, as they belonged to the count of Foix..

On the morning of Tuesday [17 November] they crossed, though with difficulty, a river called the Vixiège and entered a vast stretch of country. About 1 pm they arrived at a huge Cistercian monastery called Boulbonne. It had been founded by the grandfather of the count of Foix, and the comte himself now met the lord prince with a comfortable litter for him. The count was the governor of the whole Aquitaine[1] region. He had escaped from the Parisian prison of the crowned one of France, where he had lain for two years, and from that time on he remained loyal to the prince. That day they rode on through the lands of the comte, passing through the towns of Mazères and Calmont, which are divided by a river, at the further part of which was a castle long since destroyed. They left behind on the right the large town of Cintegabelle and the lofty castle called Auterive, which both belong to the French. But that day they burnt nothing out of respect for the comte and his neighbourhood. Indeed they crossed again the perilous waters of the Ariège, as they had done before on the day of St Simon and [136] St Jude. Also they left Toulouse untouched again. On the way down it had been one mile on their left, but on the way back it was four miles on the right. The middle-guard lodged in the large town of Miremont. Both town and castle were burnt.

On Wednesday [18 November] they passed by the castle of the count of Foix called Montaut. At the foot of the castle the English horsemen crossed the mighty waters of the Garonne in single file, to the great amazement of the natives. For the small boats, which are available for the inhabitants to cross the river on any day of the year, had been taken away by the nearby townsmen of Noé to hinder the English army. As the people in the castle reported that no one had been able to cross the river since the floods caused by daily rains, the English crossing of the Garonne was rightly attributed to the grace of God. The town of Noé was taken by assault, and the rearguard spent the night in its surrendered castle. Then with the river Garonne on their left they marched

---

[1]   'Doxitane': see n.246 above

upstream to the town of Marquefave which was surprisingly captured, the citizens marvelling as the middle-guard again crossed the waters of the Garonne. The army then came to the strong town of Carbonne. Despite its being well protected by a wall on one side and the river on the other, it had been taken by assault before the prince arrived. Indeed it provided lodgings for the victors, with the prince, as generally happened everywhere, quartered outside the town. On Thursday the army rested after their continuous exertions of the previous days, and greatly enjoyed a quiet period of recuperation.

On Friday [20 November] the prince was informed that the French had been divided into five large squadrons and were near at hand. So our men advanced for a mile from their quarters and drew themselves up for battle on suitable level ground. Then with the English army in position, some of our men cried out aloud at a scuttling hare. The French heard the cries and sent out forty spearmen to investigate. But when they saw our army in position and hurriedly returned and reported this to the French, they all fled in a blind panic, as we were later told by Frenchmen captured in the pursuit of their army. For on that day Bartholomew de Burghersh, John Chandos and James Audley were sent with twenty spearmen to spy out the French, and, coming up to the tail of the French army, they took prisoner thirty-two knights and [137] their squires, including the count of Romery. They also killed many carters and destroyed their provisions. Late in that day the prince took up his lodging in the town of Mauvezin, where four French men at arms, who fled from the English into the town church, at least lost their horses and their weapons.

On a rainy Saturday [21 November] the English picked their way to the castle of Auradé, a hard and difficult day's march. The prince spent the night in the castle and burnt it in the morning.

On Sunday [22 November], St Cecilia's day, having crossed a main highway, they discovered towards evening that the enemy were on the other side of a big mountain, near and below the town of Gimont. So the English waited where they were until midnight, and in the meantime sent sixty spearmen and archers to the right of the town of Aurimont. These men found four men at arms of the constable of the French in Aurimont and compelled them to evacuate the town. Some of the French were killed and some captured as they were chased towards Gimont. In the end the middle-guard had a poor lodging at Aurimont, while the vanguard spent the night at Celymont, a small town one mile away from the enemy.

In the morning, St Clement's day, the English carters and stewards were told to remain in the town of Aurimont, while the others, divided into cohorts for fighting, waited for the enemy on level ground, but in vain. So the lord prince reconnoitred the town of Gimont, and discovered that the enemy had fled about midnight. The French had lost the heart to fight, especially after their English enemies had put them to panic-stricken flight on the several occasions when they had caught up with them after a long pursuit by lengthy and difficult marches.

On Tuesday [November 24] after a long march they camped in the open where there was no water. The horses were given wine to drink, but were still too drunk on the next day to be able to walk straight, and many of them died.

On St Katherine's day [November 25] with great difficulty they marched beside a river, hoping to meet with the enemy. Leaving on their right the walled town of Fleurance which had once been English, they passed through the large town of Saint Lary. The middle-guard lodged in the town of Réjaumont, which was forcibly conquered and therefore burnt. They stayed there for the Thursday. A captured wandering herald at arms[1] told them that a great quarrel had sprung up between the [138] constable of France and the count of Armagnac, because, although the count had promised to enter the fighting and help the French, he had not done so, and indeed he was blamed for their disgraceful flight on several occasions.

On Friday [27 November] they crossed with difficulty a great river and spent the rest of the day marching between walled towns and strong castles. The middle-guard lodged at the town of Lagardère. This town, which was a mile from the good town of Condom, had once been laid waste by the duke of Lancaster. He had destroyed its castle and levelled the town to the ground.

On Saturday [28 November] the army crossed with difficulty a certain river and then proceeded by a difficult track through woods. Many Gascons and all the men from Béarn were now given permission to return home. The army lodged in the good, strong, peaceful town called Mézin, which had always belonged to the English. On this day the prince gave the order that they were to march with their banners furled, as they were in peaceful territory. On Sunday, the eve of the feast of St Andrew, the prince rested, so that he might receive oaths of homage from the townsmen.

On the following day [30 November], the day of that saint and apostle, they came by a long march through a vast solitude to the town of Casteljaloux, where there are three castles, one of them being situated in the marshes.

On Tuesday [1 December] the prince lodged at the castle of Meilhan, which is three miles from Casteljaloux. But several of his household passed through the vast, wooded area near the Cistercian monastery called Montpouillan, and through the forest of the king of England called the big forest and came to the large and well fortified town of La Réole. The earl of Derby[2] had recently conquered this town, as I have said earlier, and within eight weeks after the capture of the town had received the surrender of the castle.

On Wednesday [2 December] the lord prince came to La Réole. His horses and chariots crossed the Garonne at a place where no horse had ever crossed

---

[1]   The text reads *captus errancius armorum*; if *erranciu'* is an adjective, a noun is missing, and *haraldus* would fit with *armorum*, making sense of the passage. This may well be a garbled account of the episode in the letter of John Wingfield to the bishop of Winchester (Avesbury in *Murimuth*, 444), who captured the 'guide of the constable of France' and had him interrogated by the sergeant of arms of the Pope, who was in the camp on a diplomatic mission at the time.

[2]   i.e. the duke of Lancaster; Baker is giving his title at the time of the capture of La Réole in 1345.

the river in living memory. At La Réole, on the decision of the prince's council, the princes and the barons were ordered to spend the winter at different places along La Marche, to protect the country of Gascony inside it from the wiles of the French. These princes and barons guarded their appointed stations sensibly. They made frequent sallies from them and accomplished by their labours much that was excellent, not to mention the rich plunder which they brought back from enemy country [139] to sustain the youth of the army and to enrich their beloved fatherland. I do not have the time to deal with these exploits individually.

In AD 1356, the thirtieth year of the king of England, after making the arrangements I have just described, the prince decided that there should be a new gold coinage in Gascony. Then, while he was wisely occupied with the repair of destroyed buildings and other matters necessary for the preservation of the state, the frightened French invented the fantastic notion that the lord king of England had landed in Normandy, and spread this accusation far and wide. If this fantasy did not come from their dreams, it may have come from the fact that the duke of Lancaster had in the Cotentin and in many other places in Normandy reinforced with provisions and weapons the forts and castles of the king of Navarre, before directing his course towards Brittany, of which he had just been appointed captain.[1]

The common people, so it was believed, had a different idea. They thought the king of England had come to Normandy because in the previous year lord Philip, brother of the king of Navarre, had come to England to the presence of the king and had begged him urgently for help, so that he might attack those who were keeping his brother the king a prisoner, and recover by warlike means the estates which were owed by law to his brother but were being unjustly kept from him. Philip had sworn loyalty and offered homage to the king, and on the king's order had received Sir Miles Stapleton as a most reliable partner in the task he wished to accomplish, Sir Miles being utterly trustworthy, wonderfully devoted to the blessed Virgin and unusually experienced in the business of war. These two warriors, with two thousand men in coats of arms sailed to Normandy and rode across the country. They captured walled towns and other fortifications. Some they destroyed by fire, others were surrendered and ransomed. In the end they got as far as a castle which was only nine miles away from the city of Paris. Nor did they have any thought of ending this impressive expedition until a truce was made (which I shall describe in my history of the following year) and they returned to England.

Reports of all this struck the ears of the French people with complete terror, but when the same reports reached the hearing of the lord prince who was still in La Réole, he was deeply distressed at heart. Such was his devotion to the king that he was completely unable to allow his father's safety to be bound up

---

[1]   This is a reprise of the raid described on p.109 [127] above.

in the fortunes of war, while he himself was elsewhere.[140] He wished to be at his father's side, so that he could help him carry the load of a shared labour, whether heavy or light and whatever the outcome. [1]

And so he gathered together the forces which he had under his command and advanced to Bergerac, with the intention of crossing France and presenting himself before the eyes of his beloved father.[2] At Bergerac he was informed that, after his own departure from Gascony, the count of Armagnac had formed the intention of ravaging that country, and that he was not unprepared for this, as he had crowds of soldiers thronging around him. So the prince sent back to the defence of Gascony the seneschal of Gascony, Sir Bernard d'Albret, the mayor of Bordeaux and with them other Gascons and a great company of men with coats of arms.

Then the prince advanced into France, making his way through the districts of Limoges and Berry. Like a good leader, the prince encouraged his men as they marched to meet the enemy. They should not wander about unarmed. Their bodies should be equipped with weapons to protect their bodies and their souls equipped with the sacraments of penance and the eucharist. In this way they would be ready to fight with rebels against the king's peace, and, whether they lived to win honour on earth or died to win honour in heaven, they would in both places be rewarded as winners. Nor did he fail to show the skills of that wise commander, who knows the importance of assessing outcomes and of taking precautions against dangers to his men. Those famous men, John Chandos and James Audley, with assistants who all had some experience in the art of war, were sent on ahead to reconnoitre the enemy country, so that our men might not be taken off their guard as the enemy suddenly sprang upon them from ambushes in the woods. At the same time the prince himself saw to the planning of the marches and the daily moving of the camp. Just as though the enemy were at hand, he had the camp guarded at night. He set careful groups of watchmen, and would himself go round them accompanied by his nobles. On these rounds of inspection he would sometimes visit the vanguard, at other times the rearguard, and sometimes the middle-guard, for he did not want any part of his forces to be exposed to danger through lack of order.

But when he advanced into Poitou, he was told by his scouts that the crowned one had collected a large army and was at Orléans, being well aware of the arrival of the prince who in fact had not concealed his advance. Indeed the crowned one had dispatched a noble called Grismouton de Chambly at the head of a company of two hundred men in coats of arms to spy on our army. Our own scouts had fought with this company and had taken thirty

---

[1]   This is purely rhetorical: the strategy for the 1356 campaign was that a three-pronged attack should be made on France, by Lancaster in Normandy, the king from Calais, and the prince from Gascony, with the armies joining at a suitable point near Paris. See Clifford Rogers, *War Cruel and Sharp*, Woodbridge and Rochester NY 2000, 5-8.

[2]   4 August 1356. The campaign diary is in *Eulogium Historiarum sive Temporis* ed. F. S. Haydon, RS 9, London 1863, iii.215 ff.

knights and servants prisoner, the remainder being so completely wiped out that not one of them was left to tell the families what had happened to his companions.[141]

Our troops were delighted by this happy beginning and proceeded toward Romorantin.[1] Here they found the sire de Caon and the sire de Boucicaut who had been sent out on reconnaissance. The English made such a violent attack on the town that many of the French were killed by the destroying sword, while the two leaders of the enemy forces were compelled to flee to the castle. After lodging places had been secured in the town, the prince ordered the herald to proclaim that an assault would be made on the occupants of the castle in the morning. The next day our armed men crossed the ditch and attacked the castle walls in different places, some hurrying to climb them with scaling ladders, others burning down the gates. Their efforts were not in vain, for they entered the castle and killed many bands of citizens, while the two French lords flew to the main tower with several of their knights. At this point the prince ordered his nobles to gather round to discuss whether it would be better to forget about these fugitives or to hem them in by a siege and compel them to surrender. Then it was discovered that the crowned one of France was no more than ten miles away from Romorantin. So the prince judged it more sensible to stay where he was and wait for the arrival of the crowned one, who would be fiercely eager for a battle, than to go looking for the French army which would perhaps not wait for the prince, even though he himself was extremely keen to do battle with them. He also considered that an established siege ought to stir up the French to remove it. So finally he decided that he would not withdraw from the place now under siege until the besieged had surrendered or been taken prisoner, unless he was by some chance compelled to do so by the need to fight a battle.

So at the prince's order fresh ballistas were constructed and 'tortoises' to protect the ditchers. Then the Englishmen concentrated on the tasks assigned to them. Some smashed with round stones the roof and outworks of the tower. The diggers sweated and toiled to hollow out the ground under the rampart which supplied the foundations of the tower. Then they inserted fire and burnt the woodwork which had just about supported the mass overhanging the heads of the diggers while they were at work, and the whole tower, now supported on a foundation which was not there, collapsed. Amid such dangers the besieged could see no hope of salvation and, before the siege had reached its sixth day, they humbly offered their surrender, the terms of which were all arranged according to the wishes of the prince.[2]

Later the English scouts returned and reported that the crowned one of the French had moved down to Tours to put his forces into battle order. So the prince, who was eager for war because of the peace which always follows war, moved camp [142] towards the crowned one, hoping to find a new ford

---

[1]   30 August 1356.
[2]   5 September 1356

on the Loire as he had done on the Garonne. But because of recent heavy rain the unusually swollen waters of the Loire rushing down between its banks did not allow our men a crossing. A further hindrance was that the crowned one had ordered the destruction of all the bridges on the course of the Loire between Blois and Tours, so that there should be absolutely no way in which the prince and the duke of Lancaster could join forces, even though each army could easily see the fires of the other at night time. So the prince advanced, following the course of the Loire eastwards, and pitched camp by Tours.[1] He stayed there for four days, hoping that the crowned one, who was one mile away, would fight a battle. But on the fourth day he learned that the crowned one, who was now stationed at Blois, ten miles in his rear, had crossed the Loire by a bridge situated between these two well-fortified towns and was hurrying towards Poitou.

When the prince heard of the withdrawal of the crowned one, he hurried to return, intending to block his line of march, but he failed to do this. However he did take a cross-country route, which he thought was shorter, across three torrents,[2] and, after pursuing the enemy, attacked the rearguard of their army so forcefully that he took as prisoners from it the count of Joigny and the count of Châlon as well as the marshal of Burgundy. These lords were overpowered and set aside for ransom, but in this unexpected, hard-fought skirmish a great number of men in coats of arms were also killed. These events took place on the Saturday which was the day before the ensuing battle.[3] As night came quickly on, our men rested in a wood. On the next day, as they were marching towards the territory of Poitou, they were informed by scouts that the crowned one had put his forces in order and made his preparations to fight a battle. Shortly afterwards other scouts reported that the crowned one had moved his forces towards ours and advised the lord prince to choose a place for a battle and to put his army in order, to prevent the French in battle array finding the English unprepared.[4]

Immediately the prince and all the others with him, intending to fight on foot, handed over to the care of servant-boys their chargers and horses, [143] which they would pick up again for the pursuit of the enemy. But a few did ride between the armies, in readiness for the customary pre-battle tilt. The vanguard of our army was entrusted to the earls of Warwick and Oxford. The prince commanded the second division, and the third division was entrusted to the earls of Salisbury and Suffolk. In the whole army of the lord prince there were exactly 4,000 men with coats of arms, 1,000 soldiers and 2,000 archers.

The French nobility approached in all its pomp, disdaining the small numbers of the English, for their own massive force contained 8,000 men at arms, with no ordinary soldiers included, under 87 banners. Then many

---

[1] 7-10 September 1356.
[2] The rivers Cher and Indre, followed by the river Creuze twenty miles further south.
[3] 17 September 1356.
[4] For an assessment of Baker's account of Poitiers, for which he is one of the most important sources, see introduction, p.xxiv above.

of our men grumbled that a great part of our originally assembled army had recently been sent off to defend Gascony. The French had in their ranks a Scot called William Douglas[1] whom I mentioned earlier. He was a person of consequence in Scotland and had been tried and tested in the harsh trials of her wars. The crowned one had decorated him anew with the belt of knighthood, and gladly listened to his advice and trusted his judgment, because he knew that William was a bitter enemy of the English and one who had often suffered distress in battles against them. William was captain of 200 Scottish men at arms, whom he had brought to France from his homeland. These Scots were well aware that during the whole time of the current king of the English it had been the commonest practice of the English to fight on foot, for they had copied the Scots in this ever since the battle of Stirling. William himself, being a true Scot, preferred to attack our men on foot rather than on horse back, and he persuaded the crowned one and the other Frenchmen to fight in the same manner. The crowned one, who should have vetoed such shocking madness, agreed with what he thought was the good advice of the experienced William, and gladly sent his warhorses back to the city, so that they should not give any one the opportunity of a swift flight. He only retained five hundred horses covered in metal against arrows, and commanded their riders to attack the English archers at the beginning of the battle and to knock them over with the spurs of their horses and then trample upon them. But they did not carry out this order, as events will show.[2]

Both sides were now arranged in battle array, but as Sunday's dawn showed red [144] in the sky, there came to the prince a cardinal of Périgord, who charged him, by his honour for God who had suffered on the cross, his love of his mother the Virgin and his respect for the peace of the church, to refrain from shedding the blood of Christians, but to agree to postpone the battle for a time during which peace could be discussed. The cardinal promised that there could be an honourable peace through his intercession, if only he could be allowed to intercede. The prince indeed, who was completely free from any taint of tyranny, neither feared battle nor refused peace, and modestly agreed to the request of the holy father. And so, during the whole of that day set aside for the renewing of peace, the French army was increased by the addition of a thousand men at arms and a huge crowd of ordinary soldiers.

On the next day, the Monday, the cardinal came back to the prince, bringing the proposal from the crowned one of a truce which was to last for a year. The prince would not accept this proposal, but, after much persuasion from the cardinal, agreed to a truce lasting up to Christmas day. The cardinal returned to the crowned one and begged him to accept the terms of the truce which had been agreed to by the lord prince. But, although the marshal, Jean de Clermont,

---

[1]   In relation to the battle of Neville's Cross, p. 77 above.
[2]   Archibald Douglas, William's father, had been the commander at Halidon Hill in 1333, where he was killed. William had led the Scottish resistance after the capture of David II at Neville's Cross in 1346.

advised the crowned one to accept the offer, the marshal Arnoul d'Audrehem, Geoffroi de Charny and William Douglas the Scot opposed such acceptance, and the crowned one was strongly inclined to listen to these three. For they forecast that in the natural course of things the English would not be able to prevail at that time, especially as they were few in number, away from home in a strange land and pitifully worn out with the toil of their marches. Also they would be fighting against large numbers of French citizens, defending their own soil, and refreshed by receiving from their thoughtful leader all necessary provisions and a long period of rest. Also the boldness of the French against robbers ought to be increased not only by the royal presence, for they would then be experiencing for the first time the grace of one who had been crowned and anointed with the holy oil, but also by the blessing they would receive from the venerable bishops of Sens and Châlons who were fighting for the king, while those fighting on the other side would be aiming to damage the king's majesty.

When it was finally seen that the crowned one agreed with such claims, the marshal Jean de Clermont showed to a priest papal letters, on the authority of which he made his confession and was absolved. Then, in order to display his loyalty, which those with less foresight than himself had disparaged on the grounds that he had advised accepting the truce, he begged to be allowed to lead the first charge in the battle. [145] But the marshal Arnoul d'Audrehem was also trying hard to secure this privilege. His claim to it was based on a lawful right, but in truth he was doing it out of envy.

While the marshals were at loggerheads and the one striving to outdo the other, the prince heard from the cardinal's envoys that the leader of the French had no deep wish for peace, unless it was gained by the fury of the battlefield. And so, summoning his soldiers, he encouraged them with some such speech as this:[1]

'Comrades and fellow soldiers, I know that, after a display of knighthood ready to defend its own and to seize its rights by naked sword-point from him who denies them, the suspension of this previous knightly courage is accustomed to lead to danger. For delay teaches the enemy to take precautions, to think up new schemes and to look after its interests by an increase in its power or by a shameful flight. After a time those friends who have been prepared to act nobly find that their former ardour for battle is growing cold.

So no more delay now! Let each of you be minded to show his greatness in action, whether it is innate or acquired through practice. There is no place of safety to which we can escape by running away. The road to freedom must be

---

[1]   On these supposed reports of speeches on the battlefield, see John R. E. Bliese, 'Rhetoric and Morale: a study of battle orations from the central middle ages', *Journal of Medieval History*, 15.3, 1989, 201-226. The prince's speech is closely based on Sallust, *The Catiline Conspiracy*, ch.58; this is Catiline's speech to his troops before the battle in which he met his death. Sallust is said to have been the chief influence on the introduction of fictitious speeches into medieval chronicles. See *Lexikon des Mittelalters*, vii, Munich 1995, s.v. 'Sallust', 1307a. However, Bliese (203) thinks that instances of actual quotation are rare.

sought by the sword and won by the blood of the enemy and our own sweat and toil. For it is by such gifts that success desires to be deserved. You are about to fight against those who have often been beaten by you. Remember that you carry in your right hands riches, renown, glory,[1] the friendship of every virtuous knight and a famous name that will last for ever. Remember also that you will not be able to exchange warfare for peace and for the glorious life which you are longing to share with your wives and children in a happy old age, unless you are victors today.

I consider that the ground, on which we shall fight today, belonged to my ancestors as kings of England by the charter of ancient hereditary right. It should also today belong to us. It is not only the justice of my father's case, well-known to you, or the necessity of avoiding death, prison, disgrace and poverty that makes me think so. It is also that courage of yours, which so often wins battles of the few against the many and which blithely bears the heavy yoke of Mars with its absence of luxuries, that gives me great hope of triumphing over as many fancy Frenchmen as you like. In all reason this same hope should be alive in your hearts.

But if for any of you death or misfortune should prevail over your courage (which God forbid), make sure that you do not lose your life for nothing or unavenged, but that you die a good death, conquering as well as conquered like men. Do not be led away captive like cattle, to be punished by a lingering death. Think to yourselves that, if you fight firmly [146] for the justice which is our aim, whether we live or die, we belong to the Lord.[2] For he who does justly even up to death will be saved,[3] and those who suffer death for justice's sake, of theirs is the kingdom of heaven.[4]'

Having seen from their outward appearance that their minds had been greatly aroused by these courageous words and now were their master's, the wise commander turned to the company of his archers and strengthened them with the following speech.

'You have often given me good proof of your courage and your loyalty. In many fierce tempests of war you have shown that you are not degenerate sons, but of the same blood as those men who under the leadership of my father and my ancestors as kings of England found no task impossible, no place forbiddingly impassable, no mountain too high to climb, no tower too strong to capture, no army unbeatable, no armed enemy formidable. Their lively courage tamed the French, the Cypriots, the Syracusans, the Calabrians and the Palestinians. It also subdued the stiff-necked Scots and Irish, and the Welshmen who could endure all labour. It is not just my words which are urging you to show yourselves equal to your fathers. It is also the situation, the time and the dangers which are wont to make brave men out of cowards

---

[1]   Sallust, *The Catiline War*, ch.58; also 'great hope of triumphing' in next paragraph, and phrases in following sentence.
[2]   Romans 14:8.
[3]   Matthew 24:13.
[4]   Matthew 5:10.

and lively men out of lumps. It is also honour and love of your country. It is also the splendid spoils to be won from the French. So follow the standards, with mind and body concentrated on the commands of your leaders, so that, if life and triumph comes our way, we may continue in that firm friendship which 'always wants the same and scorns the same.' But if jealous fortune (which God forbid) should propel us down the final road of all flesh during the task which lies before us, it is not imprisonments awaiting the wicked which will dishonour your names. No, all of you together with me and with these noblemen, my companions, will drink from the same cup[1]. For us to conquer the nobility of France will be glory, and to be conquered (which God forbid) will not be a peril cowardly shunned, but a peril met with boldness.'

Having spoken these words, the prince noticed that there was a hill hard by on his flank. Beyond it there ran hedges and ditches, but inside it the ground was different, one part of it being pasture and also thick with bushes, but the other part being covered with vines and the rest of it arable land. And it was on the arable slope of this hill that the prince judged the French army to be positioned. Between our men and the hill there was a [147] wide, deep valley and also some marshy ground, watered by a stream. The prince's division with its carts crossed the stream by quite a narrow ford, and, climbing up the valley across the hedges and the ditches, took possession of the hill. In the protection given by this place they easily concealed themselves among the bushes, looking down on the enemy from above. The ground on which our first and second divisions were drawn up was separated from the open space, occupied by the French army, by a long hedge and ditch, with one of its ends running down into the marsh. The earl of Warwick, the leader and commander of the first division, held the slope where it ran down into the marsh. In the higher section of the hedge, some distance away from where it ran down into the marsh, there was an open cutting or gap which carters made in the autumn, and the third division under the earl of Salisbury was stationed a stone's throw from this gap.

The French perceived that the prince's banner, which a moment ago had been clearly visible, was now beginning to be moved from place to place until it was hidden from their sight by the barrier of the hill. So they concluded that the prince was fleeing from the scene, although Douglas the Scot and the marshal Jean de Clermont cried out that it was not so. But the marshal Arnoul d'Audrehem, who with these two commanded the vanguard, was mistaken in his judgment and advanced eagerly to follow the prince whom he thought to be fleeing. He was joined by William Douglas, seeking to gain the glory of fame from this new exploit, and by Jean de Clermont, who wished to clear himself of the blasphemous charge of disloyalty. As was the custom, the French were preceded by jousters. Knights from our first division, specially chosen for the jousting, met them at the bottom of the slope on which they were stationed. The marshal Arnoul d'Audrehem kept

---

[1]   Matthew 20:22.

his men in check so that he might see the result of the jousting. Meanwhile the marshal Jean de Clermont, who was hoping to advance through the gap in the hedge and to come round on the back of our first division, encountered the earl of Salisbury. As he saw the marshal advancing, the earl cleverly guessed his purpose, and so it was the commander of our rearguard who sustained the first shock of battle, as he sought speedily to close the gap in the hedge and so prevent the enemy from crossing through it. Then arose the dread noise of armed men meeting to fight one another with spears, swords and axes. Nor did the archers fail in their task, but, positioned behind a safe rampart above the ditch and beyond the hedge, they made arrows prevail over soldiers in armour, as the bolts from the [148] crossbow men flew ever more thickly and frequently.

And so on our side the third division, higher up, was manfully fighting against the enemy at the gap, while the men of the first division under the earl of Warwick, lower down on the slope and by the marshy ground, were cutting down the Frenchmen they met. At the same time the archers of the first division, who were safely stationed in the marshy ground where the French cavalry could not attack them, were having only a modest success from that position. For, as I have mentioned, the French cavalry, who were ordered to ride down our archers and so protect their own side from arrows, remained stationary next to their own men, and offered to our archers breasts so strongly protected by steel plates and stout shields that the arrows shot were either broken into pieces by these hard objects or deflected up to the heavens, from where they were as likely to fall on friend as on foe.

Noticing this, the earl of Oxford came down from the prince's squadron and led the archers round to the flank. He ordered them to shoot their arrows from here into the hind-quarters of the horses. As soon as this was done, the wounded warhorses kicked and trampled on their riders, and then, turning back against their own men, caused great havoc among the French lords, who had quite a different end in mind. Then, once the archers had driven back the warhorses, they returned to their original position and shot their arrows straight ahead into the fighting flanks of the French.

There was no break now in war's grim madness. Those lions, the earls of Warwick and Salisbury, competed to see which of them could flood the soil of Poitou with more draughts of French blood, and which of them could boast that his weapons were more deeply stained with the warm blood of Frenchmen. Nor was Thomas de Ufford,[1] a true earl of Suffolk, found wanting in his duties on that day. He was an exceptional repository of martial wisdom, and a man who from youth to old age was honoured for his bold exploits. On this day he ran in person along rank after rank, encouraging and emboldening man after man to do his best. He made sure that the young men in the heat of their valour did not advance too rashly and that the archers did not shoot

---

[1]   Baker is in error: this is Robert Ufford.

their arrows to no purpose, and his respected words added further fires to their glowing spirits.

In the conflict a not unavenged death removed Jean de Clermont from human affairs, as he fought bravely in the conflict, disdaining surrender or flight. But, as for that Arnoul d'Audrehem, English courage prevailed and forced his surrender. William Douglas escaped wounded, and also took back home with him a few other Scots of his company including his brother Archibald. For war's fierce fury had destroyed almost all the Scots, and had compelled all the others of that French first array to go down the road of an honourable death or a compulsory flight, apart from prisoners [149] taken for ransom. But our leaders made sure that the victorious English did not pursue the fugitives too far, for they thought, and rightly, that this happy beginning to the battle would be followed by uncommonly hard work after the arrival of fresh enemy forces. And so our men patched themselves up, and the first and second divisions joined into one.

Without delay the second French array advanced, led forth by the firstborn son of the crowned one of France, the Dauphin of Vienne[1]. The appearance of this array was more terrible and more frightening than the face of the first array which had been driven off, but it could not terrify our men who were greedy for glory and keen to gain revenge for themselves and their comrades wounded in the first encounter. Both sides set to boldly, and there thundered to the stars the loud shouts of those calling on St George or St Denis to decide the battle in their favour. Man fought frenziedly against man, each one striving to bring death to his opponent that he himself might live. But the speed of the pregnant lioness laying low the wolf or of the tiger terrifying the wolf was not any greater than the speed shown by our knights in their coats of arms as they routed and put to flight their armed opponents. Although this second French array resisted our men for longer than the first array, yet, after a great number of them had been killed, they wisely took that cautious step which the French, invincible in argument, are accustomed to call not a flight but a retreat to a fair position. But our men considered that victory on the field was still in doubt as long as the crowned one with his soldiers was still able to remain, lying hid in a nearby valley, and so they refused to leave the battlefield in pursuit of the fleeing French.

But Sir Maurice Berkeley, the son of Sir Thomas and a hero who was worthy of his illustrious parents, took no notice of this. For the whole of the two year expedition of the prince he had commanded troops under his banner, and had never failed on his own initiative to be among the leading men in the front line, when the horn for battle first sounded. At this hour, just as usual, he was among the first to attack the enemy, and he did thunderous deeds against the French which are worthy of everlasting praise. Finding himself in the middle of the Dauphin's troops, he dealt savage blows against those around him with

---

[1]   Title of the eldest son of the French king; in 1349, the dauphin of Viennois had no heir, and sold his principality to the French on condition that the title of dauphin should always be that of the heir to the throne.

his armed hand, and had no thought of fleeing from the French as long as he saw them still on their feet. Totally intent on what was in front of him[1] and never looking behind him for his own men or gazing up in the air for signs, he single-handedly pursued the escort which was keeping the mighty Dauphin safe. When his lance and then his sword and other attacking weapons had [150] been broken by the furious manliness of his assaults on the escort, he at the last found himself alone in the middle of a crowd of Frenchmen. Terribly wounded but still alive he was taken prisoner and retained for ransom.

Meanwhile our men placed their wounded under bushes and hedges. Others snatched from the conquered enemy spears and swords which were more in one piece than their own broken weapons, and archers hurried to pull out arrows from half-alive wretches. There was no one who was not wounded or exhausted from the extreme effort of the day, apart only from the four hundred men serving under the prince's banner, who were being kept in reserve to meet the crowned one and his division.

When the Dauphin had been put to flight in this way, one who had seen it all came to the crowned one and said, 'Sire, the field has fallen to the English and my lord, your firstborn son, has withdrawn.' In reply to him the crowned one swore an inviolable oath that he would not abandon the field that day, unless he were captured or killed, and so carried off perforce. And so he ordered his standard bearers to advance. Following behind them, a massive well-armed force of soldiers left their position in the valley and coming on to the wide field showed themselves to our gaze. So great was the despair of victory that struck our men as they saw this host that a much respected nobleman standing by the king exclaimed, 'Phew! This will be a defeat. We're going to lose.' But the lord prince, putting his trust in Christ and the virgin Mary the Christ bearer, rebuked the nobleman, saying, 'You miserable coward, you are lying, if you are blasphemously suggesting that I can be defeated while I'm still alive.' It was not only the numbers of the enemy which terrified our men, but also the thought that our own power had been considerably reduced. For besides the fact that the many wounded on our side were necessarily now out of the conflict, almost all the rest were very tired indeed, and the archers had used up their arrows. Also, as soon as the thoroughly reliable captal de Buch had seen the advance of the crowned one's army, he had gained the permission of the prince and departed with sixty men with coats of arms and a hundred archers, but many on our side thought that he had taken to flight. And so our men, though not their leaders, gave up hope of victory. They commended themselves totally to God, and, regarding their lives as nothing worth, thought only not to die alone or unavenged.

Then the prince ordered his standard bearer, Sir Walter de Wodelond, to move off towards the banners of the enemy, and with his few fresh men he joined battle with the great army of the crowned one. Then sounded the signals for battle, with trumpets [151]giving answer to clarions, tuneful horns and

---

[1]   Philippians 3:13.

kettle-drums, and the stony cliffs of Poitou sent the sound in echo to the woods. You would have thought that the mountains were bellowing to the valleys and that the clouds thundered. Nor were these mighty thunderclaps without their frightening flashes of lightning, while the sunlight sparkled on their glittering golden armour and flashes came from their flying spears of polished steel, as their points like thunderbolts split their targets. Then the threatening mass of the French crossbowmen brought back grim night to the battlefield with the thick darkness of their bolts, but this darkness was repelled by the deadly shower of arrows shot by the young English archers, driven by desperation to frenzied resistance. Also there flew through the air spears of ash, which the French greeted at a distance, as their troops, packed together in dense bands, protected their breasts with a close-fitting line of shields and turned aside their heads from the missiles. Then our archers, having emptied their quivers in vain, and armed only with shields of leather and swords, were told by the passion boiling within them to attack the heavily-armed French and to sell dearly their deaths which they thought would be the settlement for that day's work. But then with a roar the prince of Wales was upon the Frenchmen. Hewing them down with his sharp sword, he cut through their spears, repelled their blows, made their efforts a thing of nought, lifted the fallen English and taught the enemy how furious is the desperation in the breast of a man clothed for battle.

Meanwhile the captal de Buch was going around the French flank, withdrawing from the hill where he had just left the prince at the foot of its slope. He went round the battlefield without being seen and came to the low-lying place of the first station of the crowned one. Then he climbed to higher parts of the field along a path last trodden by the French, so that, suddenly breaking forth from his concealment, he showed us by the holy ensigns of St George that a friend was there. Then the prince, feeling shame, fought to break through the French line before the captain could make his attack in that quarter of the battle which was only defended by French backs. And so

> With headlong speed the prince's men in fury
> Charge the close-packed columns, forcing a way
> Through weapons and through masses of the foe,
> In search of the breast in its safe covering hid[1]

[152] as the prince charged and broke through the enemy line, laying about him with his sword. He goes into the very middle of the foe and

> On all sides fiercely whirls
> His sword, and cuts down those
> Who bar his progress; others
> Are crushed; and all he strikes
> Are to destruction hurled.

---

[1]   Slightly adapted from Lucan, *Pharsalia*, vii. 496-99.

The unhappy French were now being attacked on both sides, for in their rear they were being cut down by the captal de Buch's armed knights and pierced by the dread hail of the archers assigned to him. So then the whole formation of the French was cut to pieces.

> Here Edward storms, here hurls the prince his bolts;
> But had no wish to send to death the crowd[1]

of enemies that he could have done. Instead the prince rushed through the shattered French arrays, and, leaving the few groups of armed Frenchmen still fighting to the victories of lesser men, he directed his rapid, fear-bringing steps to the strong position of the crowned one, who was still closely surrounded by strong wedges of his guards. Then banners tottered and their bearers fell. Some Frenchmen trod on their own poured out entrails, others spat out teeth, many were fixed to the ground, and others who were standing were missing their arms which had been cut off. Dying men rolled about in the blood of others or moaned at weights which had fallen on them, and as proud souls left their cowardly bodies, they uttered dreadful groans. The blood of servants and the blood of kings ran together in one current, and, empurpling the streams of the neighbourhood, fed the fishes on rare nectar. So raged the boar of Cornwall,

> glad to find no path, but those by bloodshed won[2]

as he made his way to where the crowned one stood. Here he met with fierce resistance from the most valiant Frenchmen. The English fought, but the French fought back. Although their leader was middle-aged, he showed the anger of a youthful recruit, doing deed after deed of great note. From some he dashed out the [153] brains, while others he ran through with his sword. Of these he cut open the heads or battered the faces to a pulp, while those he eviscerated, and some he beheaded. In all of it he showed that he was not a completely degenerate scion of the royal stock of France. But at last, as fortune hastened the turning of her wheel, the prince of Wales made his way among his enemies, and, with the nobleness of a fierce lion, he warred down the proud, spared the humble[3] and accepted the surrender of the crowned one.

Meanwhile the French, scattered far and wide across the countryside of Poitou, realised that the banner of the fleur-de-lys had been lowered, and so made in headlong flight for the nearby town. But the English, in the joy of being alive and with victory in their hearts, took no thought for anyone, however badly wounded, or for any of their past labours, hard pressed though they had been, and pursued the fleeing French to the gates of Poitiers. Here, in a dangerous skirmish, they gave the French-born a good beating and routed them with great slaughter. Indeed they would have killed many more, if they

---

[1]   Ibid., vii. 534-5
[2]   Lucan, *Pharsalia*, ii. 439-40
[3]   Cf. Vergil, *Aeneid*, 6:853

had not paid more attention to taking prisoners for ransom than to the main fact of victory.

Finally our men were summoned back into one body by the sound of the trumpets. Pavilions and tents were set up in the fields, and the whole army hurried to give its attention to healing the wounded, providing rest for the weary, guarding safe the captives and feeding the famished. Then they realised that there were missing from their company men who had left them in search of the honour a knight should win, and persons full of pity were sent to search for them and to bring them back to the army dead or alive. And so all of these, sick at heart for the perils of friends that were missing, hurriedly ran to the battlefield bemoaning their fate. There, amid the piles of the dead, they found men scarcely breathing, who, overcome by the hard labour and the dripping sweat that was its witness, had poured out large quantities of their own blood that the king of England might have justice and keep intact his chief honour, and also that the army might be secure and safe. Some of these gallantly laid down their lives for their friends, and were received as victors into the kingdoms of heaven, which, as we know from the sacred promises of invincible truth, is the reward for love at its greatest.[1]

Among the half-dead who were still just breathing was found Sir James Audley. He was placed on his broad shield and was carried exhausted, wounded and bloodless to the prince's lodging by the loving arms of his exhausted, wounded and bloodstained fellow knights. Sir James' whole household gave themselves up to earnest prayers for such a precious find. [154] Even the prince himself with praiseworthy tenderness rose from the chair, where he was sitting next to the crowned one for supper. Almost in tears, he kissed the cold lips of his barely breathing friend that were rough with blood and finally laid him naked on a soft bed. For a little while he brought him back to consciousness and comforted him by asserting on his sacred oath that the crowned one had surrendered to him. Indeed the fainting hero only believed this news, which he had desired beyond measure, when the prince himself was telling him of it. As soon as he believed it, he revived.

Then the prince returned to the crowned one, and suggested that he should not think the prince had acted unworthily in rising from supper to comfort a man who was almost dead. For this knight had not spared his own blood or thought of his own safety, but had exposed both to the risk of destruction so that the English might taste the principal honour of victory. Then the crowned one, having heard a description of the knight's coat of arms which Sir James had been wearing in the battle, said that, among the other brave champions of the day, he had greatly marvelled at the awesomely brave deeds of Sir James which had continued for so long. The crowned one did not say much more during the meal, except that, when the prince with his innate kindness of heart comforted his noble prisoner, he replied in similar fashion with these words: 'Although our sorrow is inevitable, we have thought it right and fitting to

---

[1]   John 15:13 John 15:13

keep it within bounds. For although we are the prisoner of our noble cousin by the rights of war, yet we were not taken lurking in a corner like criminals or fainthearted fugitives, but, like noble knights ready to live or die for justice's sake, we were taken from our field of battle by the arbitrament of war. The rich were taken prisoner and kept for ransom, the despicable cowards ran away, and the bravest gave up their lives magnificently.'

The day after the battle the following prisoners were counted: the crowned one, who was called the king of the French by his people; also Philip, his son; also the archbishop of Sens, the count of Ponthieu, the count of Eu, the count of Longueville, the count of Tancarville, the count of Auxerre, the count of Ventadour, the count of Sancerre, the count of Vaudemont, the count of Vendôme, the count of Joigny, the count of Dammartin, the count of Saarbruck, the count of Nassau, the vicount of Narbonne, Louis d'Aubigny, the marshal Arnoul d'Audrehem, Guichard d'Angle seneschal of Saintogne, the sire Maurice Mauvinet, the sire Renaud de Guilhon seneschal of Poitou, [155] the grand preceptor or master of the Hospitallers in Spain, Geoffroi de Saint-Dizier, the sire d'Amboise seneschal of Auvergne, the sire de la Tour, the sire d'Arx, the sire de Derval, the sire de Ville-Arnoul, Jean de Maignelais, Jean de Planche, the viscount of Beaumont and the sire de Sully.

Also the bodies of these dead were found: the duc de Bourbon, the duc d'Athènes constable of France, the marshal Jean de Clermont, the sire Geoffroi de Charny, the sire de Pons, the bishop of Châlons, the sire de Landas, the sire de Ribemont, the sire de Chauvigny, the sire de L'Isle, the sire de Nesle, the sire de Sancerre, the sire de Montjouan, the sire d'Argenton, the viscount of Brosse, the sire de Duras, the vicount of Rochechouart and the sire de Château-Vilain.[1]

The prince bought all the prisoners from their owners and took them to Bordeaux, to be put in safe custody. While the prince stayed on in Bordeaux, the cardinal of Perigord, whom I have mentioned before, sent envoys to him to ask for a safe conduct for himself to come and speak with the prince. When at last his request was granted, the cardinal made his excuses to the lord prince for the fact that his unsuccessful attempts to bring about a peace on the day before the battle had enabled the French, though without his knowledge, to receive enough time to increase the size of their army; and so the lord prince could have believed that it was through his own trickery that this scheme had been devised. But at last the prince accepted the excuses of the reverend father, and the cardinal was received as his friend.

The French prisoners put pressure on the lord prince with their persistent, heartfelt prayers that he should grant them a day for peace discussions, namely the fifteenth day after the birth of Jesus Christ, so that on this day, while the English were at Blaye and the French were at Mirambeau, a final peace might be drawn up at a spot between these two towns. But the prince

---

[1]   See Chris Given-Wilson and Françoise Bériac, 'Edward III's Prisoners of War: the Battle of Poitiers and its context', *EHR* cxvi 2001 806–33 ; the list of prisoners is at 831–33

did not want to discuss these wishes of the French without the authority of the king, his father, and so he wrote him a true account of the sequence of events and sent it to his father by two men of the rank of knight, namely Sir Nigel Loring and Sir Roger Cotesford. But for two years afterwards no such wished for peace was signed.

Appendix

The alternate text for 1327-30.

As I have written earlier, the glorious king Edward *handed over* his crown to his firstborn son, Edward of Windsor. When the news of this had been established as certain, the magnates and prelates of the kingdom in a parliament at London immediately gave their consent to Edward, the firstborn *son* of Edward, as *king*, and had him crowned by Walter Reynolds, the archbishop of Canterbury, at Westminster on 1 February. He was a *young man of about thirteen*, and one who found favour with God and the whole world. At the great ceremony of his coronation there were present as many foreigners as *Englishmen*, particularly the mercenaries of queen Isabella his mother, whom, as I have said, she herself had invited from Hainault and Germany. The new king was crowned with the crown *of St Edward, the confessor* [35] . Although the crown was large and of considerable weight, the new king wore it *in a* manly fashion so that those, who *had an adequate idea of* how young the boy was and how large and heavy the crown, marvelled at it. On the same day the three sons of Roger Mortimer and many others were *made knights*.

On the eve of the feast of St Nicholas in this year master James Berkeley was unanimously elected bishop of Exeter and consecrated in Canterbury on the middle Sunday in Lent.

After his coronation the new king Edward, the third, together with his mother and those mercenaries of hers *took himself* towards Scotland. He had collected a *very* huge army of soldiers, the majority of whom *served* willingly rather than under compulsion. At York, there was a serious conflict between the citizens and the mercenaries from Hainault, in which many citizens were killed by night and part of the city burnt. After peace had been restored on *the next day*, the army moved forward towards Scotland. The Scots were waiting at Stanhope park. Although the English army was three times bigger than the Scottish and, as all knew, of a much stronger composition, the Scots, who were in league with some perfidious English nobles, *fled unharmed and with the friends of the king of England knowing nothing about it*. The king returned to England. It was a weak beginning, but the prelude to happier and better things. He sent back home the men of Hainault and the other mercenaries, who took with them as presents large sums of money and many choice jewels.

In this year lord James Berkeley, the bishop of Exeter, [36] entered upon the way of all flesh and lord John Grandison was consecrated bishop of Exeter as the pope's appointment in the Roman curia on the feast of St Lucia.

Later Edward II died, as I have described earlier.

Also in this year Charles de Valois, the son of Philip the Fair of Valois was accused of treason. He had always hated the English, and, as I have said, had led a French army against the earl of Kent in Gascony, but now he was accused of inviting the French king his nephew to hunt and dine with him in a desire to murder him, and for this unworthy act he was handed over to his executioners. The story goes that after the hunting some mace-bearers of the king entered the room where the banquet was to be held and discovered that a treacherous scheme was afoot. It was only with difficulty that the mace-bearers escaped from a struggle and told the king. So the king *turned aside* to other safer parts. *Charles de Valois was captured and convicted, but, out of reverence for his royal blood he was not hung or beheaded but was made to sit without under-garments on bare marble, which was continually sprinkled with cold water until Charles de Valois finished the day of the vengeance taken on him through the cold.*

This Charles was the father of Philip de Valois, who was afterwards king of France but unjustly, and the brother of Philip the Fair, the grandfather of king Edward III of England. This Charles thought that if he could put to death his nephew, Charles king of France who did not have an heir of his own body, then either he himself or his son Philip de Valois would gain possession of the kingdom. And because of this he devised the scheme I have described. [38] .

Robert Bruce also died in this year. He left behind a son David who was seven or eight years old, and the Scots *received him as their king.* His right of succession was as follows. Alexander, king of the Scots, had three daughters but no sons. The first was married to John Balliol, the *second to Robert Bruce, an Englishman born in Essex at Writtle, and the third to the count of Holland* . After the death of king Alexander, with the consent of Edward king of England the Scots had appointed as their king John Balliol, the husband of king Alexander's eldest daughter, and Balliol on behalf of the kingdom of Scotland *did homage to Edward, but later, at the instigation of the disturbers of the peace of the kingdom of Scotland, John Balliol renounced by his noble envoys this homage to the king of England, while none the less keeping the kingship of Scotland. And so the king of England, Edward of Winchester, with his power expelled Balliol and his son from Scotland. Balliol went abroad to France and died there. Afterwards the Scots, being rebels by nature, chose as their king the husband of the second daughter of king Alexander, namely Robert Bruce. Now he was a soldier to his finger tips, except that he laid aside his loyalty and out of love of the kingship fought against his natural lord.* [39]

Well, *with Robert Bruce dead,* the Scots planned to have his son as the next heir to the kingdom and as their king. But their plans were to be scattered to the four winds by Edward Balliol, the son of king John Balliol and the eldest daughter, *while he was in France,* with the help of God and Edward III king of England, whose famous deeds I am intending to describe.

In AD 1327, in the twelfth year of pope John and the first year of king Edward III, Charles king of France entered upon the way of all flesh. He was the uncle of the king of England and the brother of *queen* Isabella, and the third of those three brothers who ruled after the death of their father Philip the Fair. He was succeeded as king by Philip de Valois, the son of Charles, whom I have written about earlier, *who in many places*[40] *is called a tyrant of that country and the betrayer of the French. Philip de Valois the crowned one of the French held the kingdom of Navarre, thus dishonouring lady Joanna the daughter of Louis, king of Navarre and the first of those three brothers who dying without a male heir left vacant the kingship of France. Joanna's husband, Charles count of Averois, the son of Louis, who was the son of Philip, the king of France, opposed Philip de Valois, the son of his uncle and the crowned one, claiming that the inheritance of the kingdom of Navarre did not exclude women, and for that reason he demanded that his wife be given back her due inheritance. The answer to this was that the mother of his wife, as a suffocated adulteress, could not pass on the right of inheritance to a daughter, whose father was unknown. And so the lady Joan, wishing to give proof that she was the legitimate daughter of Louis the king of France, demanded that she be exposed naked to lions which for three days had been maddened by lack of food. The lions revered her as the daughter of a king and did not even touch her. And so the kingdom of Navarre which she had sought was granted to her and through her to her husband by the judgment and the piety of the peers of the kingdom of France,*

In the fifteen days of Easter of this year, in a parliament held at Northampton in the name of the king, a shameful peace was made between the English. It was agreed between them that David son of Robert Bruce, should marry Joan the sister of the English king and should rule peacefully together with her as the king of the Scots. This afterwards came to pass. Also the king of England, *a young man in the first flush of youth*, granted *charters* to the Scots, although there was a general ignorance of its conditions and contents.

[From this point to the beginning of the entry for 1328 there are no differences]

In AD 1328, the second year of the reign of the third Edward after the conquest, after the fifteen days of St Michael the king held a parliament at Salisbury, at which he made three men earls. Lord John of Eltham, his brother, was made earl of Cornwall, Roger Mortimer was made earl of the March of Wales, and Butler of Ireland was made earl of *Ormound*. The earl of Lancaster, lord de Wake and *lord Henry Beaumont and the lord marshal and others* some other nobles absented themselves from this parliament, *although they came under arms to the vicinity of the* parliament. This angered the king, but later on during the summer, at the instigation of the archbishop of Canterbury, they made their submission to the king's grace at *Bedford.*[43] *Soon afterwards the earl of Lancaster was found to be blind.*[1]

In the same year around Ascension time the king crossed the sea, leaving his brother the earl of Cornwall in charge of the kingdom, and did homage with certain qualifications for the whole duchy of Aquitaine and the countship of Ponthieu to the king of France, Philip de Valois, the son of Charles the traitor. But Philip, king of France, accepted the homage with different qualifications,

---

[1]   This is not entirely accurate: he was active in government service in the early 1330s, after Mortimer's fall from power, and as late as 1339 he was party to a treaty between England and Brabant.

namely that he was not accepting homage for the lands which his father Charles had ridden across against the earl of Kent, as I have described earlier, but was keeping these for himself and intended to keep them until he should be recompensed for the losses and expenses which his father had sustained and incurred while fighting there.

In the same year Simon, archbishop of Canterbury, held a provincial council in London.[2] Some weighty measures were passed: on Good Friday and on the commemoration of faithful souls, there should be a complete cessation from work done in service, and, on the feast of the glorious conception of the virgin the mother of God, praises should be paid to God in celebration. Also the archbishop and the other bishops present excommunicated and published as excommunicated all those who in any way had laid violent hands on Walter Stapleton, bishop of Exeter, when he was so dreadfully murdered, and also all those who had given them their help or consent or advice.[3]

---

[2] 3 February 1329.
[3] The duplication in MS Bodley 761 ends here.

Index

Printed in the United States
By Bookmasters